WW010523118

For Wendy from Bob C

HAPPY HOLIDAYS 2004

COSTUMES BY KARINSKA

Foreword by Edward Gorey

Harry N. Abrams, Inc., Publishers

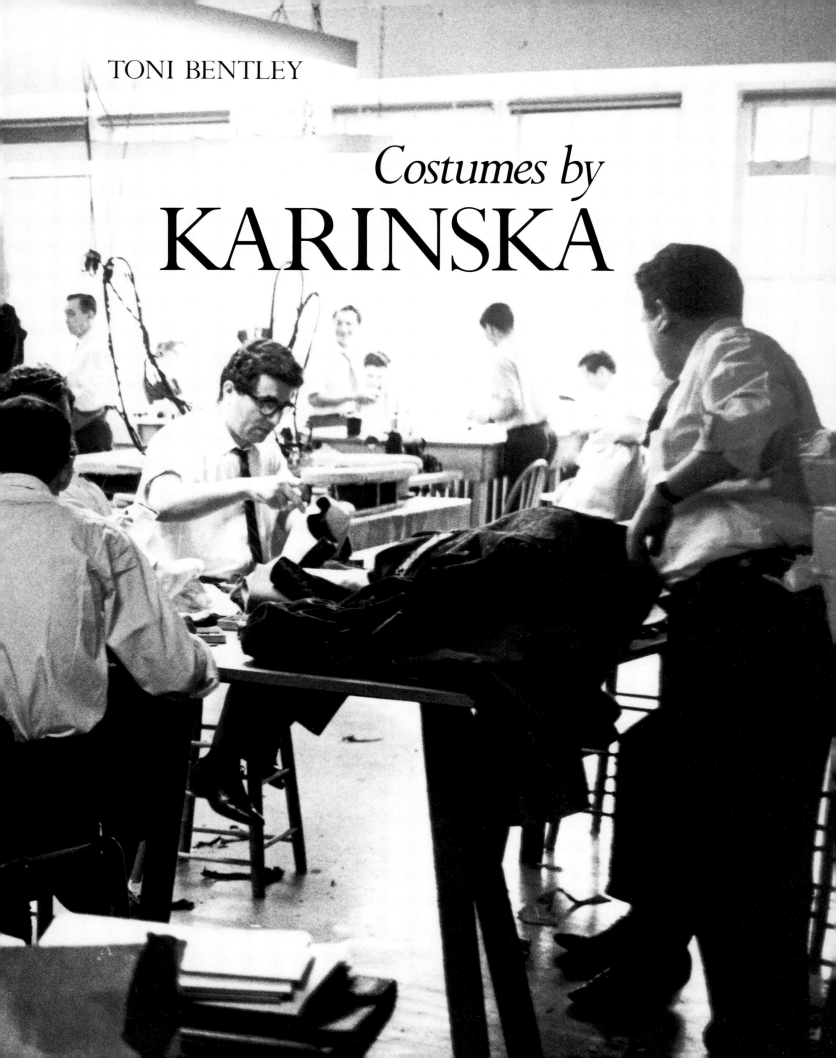

TONI BENTLEY

Costumes by
KARINSKA

FOR EDWARD BIGELOW

EDITORS: *Jennifer Stockman and Elisa Urbanelli*
DESIGNER: *Judith Michael*
The letters of Barbara Karinska and Louis Jouvet
were translated from the French by Marjolijn de Jager

Endpapers: A sample of Karinska's needlepoint. This piece, measuring 17 × 17,"
was stitched for a friend, the designer Miles White, in the course of one ocean
voyage from Europe.

Page 1: Cartoon by Alex Gard of Karinska holding a safety-pinned tutu.

Pages 2–3: Karinska's costume shop, c. 1974.

LIBRARY OF CONGRESS CATALOGING-IN-PUBLICATION DATA

Bentley, Toni.
Costumes by Karinska / by Toni Bentley; foreword by Edward Gorey.
p.   cm.
Includes bibliographical references and index.
ISBN 0–8109–3516–3
1. Karinska, Barbara.   2. Costume designers—United States—
Biography.   3. Costume designers—Europe—Biography.   4. Women
costume designers—United States—Biography.   5. Women costume
designers—Europe—Biography.   6. Costume design—United States—
History—20th century.   7. Costume design—Europe—History—20th
century.   I. Title.
TT505.K373B46   1995
792′.026′092—dc20
[B]   95–7407

Text copyright © 1995 Toni Bentley
Illustrations copyright © 1995 Harry N. Abrams, Inc.
Foreword copyright © 1995 Edward Gorey
Essay copyright © 1995 Lincoln Kirstein
Published in 1995 by Harry N. Abrams, Inc., New York
A Times Mirror Company
All rights reserved. No part of the contents of this book may
be reproduced without the written permission of the publisher

Printed and bound in Japan

CONTENTS

FOREWORD

Edward Gorey

Until I came to New York in the winter of 1953 and quickly became addicted to the New York City Ballet, Karinska was a name I happened upon now and again in the program, to which back then I had paid not nearly enough attention; so in reading Toni Bentley's manuscript for this book I was surprised and somehow elated to find that Karinska had executed the costumes for one of the first three ballets I ever saw.

A sophomore in high school in Chicago during the season 1939–40, I went off by myself to see the Ballet Russe de Monte Carlo do *Bacchanale* because of its sets and costumes designed by Salvador Dalí, who had been sprung on me by *Life* magazine. Luckily, what I had come to see was sandwiched between *Rouge et Noir* and *Schéhérezade*. Incidentally, these had designs by Matisse and Bakst, uniting in one program the three greatest, for me, of all costume designers.

Of *Bacchanale* I remember not very much except for the hackneyed score pouring away like syrup over my head, and the backdrops, props, and costumes, surrealistically over-busy and elaborate, which would have quite overwhelmed a lot more choreography than the little there was in the first place. What I particularly recall being struck by was "Lola Montez" with a whip, twirling about in enormous gold lamé bloomers encircled at their widest part by two rows of white teeth.

Now I realize that this and the other costumes must have been some of Karinska's most brilliant and ingenious translations of someone else's designs to the stage.

And as I browsed through the chronology at the back of this book I was again surprised, time after time, to come across costumes executed by Karinska that I have fondly remembered, some for over half a century, from not only ballets but also musicals, plays, and films. Two instances I can't resist mentioning. One, from 1938, the satin and ruffled dresses for the cancan dancers in *Gaieté Parisienne,* whose combinations of colors I still think were the most gorgeous I ever saw, and two, from the 1960s, a perfectly simple strapless black velvet dress for Patricia McBride; she wore it to dance "The Man I Love" from *Who Cares?* at a guest appearance somewhere or other outside of New York, and I never saw her look more beautiful.

Many of Karinska's translations of designs by others belong to the period begun by Diaghilev when ballet decor was dominated almost exclusively by famous and fashionable easel painters. Their designs, however chic and useful for publicity, often betrayed no great affinity for what went on the stage, and their sketches defied an accurate attempt to do them up in another medium. Models of sets could be adapted in a rather straightforward manner; costumes, to be derived from stylized poses and stylish renderings, presented far more difficult problems. There was no one who could solve them like Karinska, and produce such ravishing results on stage.

Perhaps her greatest triumph in this line was the remounting of *Firebird* in 1970 for the New York City Ballet, based on designs by Chagall, who may have been the most difficult of all the painters to contend with. If nothing else, his sets always upstaged whatever went on in front of them. I can still make myself faintly dizzy by recalling his backdrops for *Aleko,* in which fish and scythe ceaselessly emerged from a wheatfield and the sky was filled with an assortment of rapidly whirling suns; these go with the vaguest of recollections of some sort of gypsy pastiche going on below. Even the darkest of the *Firebird* backdrops, a forest with an upside-down reflection of itself above it, separated by a night sky, was a constant distraction.

The library at Lincoln Center subsequently held a large Karinska exhibition which included Chagall's original costume sketches, sketches by Karinska for her own use in making the costumes, and the costumes themselves. Their brilliance onstage had been a revelation to those who were used to the American Ballet Theatre production years before; now there was an even greater revelation of another kind when one saw how Karinska worked. Wispy, if brightly colored sketches, which would seem to deny any possible physical reality, were somehow turned by a sort of relentless lightness into absolutely magical stage costumes.

Still, to my mind, none of the costumes she made from other people's designs are quite as wonderful as those she designed herself for Balanchine and the New York City Ballet in the nearly thirty years that began with *Bourrée Fantasque* in 1949 and ended with *Vienna Waltzes* in 1977. One of the most persistent myths about the New York City Ballet for those who weren't there, and for some who were, is that Balanchine's ballets (and there were seldom others) took place in a setless void where cold and plotless abstractions were danced, usually to Stravinsky sewing-machine music, by insectlike creatures with tiny heads and incredibly long extremities, in black and white "practice" clothes. And if by some mischance a ballet was mounted with costumes, they soon vanished, never to be seen again, as with *Concerto Barocco* and *Four Temperaments,* although, perversely, for years afterward Maria Tallchief in her "Sanguinic" costume jetéd across the company's posters.

Of course sometimes there had to be tutus, and herein could be found one aspect of Karinska's genius. Back in the days at City Center, Balanchine wrote a piece for the program in which he used cooking as an extended metaphor for ballet, so perhaps it is not too outré to compare tutus to gravy — more often than not too thick, too thin, and liable to be lumpy. Legend here conjures up an unlikely picture of Karinska changing all that; a thin, elegant lady with blue hair, wielding a giant pair of shears, attacks clouds of tarlatan with enormous energy, and after God knows how many attempts, triumphantly cuts out the Perfect Tutu.

But there is no myth to pin down or take in all that she achieved, from the smallest pas de deux to the largest full-length ballets, *The Nutcracker* and *A Midsummer Night's Dream,* from the classic, *Symphony in C, Serenade, Apollo,* to the exotic, *Metamorphoses* and *Bugaku,* to some of the most romantic costumes ever devised, including a trio of ballets, *La Valse, Liebeslieder Walzer,* and *Vienna Waltzes.*

Genius is as unexplainable as anything else one can think of, but one is always tempted to try. Karinska's has to do, I think, with the nature of the stage, or theater, or whatever you want to call it. To paraphrase Marianne Moore on poetry, the stage is an imaginary place with real people in it. It is something I think she always knew, never forgot, and never neglected, and that is why a Karinska costume is as recognizable as Balanchine choreography.

The golden age of the New York City Ballet, and I am tempted to remark of ballet in general, came to an end with the deaths of Balanchine and Karinska in 1983. I feel it to be one of the great privileges of my life to have been able to see so much of their work. For those like myself this book will always be there to remind us what was, and for those not quite so fortunate, it will be the next best thing, a marvelous record in words and pictures of what costumes at their best are and can be.

PREFACE

When choreographer George Balanchine was asked by the Ford Foundation in 1963 what he most needed for his work, he answered with one word: "Karinska!" It was the supreme compliment from one artist to another. At the time Madame Barbara Karinska was already seventy-seven years old, but her subsequent fourteen-year exclusive association with Balanchine's New York City Ballet would mark her final glorious ascent in that mysterious land where ballet costumes are made. It is a place where she ruled without peer, possessed of, as she said of herself with characteristic grandeur, "the courage of a man and the heart of a woman."

To a dancer, the "Karinska" label in a costume's waistband (tutus have no collars) is the assurance of the very best, like "Cartier" or "Rolls-Royce." "To the New York City Ballet I gave my heart," stated Karinska, while Balanchine said of her, "I attribute to her fifty percent of the success of my ballets that she has dressed."[1] (In the course of their long collaboration Karinska clothed over seventy-five of them.) While Balanchine was giving American dance its own line, its own svelte elegance, its own unique kind of glamour, its own classical tradition, Karinska worked alongside, smoothing that line, enhancing that elegance, coloring that glamour, and framing that tradition with silk and satin.

Karinska's association with Balanchine was her longest and most deeply satisfying, but he was by no means the only dance choreographer whose visions she dressed. In a career spanning forty-five years she costumed ballets of Marius Petipa, Michel Fokine, Léonide Massine, Frederick Ashton, Antony Tudor, Bronislava Nijinska, Agnes de Mille, Merce Cunningham, and Jerome Robbins, often working simultaneously for rival companies with equal devotion. She rendered three-dimensional, functional, and portable the imaginings of such artists as Christian Bérard, André Derain, Pavel Tchelitchew, Salvador Dalí, Dorothea Tanning, Robert Rauschenberg, Isamu Noguchi, Balthus, and Marc Chagall. Karinska's ageless hands can be seen, like those of a benign Madame Defarge, weaving a delicate but indestructible thread that connects and clothes ballet in our century.

While dance was always the focus of Karinska's deepest sympathies, her costuming experiences encompassed many other genres. Before finally settling permanently in

New York in 1949, Karinska had directed ateliers in Paris, Monte Carlo, London, and Hollywood and had produced costumes for operas, ice shows, plays, and films. Her work ran the gamut of theatrical forms—from burlesque and Broadway to Shakespeare and Molière. A true sophisticate, she treated Gypsy Rose Lee's scanty trimmings with the same impeccable taste, wit, and refinement that she gave to Laurence Olivier's Becket and Birgit Nilsson's Turandot. The list of stars who have appeared in her gowns, robes, hats, shawls, vests, waistcoats, tutus, and tiaras is impressive—it includes Ginger Rogers, Judy Garland, Charles Boyer, Vivien Leigh, Marlene Dietrich, Ingrid Bergman, Leslie Caron, Gene Kelly, Olivia de Havilland, Gary Cooper, Paulette Goddard, Helen Hayes, Louis Jouvet, Jean-Pierre Aumont, Sonja Henie, Ethel Merman, Bobby Clark, Alfred Lunt, Lynn Fontanne, Renata Tebaldi, Lily Pons, Alexandra Danilova, Margot Fonteyn, Alicia Markova, Alicia Alonso, Maria Tallchief, Nora Kaye, Tanaquil Le Clercq, Patricia McBride, Suzanne Farrell, Gelsey Kirkland, Peter Martins, and Mikhail Baryshnikov.

These illustrious individuals all appeared as mere mortals, or nearly so, and do not even begin to suggest the true range of Karinska's magical kingdom, the one ruled by kings and queens, princes and princesses, and populated by butterflies, fairies, flowers, firebirds, swans, and angels. It is a place that has existed for centuries on ballet stages around the world, enhancing ballet's ethereal image and seducing big and little girls alike into wanting to be ballerinas and a public into perpetual fascination.

Karinska, like her compatriots Vladimir Nabokov, Igor Stravinsky, and George Balanchine, was one of thousands of emigrées who were flung westward from czarist Russia by the Bolsheviks in the 1920s, and she, like them, took with her an imperial standard that became the hallmark of her work. Who was this lone Russian aristocrat who, displaced from her Slavic roots, improvised on the dusty floor of a dusty room in Paris a new way to cut a ballet bodice and thus invented a garment that would later enable American dancers to move, to feel, to conquer like the nobles of a newfound land? And why did she make it her lifelong crusade to dress them for the task in fitting, flattering, and truly beautiful tutus?

CHAPTER ONE

Born Varvara Andryevna Zmoudsky on October 3, 1886, in the Ukrainian city of Kharkov, Karinska was the eldest of the ten children of Andreï Zmoudsky and his wife, Maria. Zmoudsky was a successful textile merchant whose factory sold, according to his daughter, a heavy blue-and-white fabric "to all the peasants of South Ukraine."[2] He was a highly respected, socially conscious, and wealthy man, and his household bore all the signs of western European sophistication. French and German governesses were employed for the children's education, and elegant dinner parties were served on fine imported china. Entertainment at these soirées was provided by the children in the form of elaborate homespun theatricals directed by young Varvara. Thus it was that Karinska's parents' guests were the witnesses of her first costume creations.

At this time, however, costuming was not the consuming interest that it would become; embroidery was the young girl's passion. This age-old craft of meticulous stitchery was one of Russian folk art's greatest achievements, and it was professionally taught to all well-educated young ladies from good families. For Varvara Zmoudsky it was more than just a quiet pastime; it was a world view. In its minutiae and fineness, embroidery teaches that discipline and delicacy are inseparable accomplishments, that depth and mystery can be achieved with threads of different hues and textures, and that—to the discerning eye—no detail is too small at any price. Much later, these practiced lessons would give a Karinska costume a life of its own. Embroidery was a lifelong love of Karinska's, and well into her eighth decade she could be found, after a long day at her shop, stitching a pillow or chair cover for some worthy recipient. For her it was always pure relaxation.

Karinska adored her father. As an adult, she liked to tell the tale of how he fulfilled her childhood wish to ride a swan. For one of her birthdays, her devoted Papa

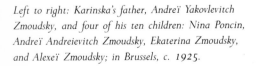

Left to right: Karinska's father, Andreï Yakovlevitch Zmoudsky, and four of his ten children: Nina Poncin, Andreï Andreievitch Zmoudsky, Ekaterina Zmoudsky, and Alexeï Zmoudsky; in Brussels, c. 1925.

arranged with the gardener to have a real swan floating in a tub of water in the house. Upon being shown her surprise, little Varvara, in her excitement, forgot her party dress and ribboned shoes and leaped for the swan, managing to land momentarily on its back. Flapping its wings, the bird clambered out of the tub, squawking in dismay, leaving the delighted little girl splashing in the water. The gardener chased after the swan while Papa sat down convulsed in laughter and Mama rescued her daughter from the tub. "I rode the swan! I rode the swan!" cried Varvara. That the result was a soggy mess of clothes and feathers did little to diminish—in Karinska's eyes, at least—the romance of Papa's gift.[3]

Karinska in the 1940s. Note the yarn corsage at her neck, typical of Karinska's detailed handiwork.

As a teenager Karinska studied law at the University of Kharkov and performed relief work in a women's prison, helping the inmates with their daily ablutions. At the age of twenty she married Alexander Moïssenko, the editor of a socialist newspaper in Kharkov. When he died of typhus several years later, leaving Karinska with a small daughter, she assumed the editorship of the paper herself, much to everyone's dismay; this was not a job for a woman. When political unrest began and the paper came under attack and lost money, Karinska closed down the enterprise and moved to Moscow. There, over the course of the next ten years, she immersed herself in numerous ventures. She set up a studio where she made and sold embroidered pillows, napkins, bags, and bonnets to the local aristocrats; she ran a very successful embroidery school; she studied painting; and, capitalizing on all her skills, she devised a way of "painting" with fabric, using appliqués of silk chiffon—even then she was drawn to making the two-dimensional three and experimenting with texture as an element of color. She became so successful at this original form of collage that her work was shown at an exhibition of industrial arts and later at a one-woman show in Moscow.

During this time she met and married Nicholas Karinsky, a lawyer and an important government figure who was then the Attorney General and Presiding Justice of the Court of Appeals of the District of Petrograd (now known as St. Petersburg). In 1916, shortly after their marriage, Karinsky adopted Irene, Karinska's daughter by Moïssenko. When the Bolsheviks finally seized power from Alexander Kerensky's government the following year, Karinska took refuge in the Crimea with her daughter and remained there a year before returning to Moscow. By this time her husband, a political refugee, had fled the country and emigrated to New York City, where he drove a taxi until his death twenty years later. (Karinska, however, knew none of this; she believed her husband was dead.) The revolution thus forced an abrupt ending to the marriage.

Karinska at her needlepoint, age 82.

Of the precise nature of either of Karinska's very brief marriages little is known except that they were her only forays into domestic partnership, and she never referred to either experience with any affection. Late in life she confessed in all seriousness, "I'm so glad I don't have a husband. He'd be old, he'd be sick. I'd have to take care of him, listen to him complain." A master at professional collaboration, on a personal level Karinska found no time or reason for compromise.

For several years Karinska survived by her wits and talents in a much-changed and impoverished Moscow, opening a salon where tea, cakes, and conversation were

Lawrence Vlady, Karinska's nephew and adopted son, and Karinska at her house in Sandisfield, Massachusetts, 1965.

Irina and Volodya, an appliquéd "painting" in silk chiffon made by Karinska of her daughter, Irene, and nephew, Lawrence Vlady, in the 1910s.

offered in the afternoons and embroidery lessons were provided in the back room. There was also a dress shop, a hat shop, an antique shop—perhaps one and the same—and another exhibition of her appliqué "paintings." As Karinska's financial situation stabilized, the government became apprehensive about her profits and offered her a Ministry post as the Commissar of Museums. As she told it, she replied, "Tovarish, I would very much like to join the government . . . but I am not educated enough. Send me to Germany to learn. . . ."[4] The ruse worked and in 1923 Karinska did in fact leave for Europe with her fourteen-year-old daughter and fifteen-year-old orphaned nephew Lawrence Vlady in tow, smuggling out the remaining family jewels

Karinska with her family in France, 1974. From left: Karinska, Irene François (her daughter), Jean-Noël Dibie (Irene's son-in-law), Martine Dibie (Irene's daughter), and Alain François (Irene's son). The two children, Dorothée Dibie and Juliette Dibie, are Martine's children, Karinska's great grandchildren.

stitched inside the lining of Irene's hat and muff; once again needle and thread were the keys to survival. Karinska, then thirty-seven years old, would never return to the country of her birth.

First stopping in Brussels, where her father and several siblings were already living (her mother had died in 1911), Karinska took an immediate dislike to the sleepiness of the city and quickly moved on to Paris. She rented a cheap, walk-up apartment on the rue de Trevise in a not very elegant part of town near the Folies-Bergère. By now Paris had a large community of Russian emigrées, and while Karinska took comfort from friendships with her compatriots, it was apparent to her that they had already glutted the job market.

Karinska's high standing in Muscovite society meant less than nothing in French society, and virtual poverty became a daily obstacle. After the money from the jewels ran out, she had only the unpredictable sales of her handiwork to help her put food on the table. She crocheted colorful wool flowers and sold them to Max Weldy, the costume designer for Josephine Baker and the Folies-Bergère, where they were used to decorate an empty corner or critical tip of a tiny costume; she crocheted shawls that friends sold in shops; and she took orders for *kokochniks*—the traditional peaked Russian headdresses decorated with pearls, gold thread, and trailing satin ribbons— for the Opéra Russe à Paris and probably also Diaghilev's Ballets Russes. Although Karinska would later collaborate with many artists who had worked with Diaghilev, during his lifetime—he died in 1929—she profited only secondhand from the great impresario who had radically changed the way the West viewed dance. During the 1920s Karinska had been given no introduction to Diaghilev and, besides, she would have had little but crocheted flowers and *kokochniks* to offer him. Her true metier, in which such decorations would find their proper perspective, had not yet found her. Meanwhile, Irene's formal education was forced to come to an end so that she could aid her mother in her work. Irene had wanted to become a pharmacist, but the family's financial needs took precedence.

Eventually more substantial commissions came Karinska's way. A chorus dancer at the Lido Restaurant—a cabaret—asked Karinska to repair her ruffled hoopskirt, and when the show's director saw the results, he sent Karinska home with the remaining nineteen hoops around her neck for similar repair. There was a commission for costumes for a production of a nineteenth-century French operetta, *La Nuit d'Amour*, and one for a touring production of Massenet's opera *Manon* and two commissions for film costumes. But still the work was sporadic and unreliable. This all changed forever in November 1931 when Colonel Wassily de Basil, a former Russian army officer who had been a director of the Opéra Russe, asked Karinska to fabricate costumes for the debut season of his newly formed ballet company, the Ballets Russes de Monte Carlo. Knowing only that she would be making ballet costumes of some sort, Karinska said yes without hesitation—even though she had never made a tutu before and had never cut a ballet bodice. The forty-five-year-old Karinska had no idea that she was about to invent the tutu that would become her trademark.

The first costume fittings were in Paris for a ballet called *Cotillon* (*The Dance*), with music by late-nineteenth-century composer Emmanuel Chabrier. The libretto was by Boris Kochno, who had been a close friend and adviser to Diaghilev, and the sets and costumes were by Christian Bérard, a young French painter who was one of the stars—along with Pavel Tchelitchew and Eugene Berman—of the post-Picasso "neo-Romantic" movement in painting. The choreographer was a young Russian named George Balanchine. Thus Karinska was thrust into a world of brilliant young artists, all on the verge of important careers, and for the first time she felt her own enthusiasm matched, required, and returned.

But before the euphoria came the fittings. Tamara Toumanova, the exotic, doe-eyed, twelve-year-old ballerina chosen by Balanchine for the principal role in the ballet, arrived with her Mama to have her measurements taken. Bérard—big, bearlike, gentle, and bearded—was present with his sketches; and Balanchine—debonair, dark-haired, and handsome—was there with his quiet confidence. Karinska, despite her inexperience, appeared, according to Toumanova, to be in full control, imperious and self-possessed, tape measure in one hand, pins in her mouth, and yards and yards of pale tulle trailing over one shoulder. Every few minutes the tulle was whipped around the child in a new draping, as Karinska, Balanchine, and Bérard discussed the varying effects and angles in a fast and furious mixture of French and Russian. Kochno, who observed this process numerous times, explained, "When she worked with Bérard he did many maquettes [sketches] for the costumes but in the end he realized the costumes with Karinska 'sur place.' He did maquettes as a point of departure but that's all."[5]

Such a scene was to become de rigueur; that semicircle of mirrors where many a barefoot dancer has stood under the unflattering lighting for a fitting was a place where the fate of a ballet could be decided well before its premiere. Forty years later Karinska and Balanchine could be found peering with unabated fascination at the curve of a décolletage, their enthusiasm undiminished by time or success.

Bérard's *Cotillon* sketches indicated a relatively straightforward costume: a bodice and a long, airy tulle skirt decorated with tiny, transparent, sparkling somethings. In Karinska's hands they became slivered moons, silver stars, and floating musical notes.

OPPOSITE:

Tamara Toumanova, age twelve, in a costume designed by Christian Bérard for Balanchine's Cotillon, *1932.*

The maquettes, while more detailed than many Karinska would work with, nevertheless indicated a general atmosphere and style more than specific material or measurements. They suggested a timeless elegance tinged with wistfulness, simple but slightly tragic. It was Karinska's job to figure out how many yards of what fabric, cut on what line, in what colors, and with what decoration, would result in a wearable costume that reflected the very elusive atmosphere in Bérard's sketches. It was in this organic translation of feeling into fabric that Karinska's genius emerged. She invented her art out of what was usually thought a menial task—executing costumes from a designer's sketches—and thereafter she became indispensable to those who collaborated with her.

It was decided that the bodices for the *Cotillon* costumes would be in various colors of velvet—"sea-green, lemon, cyclamen, rose, and lime," as one eyewitness described them.[6] Karinska bought the fabric, summoned her friend Toussia Balieff, an expert Russian seamstress, closed the door of her workroom, and started cutting. She and Toussia cut and cut, and sewed and sewed, and produced one failed bodice after another. But Karinska would not be discouraged, ordering again and again, "Cut! Cut!" Eventually, by trial and many errors, a smooth, lovely, romantic bodice emerged from the scraps like the mythical phoenix from the ashes.[7] Karinska now knew how to construct a bodice. As simple as it may appear, a tutu bodice presents a paradoxical dilemma and is a complex feat of engineering. It must be light and tight while allowing the body inside to move and breathe with freedom. Karinska's invention was to become an art form in itself that she would continue to study and improve over the next several decades. The fact that she was entirely self-taught and had no preconceptions enabled her to make the necessary leaps of imagination over earlier methods of cutting and stitching into an entirely new notion of how well a costume might fit and how beautiful it might be.

The costumes, all but completed in Paris in December 1931, were taken down to Monte Carlo in early January 1932 for their final adjustments. On the seventeenth of the month the Ballets Russes de Monte Carlo was launched in grand style, with Balanchine himself dancing the male lead in *Cotillon* opposite Toumanova in a special gala performance for Prince Louis II of Monaco. Publicity for the event was enormous and positive—it was even photographed by *Vogue*. "I think we have really accomplished something tonight," Balanchine confessed to Kochno after the premiere.[8] Bérard's sets and costumes were highly praised for their evocative beauty, and the artist in turn praised Karinska. Reviewer Adrian Stokes, an admiring observer of the company's first season, likened the atmosphere of the ballet to "a hastily convened séance," commenting, "It is rare that anything as *mondain* should be as beautiful, as strenuous, and as lyrical."[9]

Work had begun in earnest, and within the next few months Karinska—shuttling between Paris and Monte Carlo with her entourage of Russian seamstresses—made the costumes for three more ballets, all of which premiered during the company's first season in Monte Carlo that April. *La Concurrence,* choreographed by Balanchine, included decor, costumes, and a libretto by the painter André Derain and music commissioned from Georges Auric. The rather dispensable plot involved a rivalry between two tailors and required a large cast of townspeople and children (played by

Monte Carlo, 1930s. From left, front: Karinska, Alicia Markova, Boris Kochno, Comte Etienne de Beaumont, Tatiana Chamié; rear: Eugenia Delarova, Igor Youskevitch, Christian Bérard, Léonide Massine.

Karinska with her seamstresses and her nephew, Lawrence Vlady, making costumes in "the cave" underneath the opera house in Monte Carlo, in the early 1930s.

Irina Baronova in a costume designed by André Derain for Balanchine's La Concurrence, *1932.*

adults) attired in a vast array of elegant and witty costumes, many etched with swirling black filigree. *Le Bourgeois Gentilhomme,* the first of two versions of this ballet Karinska would dress for Balanchine, was based on Alexandre Benois's sumptuous designs. *Jeux d'Enfants,* choreographed by Léonide Massine, displayed scenery and costumes that were designed by Joan Miró. His charming designs were interpreted in knitted wool unitards and hoods with asymmetric stripes and swirls in primary colors that perfectly complemented Kochno's libretto about a child's playroom come to life, and the ballet presented a stark modern contrast to the ornate finery of *Le Bourgeois Gentilhomme.*

All these ballets, the first with which Karinska was associated, were examples of Diaghilev's method of theatrical collaboration: choreographer, composer, painter, costumer, and librettist—all artists in their own right—worked hand in hand to create one unified vision. It was a process that became increasingly simplified—often for financial reasons—as the century proceeded, with Balanchine leading the way with his pared-down, abstract ballets.

Over the course of the next two decades Karinska would costume twenty new productions for the de Basil company, working alongside such artists as Raoul Dufy, Etienne de Beaumont, André Masson, Tchelitchew, Giorgio de Chirico, Pierre Roy,

Sketches by Jean Hugo for Les Cents Baisers,
and Irina Baronova and Paul Petroff in the costumes,
1935.

Natalia Gontcharova, Oliver Messel, and Cecil Beaton. Thus Karinska's teachers and collaborators were neither sewers, couturiers, nor even costume designers but rather many of the great visual artists of the day. This is an important distinction whose effect on Karinska's work—her approach and her standards—cannot be overestimated. It provided an education in style, taste, and sophistication upon which all her future work would be based.

She also recostumed old productions and traveled with the Ballets Russes as wardrobe supervisor on their tours. Arnold Haskell, then a young man who invented and then exemplified the word balletomane, was along for the company's first American tour in 1933. Inspired by Karinska's stalwart behavior in the midst of a shipful of seasick dancers, he wrote this portrait for his 1977 memoir, *Balletomania*:

In the Green Room, Madame Karinska is in complete control, trying on costumes and superintending a whole company of tailors. I feel that she should be on the stage and not under it; as beautiful as any of our dancers, during the journey she earned the name "Princess." No matter how rough, there was the Princess at eleven each morning, walking up and down the deck as calm and elegant as if she had been in the Bois [de Boulogne]. This businesswoman-artist from Russia has stormed the city of dressmakers and won. The work of the great decorative artists of the day is entrusted to her; and they admire her beauty, enjoy the wit of her conversation, and trust her completely.[10]

Ever true to her profession, Karinska was always impeccably dressed in what was to become a uniform that she would wear tirelessly her entire life. Although she did not like Coco Chanel personally (they had occasion to meet more than once through mutual friends), she adored the designer's suits and in her later years always wore a classic dark blue one (she owned many, sometimes replicating them herself, sometimes ordering them from Paris) together with a silk blouse with a large soft bow at the neck and a pillbox hat and veil. This relatively simple garb was gussied up with a profusion of rather heavy, dangling jewelry—often large amethysts or religious tokens. The fourteen-year-old Irina Baronova, a young ballerina with the Ballets Russes, was so impressed with Karinska's chic that on her first tour to America she emptied Bergdorf Goodman's paste cabinets with her paycheck and arrived at the theater one evening with her small, young frame weighted down by gigantic clanging jewelry. It was her homage to Karinska, and no one, including the object of this homage, said a word; they just smiled.

§

It was around this time that Karinska made her first tutu for an American dancer. Twenty-three-year-old Agnes de Mille was about to make her Parisian debut on a rather shabby rented stage in a concert performance featuring some of her first choreography, but her costume for the solo entitled "Stagefright" had wilted from age and use. When de Mille inquired at Madame Egorova's studio (where she was taking class) where she might take the tutu for repair, she was given an address on the rue de Trevise. "Karinska was charming and businesslike," said de Mille. When she returned to pick up the finished tutu, it was sitting in lonely splendor in the center of Karinska's large round dining table, covering it like a huge yellow sunflower.[11]

OPPOSITE:
Le Triomphe de Suzanne. *A self-portrait,*
with Karinska, by the designer and painter Tom Keogh.
The title may refer to Karinska's admiration
of Saint Suzanne.

Le Triomphe de Suzanne

By November 1932 critical success and earnings allowed Karinska to establish her first official atelier at 9 rue Roy in Paris's fashionable eighth arrondissement. She registered the studio in her daughter Irene's name—a gesture full of foresight, considering that within a relatively short time she would leave France and Irene would take over the atelier. (During the next few years programs would often credit "I. Karinsky" for costume execution, though it was clearly Karinska's work.)

The following spring the shop was flooded with commissions. There were three new ballets for the Ballets Russes in April, all choreographed by Massine, the company's new ballet master. These were the controversial symphonic work *Les Présages,* designed by André Masson; *Beach,* designed by Raoul Dufy; and *Scuola di Ballo,* designed by Etienne de Beaumont. Despite the enormous success of Balanchine's tenure at the Ballets Russes—or perhaps because of it—differences had arisen between the young choreographer and the management team of de Basil and René Blum, and Balanchine had departed, with Kochno, after only several months' work.

In June 1933 Paris audiences were presented with two rival companies, the Ballets Russes and Kochno and Balanchine's new venture, Les Ballets 1933, the first company Balanchine had directed. Because of its then-radical declaration of new artistic priorities and innovations, this small company has had an influence on ballet in this century as deep as its existence was brief. Starting with a total lack of funds, the troupe had scarcely a hope of finding a theater until Edward James, a wealthy British patron, decided to sponsor the fledgling company—a generous gesture inspired, in part, by his desire to win back his estranged wife, Tilly Losch, who was slated to appear in several of the ballets. Personal reasons notwithstanding, the beautiful Théâtre des Champs-Elysées was booked, and a formidable group of artists was assembled to design the ballets. Derain executed charming designs for *Les Songes* and *Fastes,* Caspar Rudolph Neher designed hard-edged cabaret costumes for *Les Sept Péchés Capitaux,* Tchelitchew devised dark and dramatic swathed robes to signify "the restraining forces of the earth"[12] for *L'Errante,* and Bérard designed exquisite, aerial tutus and sprouting head feathers for *Mozartiana.* In his ideas for the sixth and least successful ballet in the repertory, *Les Valses de Beethoven,* another young designer provided little competition for the other artists, as recounted by Diana (Gould) Menuhin, one of the ballet's unhappy performers.

A rich and not very gifted South American called Emilio Terry designed a dotty decor and hideous costumes. There were four elements: Earth, Air, Fire and Water. I was Earth in a deplorable sort of chiton in Bovril-colored chiffon (Old Mother Manure, I called myself). Standing dismally for hours while the magnificent Karinska, the dressmaker, dripping with amethysts, would drape and redrape, muttering the while, somewhat hampered by a mouthful of pins: 'Ach, Boje moi! Kak oojus' [*sic*], which meaning 'Oh my God, how awful' did nothing to cheer me on my way.

On the opening night, trembling with nerves, we were still awaiting the head-dresses backstage, the audience clapping with impatience and panic all around. At last Karinska arrived in a flurry and a taxi. She handed me a monstrous sort of cairn at least two-foot high and made of plaster and mud. I put it on my head, tears pouring down my face . . . and ran, knees knocking, to take up my lonely position onstage. . . . [13]

Tamara Grigorieva in Léonide Massine's
Les Présages, *1933.*

Scuola di Ballo *designed by Comte Etienne de Beaumont, 1933.*

OVERLEAF, LEFT:
Sketches by André Derain for Les Songes, *1933; (above, left to right) the Knave, the Acrobat; (below) the Ballerina, a Coryphée.*

OVERLEAF, RIGHT:
(Above, left to right) Roman Jasinsky as the Acrobat; the cast in the ballet, with the Knaves on the left and right and Tamara Toumanova, as the Ballerina, lying on the stage; (below) the five Coryphées: Nathalie Leslie, Tamara Tchinarova, Tamara Sidorenko, Tatiana Semenova, and Galina Sidorenko.

23

Sketch by Christian Bérard for Balanchine's Mozartiana *and Tamara Toumanova and Roman Jasinsky in the finished costumes, 1933.*

Sketch by Pavel Tchelitchew for Tilly Losch's costume in Balanchine's L'Errante *and Daphne Vane in the American Ballet production, 1935.*

Lincoln Kirstein, the future cofounder, with Balanchine, of the New York City Ballet, was in the audience for those historic performances of Les Ballets 1933 and, monster headdresses aside, put the overall atmosphere in perspective:

[The company's] dozen or so evenings of ballet in London and Paris in the summer of 1933 were, in reality, the swan song of the Diaghilev period. Here was real artistic discovery, real theatrical invention, true collaboration on Diaghilev's own ground, even without him. It could not have been greatly different even had he been alive to supervise the scene, for every new talent of the day, with the possible exception of Salvador Dalí, and the surrealists (who had refused on ideological grounds to be included), was somehow involved.[14]

It was during the costuming of the six Balanchine ballets that comprised the short-lived company's entire repertory that Karinska and Balanchine's friendship and mutual artistic regard was sealed. They would not, however, work together again for seven years. In late 1933 Balanchine, at Kirstein's invitation, came to America to found an American ballet company, while Karinska remained in Europe, where her work took a new direction.

CHAPTER TWO

Lady Iya Abdy in a costume designed by Balthus from Les Cenci, *a play by Antonin Artaud, 1935.*

OPPOSITE:

Louis Jouvet as Arnolphe in Molière's L'Ecole des Femmes, *1936, designed by Christian Bérard. In an innovative move, Karinska used netlike horsehair fabric to achieve the desired historical affect of the actor's overcoat, yet keeping the costume lightweight.*

In April 1934 Louis Jouvet, the charismatic actor, producer, and director who was to become a great force in French theater and film — introducing the impressionistic plays of Jean Giraudoux and reintroducing the plays of Molière — was directing the premiere of a play he had commissioned from Jean Cocteau. *La Machine Infernale* was to be a version of the Oedipus legend presented as never before, with a tone described by Colette as "intimate phantasmagoria."[15] Cocteau introduced Jouvet to Bérard, who would design the sets and costumes, and Bérard in turn introduced Jouvet to Karinska. It was decided that Karinska would execute the men's costumes and that Jeanne Lanvin, a much better known couturier at the time, would execute the women's. Whatever Karinska's true opinion about this division of labor, her response indicated only a concern that the result would not be homogeneous: she suggested that Lanvin should make all the costumes. As a result, Karinska was given the entire commission.

The production is, for many reasons, a landmark in the history of French theater. Featuring young Jean-Pierre Aumont as Oedipus, Marthe Regnier as Jocasta, and Pierre Renoir as Tiresias, the play stunned Paris. Cocteau wrote of Karinska in the program:

I intend to express my thanks to Madame Karinsky and the Messieurs Rodier as true poets. [Rodier, the textile design firm, provided the fabrics and draperies in Act II.] With a masterful eye, Madame Karinsky has seized the gouaches of Bérard, from the queen-idol Jocasta to the young messenger of Corinth who crosses plague-ridden Thebes with the sun-drenched wings of misfortune, and transports them in this world and in this age of myth in which precision is no more than the sense of truth in itself, a kind of mysterious balance between life and death. . . . It seems to me that this surpasses by far the role of mere costume-designers; and this deserves our respect and our gratitude.[16]

Later that year Karinska collaborated with Jouvet on the costumes for two more plays — Jean Giraudoux's *Amphitryon 38,* designed by A. M. Cassandre, and *Tessa,* Giraudoux's adaptation of Margaret Kennedy's novel *The Constant Nymph,* with costume designs by Dimitri Bouchène. In this present-day story about the terrible and sometimes tragic price of love, Karinska for the first and only time dressed Jouvet in simple contemporary clothes, including sweaters, trousers, and black tie.

A year and a half later, plunged back several centuries, Jouvet was again dressed by Bérard, care of Karinska. This time, however, he was given reason to voice serious concerns about his costume. For Arnolphe, the bumbling husband in Molière's *L'Ecole des Femmes,* Bérard made a sketch depicting a long ornate overcoat that somehow allowed the breeches underneath to show through. Whether this strange

Collaborators on Jean Cocteau's La Machine
Infernale, 1934. *Top from left: Maurice (who built
the sets), Cocteau, Eric Erickson (fashion illustrator
for* Vogue*), Horst; middle from left: Mariel Khill
(a friend of Cocteau's who appeared in the play),
Madame de Séréville (an editor at French* Vogue*);
bottom from left: Karinska, Christian Bérard (who
designed the sets and costumes), Mrs. Erickson (wife
of Eric).*

*Jean-Pierre Aumont and Robert le Vigan in the
production, which Colette described as "intimate
phantasmagoria."*

OPPOSITE:
Pierre Fresnay in Edouard Bourdet's play Margot, 1935.

Pierre Dux and Lise Delamare in the Comédie Française's production of Corneille's L'Illusion Comique, 1937. The folded ribboned rows of Dux's breeches reappeared on Broadway—nine years later—in shameless profusion as Bobby Clark's coat in The Would-be Gentleman (see page 58).

Alfred Adam, Madeline Ozeray, and Romain Bouquet in Jean Giraudoux's Electre, 1937. The yarn details on the costumes were a Karinska trademark.

detail was by conscious design or artistic license is not known, but Karinska proceeded to work as she always did with an artist's maquette—with absolute precision and independence. By now an expert in textures and fabrics, she was able to reproduce this transparent coat using horsehair, a flexible, lightweight, woven material that was usually used invisibly in the linings of men's jackets, for styling hats, and for hemming dresses to lend body and shape without adding weight. Horsehair had always been a sewing aid, not an end in itself—until Karinska's exhaustive search for special effects led her to bypass the rules.

Jouvet as Arnolphe, in his long rippling wig and transparent coat, became the actor's signature image. The play ran for 446 performances in Paris. During the German wartime occupation of the city, Jouvet and his company toured with it in South America and later, in 1951, brought the play to the United States. And always there was the horsehair, yards of it for all to see, visible in all its glorious invisibility. It was to become one of Karinska's well-known "secrets," and over the next several decades she lovingly and tenaciously put horsehair center stage. The unconventional transparent fabric could be found in costumes and headpieces from opera to Broadway to ballet.

The following year Karinska prepared the costumes for two more Jouvet/Bérard productions, Pierre Corneille's L'Illusion Comique and Giraudoux's Electre. It was these numerous collaborations with Jouvet that Karinska always looked back on as her first real successes. Under such circumstances of great mutual respect for each other's craft her own abilities flourished. Her allegiance to and personal adoration of Louis Jouvet—and her steadfast belief in his integrity as a director—may now be seen as having been a significant prelude to the association she would have later with Balanchine.

Although Karinska did not work with Jouvet after 1937, affectionate contact between them was maintained through letters. In 1949, after the sudden death of Bérard, Jouvet was frantic about his upcoming production of Tartuffe, which Bérard was to have designed. While ultimately unable to create the costumes (she was busy making her own first designs for Balanchine in New York), there was extensive correspondence between Jouvet and Karinska—his typed, hers in a sweeping theatrical hand—in which the two discussed who might fill Bérard's shoes. The search was long and desperate and demonstrates the stoic desolation of collaborative artists who have lost a soulmate . . . but must get back to work. (Everyone from Karinska, Derain, and Tchelitchew to Eugene Berman, Esteban Francés, and Emilio Terry was considered. Ultimately, George Braque designed the sets, and Karinska's daughter, Irene—in collaboration with her mother—made the costumes.)[17]

When Karinska heard of Jouvet's unexpected death in 1951 she was in France with her grandchildren. After weeping for several days she erected in her home a small altar of photographs and candles, an homage to this man who changed her life. Those who knew Karinska in her later years speak of having had an overwhelming sense that, though she did not speak of him often, Louis Jouvet had been a pivotal influence for her. If her behavior suggests the possibility of a love affair between the two, it is because their mutual love of theater carried the passion and dedication that is usually reserved for more personal entanglements of the heart.

§

In early 1936 Karinska had begun to work in London, leaving her Paris shop to be run by the twenty-five-year-old Irene. Her reasons for moving were various: she found more work in England at the time; the Ballets Russes was having frequent seasons at Covent Garden; the new Markova-Dolin company gave her commissions as well as some financial backing for an atelier; and the London couturier world was welcoming, while Chanel and Schiaparelli dominated the Parisian scene. Also, Léon Blum's short-lived socialist government had come into power in the spring of 1936, and Karinska's business probably suffered—as did Chanel's—from the sudden proliferation of labor strikes. As a White Russian, however apolitical, Karinska may have been a special target for the extreme left wing of the labor movement, and in any case she would have feared the general economic disruptions in France during those years.

Karinska's first notable commission in England came from a young Cecil Beaton, who, as a great admirer of Bérard's and Tchelitchew's, was adamant about having Karinska execute his first theatrical designs. "The First Shoot, A Tragedy," a ballet made for the great British impresario Charles B. Cochran's 1935–36 revue *Follow the Sun*,[18] marked the beginning of a long friendship and collaboration that would culminate thirty years later at New York's Metropolitan Opera in productions of *Turandot* and *La Traviata*. But their initial collaboration was much more modest—and definitely more amusing. The dancing was choreographed by young Frederick Ashton to music by William Walton. The libretto was written by Osbert Sitwell, who explained his intent to Beaton this way:

Sketch and costumes by Cecil Beaton for The First Shoot, A Tragedy, *a ballet in a C. B. Cochran revue, 1936.*

We want to observe in everything that faint line of parodied resemblance to the "Lac des Cygnes" (pheasant feather opposed to swans) . . . to be done by sudden bursts of idiot mirth in the middle of melancholy, love-soaked passages. . . . Anyhow, we must make it magnificent, and not to be forgotten![19]

While it is by now well forgotten, Beaton, in his memoir *Ballet,* re-creates the event with affection.

To my surprise the whole thing turned out to be delightfully straightforward. To begin with I had worked out the general scheme with Frederick Ashton on a piece of notepaper, sketching in the dancers in conventional ballet skirts. But the choreographer said at once, "No tutus!" I simply removed the skirts on the design, and the effect was charming.

I was fortunate in that the costumes were made by Madame Karinska, the dressmaker who had made tutus for all the Diaghilev dancers, and for Pavlova herself.[20] Karinska has that rare genius for being able to interpret an artist's sketches in such a way as to produce exactly the effect required, while at the same time making costumes in which dancers can perform without the freedom of their movements being in any way hampered.

When I saw what she had made of my sketches, I was both astonished and delighted. The caped coats and suits of plus-fours worn by the male members of the balletic shoot were of theatrically interpreted tweeds which Karinska fabricated with large painted checks and bold stripes, emphasized by heavy stitching in coarse wool. On the dresses worn by the chorus, who represented pheasants, she stitched pieces of mica (her own idea) to reproduce the sheen of feathers.[21]

A few weeks after the revue opened at the Adelphi more Beaton/Karinska costumes could be seen on display at the nearby Sadler's Wells Theatre. There Ashton was enjoying his first season as the choreographer for the Vic-Wells Ballet (later the Royal Ballet). In *Apparitions* he created a neo-Romantic work to the music of Franz Liszt that starred Robert Helpmann as the Poet and the sixteen-year-old Margot Fonteyn, in one of her first important roles, as his unattainable vision of love. Beaton designed an exquisite ball gown for Fonteyn that featured masks and skulls buried among its flowery excesses.

The ballet was a big success and did much to establish the young British company as a viable alternative to the Ballets Russes. It was deemed by composer Constant Lambert, who devised its murky libretto, to "knock spots off any ballet since *Cotillon.*"[22] The subject of poets and their elusive muses was a popular one, and if several ballets—Massine's *Symphonie Fantastique* with designs by Bérard for de Basil's company or Bronislava Nijinska's *The Beloved One (La Bien-Aimée)* revived for Markova-Dolin, for example—evoked similar Romantic atmospheres, it was no accident: all had been costumed by Karinska. With her unwavering quality, she was, ironically, beginning to form links among rival companies.

§

In a letter to Beaton, who was absent for the premiere of *Apparitions,* Constant Lambert commented on what was to become as predictable a Karinska trademark as the quality and fit of her costumes. She was late, always late.

The dress rehearsal was too depressing. Half the costumes were unfinished, the atmosphere was dead and one felt the awful weight of middle-brow opinion against the whole thing. But when we opened there was the most marvelous atmosphere in the house . . . and the ballet went over as a whole with real dramatic suspense all the time. . . . I am sure you would have

Sketch by Cecil Beaton for Frederick Ashton's ballet Apparitions *and Margot Fonteyn (opposite), at age seventeen, in one of her first leading roles, 1936.*

RIGHT:
Karinska fitting Tatiana Riabouchinska for Le Pavillon, *with Cecil Beaton, the designer of the ballet, 1936.*

Anatole Vilzak in Don Juan, *c. 1936.*

Tatiana Riabouchinska in Le Coq d'Or, *1937.*

been delighted with how your work looked. Karinska, although dreadfully behindhand, did the costumes superbly.[23]

Later that year Beaton was commissioned by the Ballets Russes to design a ballet choreographed by David Lichine entitled *Le Pavillon* and here, in conspiracy with Karinska, her reputation for tardiness was used as an alibi. Kochno's libretto specified a glade to be filled with dancers representing various flora, birds, and insects, and Beaton had designed some very blue costumes onto which various wings, skirts, and flowers were to be added. Kochno thought the simple blue underskirts perfect and insisted they be left unadorned for the premiere. Hurt, Beaton went to Karinska after the premiere and, paying her out of his own pocket, arranged to have the costumes secretly altered to match his original vision for the next performance.

She agreed and immediately got to work on the brilliant bird wings, flowers and overskirts. When they were ready she surreptitiously removed the costumes from the dressing-rooms, completed the alterations, and returned them only ten minutes before the ballet was due to start. I enjoyed watching the consternation among the corps de ballet when they saw their new costumes. Some, in fury, tried to wrench from the skirts the glittering bird-wings that had been added. But Madame Karinska had done her job thoroughly; the new additions were made with the idea of a long tour in view and were fastened securely.[24]

While Beaton felt that his reputation had been salvaged, de Basil was furious about the disobedience. Sono Osato gives a third point of view, the dancers':

The overall nature of the work shifted from the pretentious to the outright ridiculous when Beaton's set appeared at the first orchestra rehearsal. It looked like a ladies' room of a swanky nightclub rather than the trysting place for a poet and his beloved. Irina [Baronova] put it bluntly, "Look like pissoir!"
We wafted around this dubious setting as Spirits of the Garden, striving to look

"spiritual" while nearly being choked by the elastic bands under our chins that held large flowers onto our caps. The constricting headdress made it impossible to hear as well as to swallow.[25]

Pleasing both dancer and designer, usually one of Karinska's specialties, was evidently impossible on this occasion. Beaton, however, was so entranced with Karinska's small nature re-creations that he asked her to make artificial flowers grow out of the grass-green carpet, and birds perch on the curtains, at his country house at Ashcombe. A year later she made costumes and masks for a "fête champêtre" at the house. The tables were dressed as ballerinas, and the masks were distorted birds and flowers from Salvador Dalí's imagination.[26]

Images of tardiness abound in Karinska lore. The costumes were so late for the premiere of the Ballets Russes production of *Le Coq d'Or* at Covent Garden (the royal family was in attendance, among other notables) that while the nervous dancers waited in tights, makeup, and headpieces, de Basil, in desperation as the intermission extended to almost an hour, called the fire department. Minutes later, Karinska, her assistants, and the costumes were delivered in ambulances, sirens blaring, to the stage door. But that was not the end of it. Many dancers went onstage with pins still holding the seams together—which made for prickly dancing and blood-spotted waists—while Karinska and her helpers stood in the wings, needles and thread in hand, for mid-performance repairs. Nevertheless, the ballet was a huge success, with endless curtain calls, and Karinska's reputation for magnificence was only enhanced by the last-minute drama.

Alicia Markova describes the exquisite Bérard/Karinska creation for her role as Spirit of the Air and Sky in the Massine ballet *La Septième Symphonie*:

A ravishing costume of all-over white silk tights with, over them, a sensational chiffon skirt which was cut "on the cross" with invisible white horsehair woven in to it so that the fabric moved like clouds. The silk chiffon of the skirt was a clear sky-blue with faintest pink clouds appliquéd on to it. It fastened at the waist with a blue and pink band, while a cloud was also appliquéd on my breast, covering one shoulder. The costume was a work of art.[27]

. . . When it was finally assembled. The skirt—without bodice or headpiece—arrived ten minutes before the curtain was to rise, and Bérard himself had to perform an instant cut, wrap, and stitch job to finish the costume. Tamara Toumanova's mother went even further when her daughter's costume for a flying-across-the-stage-on-wires sequence in *Symphonie Fantastique,* also designed by Bérard, had been entirely forgotten. She simply wrapped her daughter up in yards of loose tulle and sent her hurtling on her way. This was not the only missing costume that evening, as Sono Osato recounts in her memoir *Distant Dances*.

We arrived at the theater early that night to dress, only to be told that most of the costumes had not been delivered yet from Mme. Karinska, the costumer. Onstage, the dancers in the first movement had been dressed as visions of melancholy and gaiety, while the rest of us paced anxiously in the dressing room, wearing only shoes, tights, and makeup, with our jitters mounting as each bar of music came closer to the unclad entrance. At the last minute a

David Lichine in Protée, 1938. The costumes and scenery were designed by Giorgio de Chirico.

Igor Youskevitch and Alicia Markova in Christian Bérard's costumes for La Septième Symphonie, 1938. Markova recalls the "sensational chiffon skirt which was 'cut on the cross' with invisible white horsehair woven in to it so that the fabric moved like clouds."

caravan of taxis came screeching into Floral Street. Karinska's assistants jumped out, arms bulging with white hoop-skirts and tall, transparent headdresses. As they rushed into the dressing room, we snatched our gowns out of their hands, pulled them over our heads, and ran through the basement in a flurry of pale petticoats, reaching the stage just as the lights came up on the second movement.[28]

On the other hand, Karinska was able to work very quickly when the pressure was on, as proven by the time her atelier remade the entire wardrobe for Fokine's *Don Juan* in only nine days when the original had been burned in a fire just prior to the premiere.

§

By 1937 Karinska had split from Madame Hayward, a well-known dressmaker with whom she had shared her London atelier, and—with the support of the Markova-Dolin company and their patron Mrs. Laura Henderson (who owned The Windmill, a variety theater)—established her own workrooms at Reynold's House, an elegant Georgian town house not far from Covent Garden. Her reputation was by now considerable on both sides of the Channel, both on and off the stage, and the fashion world was taking note. A *Harper's Bazaar* reviewer applauded Karinska's chic, quilted-satin "bedroom booties" and said of her: "Defiant and headstrong, never taking one word of advice, she is now the most exciting and ingenious, the most wildly imaginative costumer in Paris."[29] Lesley Blanch, writing in British *Vogue*, listed Karinska as one of five exceptional "Women of Achievement" and described her as "a contradiction in terms, for though she is in appearance the personification of the Rococo, an ornately pretty frivolous and mercurial creature, in her work she represents an executive force which has become one of the most powerful influences in the art of theatrical costume today." Blanch continued:

Why should her costumes make everybody else's look like well-intentioned Parish Hall Charades? I think the secret lies in the emotional, almost telepathic sympathy of her interpretations. The mood of a costume is as important to her as its epoch. She knows the value of deliberate under- or over-statement. She will echo the stylization of a production by the stylization of her costumes.[30]

During these years Karinska took on commissions in every possible period style. She dressed Charles Boyer in archducal garb for the film *The Tragedy of Mayerling*, Marlene Dietrich in both gowns and rags for *Knight Without Armor*, the young Vivien Leigh in Elizabethan neck ruffles for *Fire Over England* (the film in which Leigh met Laurence Olivier), and Merle Oberon in Greek drapes for the unfinished *I, Claudius*. For Cochran's 1937 Coronation Revue *Home and Beauty* she executed the costumes for various acts, including those of the Lovers, Belles, and Beaux in "At the Music Room Window," negligees for "Julika Kadar's Bedroom," and robes for Abbots, Knights, and Angels in "The Tapestry Room." She also dressed "Mr. Cochran's Young Ladies" in such numbers as "Peckin' and Posin'" and "The Greeks Had a Word for It," performances staged by the brilliant American dancer Buddy Bradley and Antony Tudor, the British choreographer, for Cochran's late-night supper shows at the Trocadero Grillroom at Piccadilly Circus.

Vivien Leigh, Laurence Olivier, and Robert Newton in the film Fire Over England, *1937.*

At the height of all this success the fifty-two-year-old Karinska fell in love. According to John Braden, a close friend in her later years, her beau was a man named Vallejo Gantner, a debonair American—many years her junior—from a wealthy San Francisco family. Gantner had been living in London making the social rounds and pursuing an acting career. When he returned to San Francisco in early 1939 Karinska followed. Under the auspices of a ballet company tour, she sailed to New York and traveled by train to the West Coast. Gantner's family—owners of a lucrative swimwear business—had their own plans for him and they did not include marriage to an older Russian divorcée who labored in the theater for a living. Soon an announcement was made of Vallejo's engagement to an appropriate young debutante, and Karinska found herself in America with neither work nor the prospect of finding any as Europe headed into war against Hitler.

While Irene continued to manage the Paris atelier, Reynold's House, due to Karinska's absence, was closed on April 1, 1939. As she told it later—leaving out the story of her affair with Gantner—her permanent transfer to American soil was not by her own design but rather, like her exodus from Russia, because of the political circumstances of the day. She had no money to speak of, and her reputation in London and Paris meant little in American theatrical circles. So once again, as she had sixteen years earlier upon arriving in Paris, she started over. That she was able to virtually reconstruct her life several times was a great source of pride for Karinska. "Who could have done what I did," she would remark to her friends on rare occasions of self-assessment. While the move to America was the last time Karinska had to adapt to a new culture, she would go bankrupt several more times, thanks usually to the expenses of her work—an area in which she would not compromise, often going so far as to subsidize productions herself to achieve the quality she required.

CHAPTER THREE

From this point forward the story of Karinska's life becomes the story of her work. In this regard the new world proved a surreal one. Her first commission in the United States, in May of 1939, was for, not a tutu, but a sixty-foot-long serpent that was to feature as one of many creatures floating in the subconscious fetal world of Salvador Dalí's extraordinary exhibition at the 1939 World's Fair in New York. The young Spaniard had taken the city by storm, first in a show at the Julien Levy gallery, then in his famous surreal window displays at Bonwit Teller (during the staging of one of these he fell through a window in a rather real way), and now in this showcase of the watery gurglings of the womb. Karinska's dragon—hurriedly devised from a suede carcass filled with rubber balls and covered with scales—was transported to Flushing in two tandem taxis and later, after the fair, was sold to China, presumably for festivities of a more conventional sort. This was not the last Dalí/Karinska collaboration, and in the next her sculptural ingenuity would be tested to its limits.

When Serge Denham's Ballet Russe (a different company from de Basil's)[31] arrived in New York late that autumn—having beaten a hasty retreat from London when war was declared against Hitler on September 3—they were without the costumes for a scheduled November premiere, and Karinska, who had made many costumes for them in Monte Carlo, was summoned. Prior to the company's departure Coco Chanel had been at work executing Dalí's designs for the troupe's production of a new Massine ballet entitled *Bacchanale,* set in the elaborate world of mad King Ludwig II of Bavaria to the music of Richard Wagner. With only copies of the original sketches to go by, Karinska, undaunted by the difficulty of realizing in material Dalí's painted inventions, re-created sixty costumes in one week.

The ballet was dubbed the first "paranoiac performance" but in truth the atmosphere was "more hysterical" than paranoiac.[32] The costumes were late, of course, and when they did arrive, after an extended intermission of forty-five minutes and several repetitions of the overture, shock and confusion reigned. Not only did many of the elaborate structures sport enormous breasts and other unmistakably sexual adornments, but the dancers literally could not see how they should fit inside them. The production was a cause célèbre, not only for its balletic artistry, but for its visual impact. Here Karinska did not concern herself with any established notions of beauty. Instead she demonstrated her enormous knowledge of malleable materials, soft fabrics being only the most conventional of the textiles she chose. The production was an exercise in architecture and sculptural molding—appliqué in the fourth dimension.

Sketch by Salvador Dalí for Bacchanale and,
as finished costumes, the Umbrella figure (above)
and three tree figures (left), 1939.

OVERLEAF:

Ballet Russe de Monte Carlo, c. 1945. © Irving Penn

1. Lawrence Vlady, Costumer
2. James Griffith, Master Carpenter
3. Sophie Pourmel, Directrice of Costumes
4. M. Hornyak, Assistant to Director
5. Yvonne Chouteau, Dancer
6. Claire Pasch, Dancer
7. Joy Williams, Dancer
8. Maria Tallchief, Dancer
9. Alexandra Danilova, Prima Ballerina
10. Emanuel Balaban, Conductor
11. George Ford, Company Manager
12. Rachel Chapman, Pianiste-Repetiteur
13. Frederic Franklin, Principal Dancer and Maître de Ballet
14. S. J. Denham, Director
15. Nicolas Magallenes, Dancer
16. Nathalie Krassovska, Dancer
17. Leon Danielian, Dancer
18. Todd Bolender, Choreographer
19. Ruthanna Boris, Dancer
20. Michel Katcharoff, Dancer
21. Eugene Berman, Designer
22. Jerome Moross, Composer
23. Ivan Boutnikoff, Conductor
24. Lewis Smith, Chief Electrician
25. Barbara Karinska, Costumer
26. George Balanchine, Choreographer
27. Boris Aronson, Designer
28. Agnes de Mille, Choreographer
29. Vittorio Rieti, Composer
30. Jean Cerrone, Executive Assistant

There was a woman with a rose-colored fishhead. Lola Montez wore harem trousers with a hoop skirt decorated with false teeth. The Knight of Death turned out to be an immense perambulating umbrella. Later, when Ludwig died, a whole set of umbrellas opened on stage. Prudish audiences blushed to behold the male ensemble with large red lobsters (as sex symbols) on their tights, and Nini Theilade, portraying Venus, created a sensation because she seemed totally nude. In actuality, she wore flesh-colored tights from her neck to her toes.[33]

Three days later, in an attempt to give their American audience an American theme, the company premiered *Ghost Town,* with music by Richard Rodgers. While

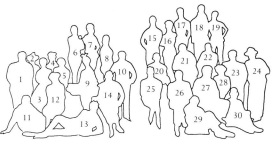

41

Mrs. William Rhinelander Stewart, photographed by George Hoyningen-Huene for Harper's Bazaar, *in a white silk jersey gown designed by Karinska for the Beaux-Arts Diamond Ball on January 26, 1940. The baroque scrolls were made from baked rubber, echoing Karinska's work on Salvador Dalí's designs for* Bacchanale *the previous year.*

OPPOSITE:

Sketch by Kenneth Paul Block of an Edwardian gown designed and made by Karinska for Gloria Vanderbilt.

Pale blue chiffon gown with black lace cockle shells, designed by Karinska, photographed by George Hoyningen-Huene for Harper's Bazaar, *1940.*

WATCH FOR THESE TWO NAMES

Karinska, famed designer of costumes for the ballet, now creates for the private world as well. Below: she places black lace cockle-shells on a pale blue chiffon dress

Jewels on both pages from Mermod-Jaccard-King, St. Louis

one critic found it "as American as a Russian Grand Duchess in dude ranch clothes,"[34] it was a significant production for Karinska: it was her first taste of Americana, a genre that fascinated her and which she would clothe to perfection later in Agnes de Mille's *Rodeo* and, very differently, in Balanchine's *Western Symphony*.

§

Baron Nicolas de Gunzburg, a professional acquaintance from Karinska's Parisian days, had also escaped to New York, and it was in collaboration with him that Karinska would embark on one of her most extravagant—albeit short-lived—ventures. The baron was an aristocratic Russian who had to his credit a European education, money, and impeccable taste in women's clothes. He had been one of the most dashing young boulevardiers and orchestrators of evenings of elegant fun in prewar Paris, including the Bals des Valses (A Night at Schönbrunn), which he hosted in June of 1934. The festivities on this legendary evening began at midnight on an island in the Bois de Boulogne, to which guests dressed as historical figures from the Imperial Hapsburg court of Vienna were wafted in a boat lined with hay. De Gunzburg appeared as Archduke Rudolf, Denise Bourdet as his beloved Marie Vetsera, Prince Faucigny-Lucinge as Emperor Franz Josef, Baba Lucinge as Empress Elizabeth, Carlos de Beistegui as Ludwig of Bavaria, and the photographer Horst as a Hungarian Black Hussar. The costumes were all designed by Bérard and executed by Karinska.[35]

Thus already familiar with her talent, de Gunzburg now teamed up with Karinska and the aristocratic Princess Natasha Paley to open a couturier house with backing from Paley's husband, producer John Wilson. The trio of sophisticated Russians caught the fancy of the press and the public alike, and when the shop opened in the summer of 1940, on 56th Street just off Fifth Avenue, reporters from *Vogue* and *Harper's Bazaar* were in attendance to witness the great unveiling. It was Karinska's first and last retail shop. (In both Paris and London her business had been conducted in a salon—as was the custom of couturiers at the time—behind a door marked only by a discreet brass plate.[36]) Behind the show curtains, however, there was great consternation; things were not ready, and Karinska was to be found madly crocheting lace collars, cuffs, and hems to provide original ornament on some rather less-than-original little black dresses.

The press, fortunately, reported only triumph, and for the following eight or nine months "Karinska, Inc." appeared to be a total success, with frequent full-page photographs of her gowns—clearly not those little black dresses—often modeled by the gorgeous Princess Paley. There was a line of silk lingerie with handmade lace and cockleshell-shaped bosoms; there was a Giorgio de Chirico–style strapless gown designed for Mrs. Rhinelander Stewart made of "white silk jersey with baroque scrolls made of baked rubber"[37] (perhaps influenced by Karinska's recent cram course in Dalí dimensions); there was a shawl of "chartreuse celanese rayon jersey, embroidered with colorful yarns" that, according to a *Bazaar* account, "launched one of the most successful fashions in years."[38] And, finally, there were numerous witty accessories—a "snappy" and "tantalizing" purse, glove, and umbrella set of snakeskin, black suede, and silk, and—in an unmistakably Karinskaesque touch—the

Baron Nicolas de Gunzburg and Natasha Paley Wilson, Karinska's associates, in the window of their shop, "Karinska's," located on East 56th Street between Madison and Fifth avenues.

crocheted wool flowers once sold to the Folies-Bergère for barely a sou and later sewn into Cecil Beaton's grass carpets again raised their dainty heads. They were to be found growing on shoes, shawls, muffs, and even a necklace "in all the colors you've ever wanted,"[39] according to *Bazaar*. A bargain department was even established downstairs for those who "have passed Karinska, Inc. several times with dejected longing because her beautiful clothes, which have won so much acclaim this year, are far beyond your budget."[40] And then, as suddenly as it had appeared, Karinska, Inc. vanished.

The reasons were financial. More money went out than came in, and while Karinska spent her private life fluctuating between wealth and bankruptcy, it was no way to run a business. Karinska was not then, or ever, interested in profits, and her skills in cost-effectiveness were nonexistent. She did not believe in compromising or limiting anything—money, fabric, labor, decoration, or time—that might hamper

Mrs. John C. Wilson—the Princess Natasha Paley—
in a black crêpe and satin gown designed by Karinska.
This 1940 photograph was taken for Vogue *by Horst*
P. Horst at Karinska's shop.

the production of the most beautiful clothing she could imagine.

"All she knew was that if she wanted it, she wanted it," says Kermit Love, the creator of "Sesame Street's" Big Bird, who in 1940 worked as a prop boy for the photographer George Hoyningen-Huene when he photographed Karinska's couture creations and later worked with Karinska as a designer on many theater and ballet productions. "She always overbought. If Olga Petrovna [one of Karinska's cutters] said, 'I need twelve yards,' Karinska would buy twenty on principle. Many thought it unforgivable expenditure." Her style—even for expensive gowns—was just a little too theatrical, a little too ornate, for the arbiters of current sartorial taste in a world at war.

The store closed its doors, but Karinska remained living in an apartment upstairs, continuing her work on theatrical commissions downstairs. It is unlikely that she mourned the failure of this brief foray into the world of haute couture, and she would

Sketch and costume by Pavel Tchelitchew for Tamara Toumanova in Balustrade, *1941.*

later speak with some disdain of the society people she had clothed. Her heart lay on the stage, and she yearned for something more than the personal acclaim accorded fashion designers. Karinska wanted her work to be the star, under the lights, exhibited to greatest advantage on the bodies of artists she admired—dancers, singers, or actors—in productions directed by artists she respected. She was a true collaborator, with enough self-assurance to recognize that another's genius would enhance her own, not compete with it, overshadow it, or negate it. And while in the theater there were also always cash problems, they rarely compromised her work—which was often for productions, especially ballet, that were decidedly not-for-profit.

§

As soon as Karinska had arrived in New York in early 1939 she had looked up her old friend George Balanchine and expressed to him her willingness to work on anything he might be doing. Since coming to America Balanchine's life had been eventful. With Lincoln Kirstein he had opened the School of American Ballet in New York City and begun the American Ballet Company which had sporadic seasons and equally sporadic success from 1934 until its demise in 1937. Without a company of his own, Balanchine had freelanced, staging operas, ballets, films—such as *On Your Toes* and *Goldwyn Follies*—and musicals on Broadway—including *The Boys From Syracuse, I Married an Angel,* and *Louisiana Purchase*. It was on a Broadway stage, for *Cabin in the*

Sketch by Miles White for Agnes de Mille's Fall River Legend, *and Nora Kaye in costume, 1948.*

Sky—starring Ethel Waters and Katherine Dunham—with a score by Vernon Duke, that Karinska and Balanchine would finally work together for the first time on American soil. It was ironic, yet perhaps rather fitting, that this quintessentially American musical had brought the two imperialist Russians together again in their adopted country. Their next collaboration, however, was something rather less accessible and a great deal more exotic.

Balanchine agreed to stage a new ballet for de Basil's Ballet Russe to premiere in New York in early 1941. The short-lived *Balustrade* was an entirely Russian affair, with the music of Igor Stravinsky ("Concerto for Violin and Orchestra"), designs by Pavel Tchelitchew, costumes executed by Karinska, and Tamara Toumanova dancing the central role. At its premiere, held on Balanchine's thirty-seventh birthday, the ballet made a startling visual impact and received blistering reviews. After only one additional performance it disappeared forever.⁴¹ While Balanchine denied the existence of a plot, the atmosphere created by a low white balustrade marked by two blood-red skeletal trees, a surreal garden, otherworldly creatures, and sensual

Anna Istomina and Robert Pageant in Kermit Love's designs for Agnes de Mille's ballet Rodeo, 1942 *(photo 1944).*

movement cast a definite spell. Toumanova was dressed "in a stunning black jewel-encrusted costume . . . with a fringed georgette skirt drawn between the legs, black silk tights embroidered with sequins and brilliants and long black gloves with pendant crystal drops at the finger tips."[42] With a pale half-moon crowning her head she was the epitome of sinewy sexy elegance. It was too much for many of the viewers. One critic reported that the costumes "look vaguely like what a bat would wear if dressed by Hattie Carnegie,"[43] while the great dance writer and critic Edwin Denby declared that the costumes had a sort of "super-Hollywood pruriency" that removed from "this erotic dance its mysterious juvenile modesty."[44]

Little black costumes were again in demand the following year, when Karinska was hired by theater and film designer Irene Sharaff, at Balanchine's suggestion, to execute her designs for a new Mike Todd revue on Broadway. This, a stormy meeting of minds at best, was to be the first of many Sharaff/Karinska collaborations as well as the first of several Todd productions in the course of which Karinska banged heads — and pocketbooks — with the flamboyant, brilliant, and difficult producer of the film version of *Around the World in 80 Days*. According to some, Todd lacked taste himself but had the genius to hire it — although rarely was he prepared to pay for it.

Star and Garter introduced burlesque to Broadway and featured "tall dames and low comedy"[45] in a production carefully designed to avoid the censorship of Mayor La Guardia's watchdogs. Mounted at the prestigious Music Box Theatre, it starred the

Sketch by Jo Mielziner for Pillar of Fire *and Diana Adams in the costume, 1942.*

comedian Bobby Clark, Carrie Finnell—who could whirl the tassels on her huge breasts in opposite directions simultaneously, to the delight of all—and Gypsy Rose Lee, all surrounded by lavish sets and costumes. Kermit Love describes the show as "one of the most sumptuously understated things I'd ever seen" and remembers thinking, "'Boy, if this is burlesque I'll spend the rest of my life here.'" He was not alone in this opinion: the show remained sold out for almost two years.

For the performers in the show Sharaff and Karinska devised some memorable and very innovative costumes: one for Georgia Sothern had to be in multiple parts that would fly away into the wings at perfectly timed moments in the choreography. As for Gypsy Rose Lee:

She shed several crisply starched petticoats and finally stood in a small G-string made of flowers crocheted in wool of pastel colors, with an extra flower on the tip of each breast . . . She had invented a trick of pasting the crocheted flowers on her nipples in such a way that the tightly woven stem of each flower untwirled at a light tap of a finger. This gave a fillip to her curtain call and of course the audience applauded wildly.[46]

The striptease artist adored Karinska and told Kermit Love that she felt that Karinska understood her body, her style, and her attitude. Karinska saw Gypsy as a nineteenth-century lady, not a twentieth-century stripper. Gypsy was not the first or last female performer to express confidence in Karinska's ability to enhance her looks. And Gypsy's extreme lack of clothing underscored the crucial importance of every stitch.

Star and Garter was not Karinska's only foray into the world of chorus girls and their accoutrements. Around 1943 Love designed several shows that Karinska executed for Lou Walters's Latin Quarter, a successful nightclub in the Broadway theater district. One of these was nearly sidelined by what Love terms "the biggest battle" he ever had with Karinska.

She could not understand that the sizes of the girls' headdresses were determined by the fact that they had to go up a spiral staircase to get to the dressing room. We had a "parade of nations," and, of course, the Eiffel Tower did not look big enough to her. I kept having to explain to her, "But you see the Eiffel Tower must stay downstairs while the girl is upstairs." Finally she came to a rehearsal and sadly confessed, "We made it too big."[47]

The nightclub world was one that Karinska, for all the sophistication of her upbringing, enjoyed. It required both an intuitive understanding of the morphology of the female body—where it curves, where it bends, which angles are good, which need to be camouflaged, which need to be accentuated—and an equally passionate interest in its inherent mysteries. It is here that the qualities of a great tutu and a great G-string converge. While Karinska's costumes conferred subtlety, femininity, and elegance on burlesque, they brought sex, sinew, and exposure to ballet.

§

In 1942, taken with Love's enthusiasm, Karinska asked him to work in her atelier and he became intrigued by her.

I'd seen a lot of ballet, but I'd never been touched by ballet until I met Karinska. Even in the early days you weren't touched by Balanchine. He would appear at rehearsals and he would rehearse things for the old Ballet Russe, but he didn't carry any mystery with him. Karinska did.

She lived upstairs, on the top floor of the building [on 56th Street], and to be asked to bring a cheese sandwich up there was like being elevated to some extraordinary Olympus. You

OPPOSITE:
Gypsy Rose Lee, Karinska, and Irene Sharaff in a publicity shot for the Mike Todd revue Star and Garter, *1942.*

Sketch by Stewart Chaney for Shakespeare's Twelfth
Night *and Maurice Evans and Helen Hayes as Viola/
Cesario in costume, 1940.*

would go in and you would call her and there would be nobody there, and then Gili would
come and attack you. A great brown poodle. Monster brown poodle. [This dog was once the
subject of a lawsuit brought by one bitten recipient of his attentions, but Karinska charmed
the judge and saved Gili's life.] And then you would call, "Madame Karinska!," and she would
say, "I'm watering my geraniums!," and you would see her watering these absolutely dead
plants on her roof in the middle of winter. Three months later you'd go up again and the
whole place would be a profusion of blooms. So one always attached to her this extraordinary
sense of a miracle worker. She had the eccentricity of someone who was possessed with a way
to do something that in her mind had never been done before. I think it came from her not
really knowing how to do it, from this incredible will to explore: there has to be an answer,
there must be a way, there must be a different approach. That was her ability. In later life she
had built up a vocabulary of ways to do things. But in the early days that vocabulary was not
clearly established.[48]

Karinska's ability was certainly challenged that summer when Love was given
the commission to design the costumes for Agnes de Mille's new ballet, *Rodeo,* for the

Ballet Russe de Monte Carlo at New York's Metropolitan Opera House. Denham, the company's director, announced to Love, "We have no money, but Karinska will work with you and you will do it."[49] And so they did—cheaply. But in all its many reincarnations this seminal American ballet has never again been, in Love's opinion, so beautifully dressed. Set in the colorful, brawny world of cowboys and cowgirls, the production marked several firsts for Karinska—one of these being the use of button-up blue jeans. The fabric greatly intrigued the lady from Kharkov, and each day she would descend to the basement of her building on 56th Street—where Love was bleaching yards of denim in great boiling vats—to observe the rigorous treatment that this particular material withstood, only to improve in color and texture. For the girls' skirts in the ballet Karinska used cretonne, a kind of unbleached muslin previously considered unworthy of exposure. Love recalls Karinska's delight when the unconventional was again used to such spectacular effect, giving both the ballet and the fabric a whole new life. Like a kind of textiles scientist, she was always experimenting with fabric, ignoring convention—moral or material.

The premiere of this ballet—which tells the story of a cowgirl learning how to be a girl—was received with almost unqualified praise, and *Rodeo* has now taken its place as a classic in American dance. The day of the premiere, however, was fraught with tension. De Mille recounts the episode in her book *Dance to the Piper.*

Dooley Wilson and Ethel Waters in the Broadway production of Cabin in the Sky, 1940.

The afternoon of the opening, we had dress rehearsal. That is, the scenery was up. . . . There was not a costume in the house. . . . It was a tradition of Karinska's that her clothes arrive piecemeal in a flotilla of taxis during the evening, some still with bastings and pins, and a half score of seamstresses in attendance to do last-minute sewing on dancers in the wings. The clothes were worn without trial of any sort. It is a tribute to her expertness that no accidents ever resulted. The wear and tear on the cast's nerves was, however, simply dreadful. Karinska has executed three ballets of mine [*Three Virgins and a Devil, Rodeo,* and *Fall River Legend*]. I have never had anything like complete costumes at the dress rehearsal. Why does anyone hire her a second time? Simply, she is without peer in her field.[50]

Six months later, this time for the newly formed American dance company Ballet Theatre, Karinska was not the only one keeping the curtain from rising on a premiere. Although she had already dressed *Gala Performance* and *Pillar of Fire* for British choreographer Antony Tudor, his 1943 production of *Romeo and Juliet,* designed by Eugene Berman, was the most complex by far. When the evening of the opening arrived, Tudor had not even finished the choreography. Sol Hurok, the company's presenter at the Metropolitan Opera House, was adamant; he would wait for neither costumes nor steps, and the premiere took place as scheduled, a distraught Tudor stepping before the curtain to offer the expectant audience a disclaimer. Though both Karinska and Tudor completed their work by the following performance, it was the costumes that had the last word: "The work is less a ballet by Antony Tudor," wrote John Martin in *The New York Times,* "than a pageant by Eugene Berman, whose beautiful but unyielding setting and sumptuous costumes quite swamp the stage."[51]

Sketches by the designer Miles White for the Broadway production of The Pirate, *and Alfred Lunt and Lynn Fontanne in costume, 1942. Karinska used lace doilies as her inspiration for Fontanne's gown.*

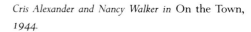

Cris Alexander and Nancy Walker in On the Town, *1944.*

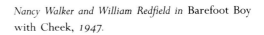

Nancy Walker and William Redfield in Barefoot Boy with Cheek, *1947.*

OVERLEAF, LEFT:
Bobby Clark wearing his ribboned coat in Mike Todd's production of The Would-be Gentleman, *1946.*

OVERLEAF, RIGHT:
Bobby Clark and chorus girls in As the Girls Go, *wearing costumes designed by Oleg Cassini, 1948.*

57

Lucas-Monroe 14.

OPPOSITE:

Alice Pearce, being fitted by Karinska, and costume
designer John Derro, working on Small Wonder.

Nydia Westman, Estelle Winwood, and Martita Hunt
in The Madwoman of Chaillot, 1948.

Mary McCarty and others in Small Wonder, 1948.

Eddie Albert, Allyn McLerie, and Mary McCarty
in Miss Liberty, 1949.

RIGHT AND OPPOSITE:
Showgirls in Mike Todd's Peep Show, designed
by Irene Sharaff, 1950. Karinska's Folies-Bergère
experience with small, well-placed decorations
reemerged here in its full glory.

Lilo and Peter Cookson in Can-Can, *with music
and lyrics by Cole Porter, 1953.*

ABOVE RIGHT:
Don Ameche and Hildegarde Neff *in* Silk Stockings,
1955.

RIGHT:
Edie Adams and Peter Palmer *in* L'il Abner,
designed by Alvin Colt (costumes only), 1956.

OPPOSITE:
Joan McCracken *in a publicity shot
for* Me and Juliet, *1953.*

Olivia de Havilland in Romeo and Juliet *on Broadway, 1951.*

Eva Le Gallienne as Queen Elizabeth in Mary Stuart, *1957.*

OPPOSITE:

Laurence Olivier and Anthony Quinn in Becket *on Broadway, 1960.*

67

CHAPTER FOUR

While in London, Karinska had worked with a brilliant young American designer named Raoul Pène du Bois — son of painter Guy Pène du Bois, and brother of illustrator William Pène du Bois — on several of Cochran's revues. Later, in America, Pène du Bois asked Karinska to create some of the costumes for the Rodgers and Hart musical *Too Many Girls,* produced by George Abbott. This was Karinska's introduction to Broadway, a place that would provide her with consistent work for several decades.

Sometime in early 1943 Pène du Bois was responsible for introducing Karinska's talents in another theatrical arena; as a result of his coaxing, she found herself in Hollywood working for the movies. It was not always a happy environment for Karinska's uncompromising nature, but it was eventful, amusing, lucrative, and, ultimately — when she earned an Oscar for costume design in 1948, the first year that award was given — a milestone of sorts. Though making movies during wartime involved numerous fiscal and material restrictions, the first movie Karinska worked on turned out to be Paramount's biggest costume picture to date. Flush with the success of the Bing Crosby/Bob Hope *Road* pictures, the studio put out an extraordinary two million dollars for a Ginger Rogers/Ray Milland musical. Directed by Mitchell Leisen, with music by Kurt Weill and lyrics by Ira Gershwin, *Lady in the Dark* sounded promising enough, but Rogers's publicity slogan, "The minx in mink with a yen for men!" provides a better idea of the result.

With a design team consisting at various times of Paramount's chief costume designer, Edith Head, and Leisen himself — in addition to Pène du Bois — it is difficult to assess exactly who did what, although it appears that Karinska was brought in to execute some of the more fantastical gowns for Rogers. There was a wedding dress that consisted of no fewer than 124 yards of chiffon and silver lamé — with a hem appliquéd with satin scallops, sequins, and pearls — and a huge headdress supported by a concealed wire frame. "Just to show you how Karinska does things," said Virginia Ritter, the milliner who worked with Karinska on the project, "the wires were wrapped in tulle, and pearls were sewn on by hand."[52] This costume, almost absurd in its extravagance, elicited giggles rather than awe from the audience, though it did enjoy a second life in store windows across the country, on display as publicity for the movie.

But it was another outfit for Rogers that has become a legend. Edith Head tells the tale of the famous mink skirt, whose pelts were subjected to their own screen test before final casting, in *Edith Head's Hollywood.*

OPPOSITE:

Ginger Rogers in the legendary mink skirt from Lady in the Dark, *1944.*

Mary Todd Lincoln photographed by Mathew Brady in her inaugural gown (1861), and Karinska's reproduction of the gown, an example of her talent for period re-creation. The gown was made for "White House Happening," Lincoln Kirstein's dramatic pageant of the Civil War held at Loeb Center, Harvard University, 1967.

As Liza Elliott in *Lady in the Dark*, Ginger was the fashion editor of the world's greatest fashion magazine. Her costumes were superlative. She was constantly having daydreams that she was a glamorous sexpot instead of a tailored-editor type, and the dreams created a perfect plot excuse for fabulous gowns. One of these sequences involved the circus, and Ginger wore one of the most expensive costumes in Hollywood history. It has come to be known as the mink dress, but actually it was a mink overskirt which was lined with sequins, worn over a matching sequinned bodysuit. There was also a mink bolero and muff. It cost about $35,000 to make in those days, and couldn't be made today without a limitless wardrobe budget.

Over the years there has been a great deal of controversy over who designed that costume. Some people have even said that I had nothing to do with it, which is ridiculous. Mitchell told me exactly what he wanted, I interpreted what he had to say, as I would with any director, and my staff made the gown. Mitch had originally requested that the mink skirt be lined with *faux* rubies and emeralds, but when that huge expanse of mink was backed with stones, Ginger couldn't even lift it, let alone dance in it. We relined the skirt with sequins in a paisley pattern and it moved beautifully. Since the skirt was open down the front it bared her beautiful legs, which was always a goal when you worked with Ginger Rogers.[53]

In claiming responsibility for this outfit, Head illustrates the lack of proper accreditation that existed for costuming in movies, as well as the prerequisite competitiveness—a quality Karinska could certainly match on her own terms when necessary, though in Hollywood her name was more often than not a casualty of contracts. Although Karinska's name does not appear in the credits for *Lady in the Dark*, many witnesses claim that she was the one who finally solved the problem of the mink skirt that had to move as Rogers danced. Her lightweight yet sumptuous solution serves as a perfect illustration of her ability to provide both visual splendor and practical comfort—the two usually being mutually exclusive.

Despite its fame, Karinska always referred to the mink dress as "an embarrassment in her career," according to Kermit Love.

She hated Hollywood, and she hated Ginger Rogers. It upset her that she had done some lovely, draped flowing things inspired by couture with a wonderful body look, a little mysterious, whereas Ginger wanted everything built like a piece of armor plate. She wanted a defined bosom, a *guêpiered* waist with the bosom on top, and nothing Karinska could do would satisfy her. . . . There was a great deal of dissension throughout the whole making of that movie. They really battled.[54]

It was not all trial and tribulation, however, and a more than friendly letter from Ray Milland, written in perfect French, implies that there may even have been some flirtation going on behind the cameras. However, Willa Kim, Karinska's assistant at the time, thinks Milland was more interested in being introduced to a particular ballet dancer back East than in Karinska herself. Be that as it may, he appears the perfect gentleman, writing, "Querida Karinska . . . Je suis triste parce que j'ai perdu votre compagnie charmante et délicieuse."[55] In any case Karinska was soon taking his measurements for another costume drama.

Again directed by Leisen and designed by Raoul Pène du Bois, *Kitty* was a black comedy version of *Pygmalion* set in the eighteenth century. Paulette Goddard starred as the street urchin who works her way up the social strata by means of several fortunate marriages—"I'm not going to entertain him, I'm going to marry him," she

Basil Rathbone, Joan Fontaine, and Arturo de Cordova in Frenchman's Creek, *1944.*

declares before hooking another victim. With a beautiful Goddard going from bare feet and rags to peaked wigs and luscious gowns, the story gave Pène du Bois and Karinska opportunity for a full and ever-widening array of décolleté clothes for the star. These range from a simple, fitted, black dress with a quarter-inch of pale lace peeking out from a very well-contained bosom to a ball gown with enormous side paniers, a tapered bodice, and a less well-contained bosom, to Kitty's final appearance, her head framed in a wide circle of pale sheer gatherings; this nonsensical head decoration, suggesting a halo, signifies Goddard's having finally ascended to her true status as a lady. Milland, as Sir Hugh Marcy, is Kitty's true love, a handsome and arrogant gambling man with no money—though he is always beautifully turned out in Nelson-style tricorne hats, waistcoat and tails, silk breeches, ruffles at the wrists, and the requisite lace handkerchief hanging jauntily from his right-hand breast pocket.

While most period films of the day still adhered to current fashions in their re-creation of another century, Edward Maeder, author of *Hollywood and History: Costume Design in Film* (1987), points out that, "In *Kitty,* a masterpiece of period costume, the only item that related directly to the 1940s was a small set of side hoops made of ruched satin. In eighteenth-century England structural undergarments such as these were usually made of linen or cotton and were merely practical, not beautiful. But drawing attention to such unfamiliar garments heightens the period effect."[56] This exaggeration of detail in order to, ironically, produce visual and atmospheric accuracy is an imperative truth of theatrical design. Absolute accuracy simply would not translate onto the big screen or stage. But mere exaggeration is not enough; the secret lies in knowing and understanding period style so well that the leap to an extreme illustrates the original and does not appear to update it. It is all about illusion, and it is here that Karinska was a master, always conducting meticulous scholarly research, as her extensive library of books attests, before she undertook any project in fabric.

Feminine fancy took on new meaning in the next Leisen/Pène du Bois movie Karinska worked on for Paramount. In this film the female star, Joan Fontaine, required no fewer than fifteen costume changes. Set in 1668 in London and Cornwall, *Frenchman's Creek* was described accurately and uncharitably by James Agee as "Daphne du Maurier's little bathroom classic.... This film, like the 'novel' it improves on, is masturbation fantasy triple-distilled."⁵⁷ Clearly, it was the perfect setting for a fabulous costume parade with endless lush gowns, petticoats, nightgowns, shawls, brimmed hats, and adorable lace hair decorations (a Karinska specialty) that climaxed in a bright orange, shimmering gown with a beaded neckline that perfectly matches the fiery ringlets of Fontaine's wig. Perhaps the most appealing of her costumes, however, is *en travestie,* when Fontaine is dressed in white shirt, knee breeches, and head scarf as she boards incognito the boat of her would-be lover.

Arturo de Cordova, as Fontaine's fantasy man, has the requisite bare-chested look, while her older foolish husband is seen in one scene sporting a pair of ridiculous ruffled culottes that recall those of Jouvet's Arnolphe in *L'Ecole des Femmes* and prefigure Bobby Clark's fabulous costume for Mike Todd's Broadway production of *The Would-be Gentleman* in 1946. While Karinska's specialty might have been in enhancing the feminine, she repeatedly demonstrated a wit in her work for both men and women that she did not always exhibit in private life.

Wit and beauty aside, costumes not only cannot save a bad movie, but they have on occasion appeared to add fuel to the subsequent roasting process. In a good film, however, the costumes become part of the whole, inseparable from the performances and the narrative. This is certainly the case with Karinska's work for George Cukor in *Gaslight*. Officially an employee of Paramount that year, with her offices on their lot, Karinska was apparently loaned out to Metro-Goldwyn-Mayer when they ran into difficulty with the elaborate Victorian gowns for Ingrid Bergman in *Gaslight*. As David Chierichetti explains in his book *Hollywood Costume Design,* the first costumes for Bergman were consummately copied from Victorian engravings; but Cukor was not satisfied with them.

Irene [Lentz Gibbons, head of wardrobe from 1942 to 1949] brought in Madame Barbara Karinska.... She designed and executed the most intricate bustles and flounces MGM had ever seen, then stayed on to do the fantastic *Kismet* (1944). Both times Irene was listed as the designer, but studio employees now say that she really had no part in them at all.⁵⁸

As was the case with many studio department heads, Irene received credit for the work of subordinates, but Karinska's dissatisfaction with Hollywood never seemed to include resentment over this particular practice. Her reputation in ballet and theatrical circles was assured, and in Hollywood she was widely recognized as the preeminent specialist in period re-creation and technical executions.

By the end of 1944 Karinska had worked on five films and had been paid the then enormous sum of $10,500 by Paramount; even in the costume department during wartime, Hollywood salaries still managed to defy the odds in their superfluity of zeros. With an additional five thousand dollars earned from her dance and theater

OPPOSITE:
Paulette Goddard and Ray Milland in Kitty, *1945. This elaborate costume drama took drawings by Hogarth as its design inspiration.*

OVERLEAF, LEFT:
Ingrid Bergman and Charles Boyer in Gaslight, *1944. Dissatisfied with the precise period re-creations initially executed, director George Cukor brought in Karinska to redesign the costumes.*

OVERLEAF, RIGHT:
Marlene Dietrich as the dancer, Jamilla, in Kismet, *1944. Dietrich's legs were painted in gold for this scene, producing a stunning effect on screen, although in reality her legs turned green from acute hypothermia due to lead poisoning.*

RIGHT:
Paulette Goddard, Victor Varconi, and Gary Cooper in Unconquered, *1947.*

Judy Garland in Vincente Minnelli's The Pirate, *1948.*

work in New York she was — for the first time since before the Russian Revolution — wealthy, and while this was never her aim, she always had good use for money when she had it.

She bought a house on the beach in Malibu and an Oldsmobile, which she fed exclusively with Shell brand gasoline — having taken the chance remark of a salesman as gospel — and which, to the terror of her passengers, she drove in a wild and eccentric manner. Having decided that left-hand turns were too complex, Karinska made her way around Hollywood by means of a complicated system of right-hand turns. She once drove into her garage and straight out the back of it onto the beach, leveling a neighbor's palm tree in the process. "What a terrible place to put a tree!" she remarked, and thought the neighbors "very rude" when they complained about its destruction.

Over the next few years Karinska worked on several more film projects. In 1947 she helped dress Cecil B. DeMille's *Unconquered* featuring Gary Cooper as an American frontiersman in fringed suede jackets and Paulette Goddard, "stripped down to within one inch of the Johnston Office,"[59] as a kind of white slave who is "whipped, sold as a bonded servant on the auction block, tied to a stake by savage Indians, taken on a wild ride over a waterfall, and, in a rare moment of tranquility, compelled to scrub a barroom floor while various barflies tried to seduce her."[60] It was another nineteenth-century period re-creation for Karinska, this time on the barbaric side of the Atlantic. She was later to admit that of all the movie stars she dressed, "Cooper was my favorite."

For his screen version of S. N. Behrman's story *The Pirate,* Vincente Minnelli, himself an expert costume designer, called upon Karinska's services.

I'd worked on several New York shows with Karinska, the great costume designer who'd started out with Diaghilev and the Russian Ballet. She had the uncanny talent of transforming the elements of Braque and Picasso [*sic*] sketches into magnificent costumes. It would be no great challenge for her to suggest the many cosmopolitan influences — East Indian, Chinese, and European — of Martinique in the 1830s. She brought out a young artist — Tom Keogh — with her. When he later moved to Paris, he became a most important international painter.

I showed them my collection of prints and drawings of the period, and they proceeded to execute a very muted look, which I felt would counterbalance the more outlandish elements of the story.[61]

The vivid costumes that resulted were anything but "muted" and served, rather, to overextend the "outlandish" plot. Starring Minnelli's wife, Judy Garland, Gene Kelly, Gladys Cooper, and the Nicholas Brothers, the film centered around Garland's love for the pirate Macocco. Unlike Joan Fontaine's buccaneer in *Frenchman's Creek,* this one is in reality a fat, old, retired pirate, impersonated in more youthful guise by Kelly, a song-and-dance man from a traveling troupe who falls in love with Garland. Garland's dresses are luxurious, theatrical gowns featuring seamed bodices, enormous puffy sleeves, decorative lace décolletages, and fancifully draped skirts and aprons. Kelly wears nutty striped "pirate" breeches and purple-and-red lined capes, while the ensemble scenes feature swirling layers of spinning skirts in vibrant hues.

Karinska's Oscar for Costume Design
for the 1948 film Joan of Arc.

In the end the film was applauded far more for its "color"—Technicolor, costume color, Caribbean color—than for any dramatic sense or popular success.

Karinska's next film, for her the most important by far, for reasons spiritual as well as temporal, was also one of the least successful that she worked on. The producer, Walter Wanger, impressed by Laurence Olivier's 1944 production of *Henry V,* wanted to create a historical drama of equal quality and prestige in America. With Ingrid Bergman Wanger formed a production company, Sierra Corporation, and soon had signed director Victor Fleming (of *Gone With the Wind* fame) for their first project, slated for release in 1948—a screen adaptation of Maxwell Anderson's successful Broadway play *Joan of Lorraine.* From the beginning, everything—including the hiring of Pène du Bois and Karinska, with their reputations for superb historical costume re-creations—was geared toward the making of a film of epic scope with intellectual integrity, historical accuracy, and, simultaneously, great popular appeal. But Wanger's grand gamble failed. By the time it was finished the movie was the most expensive production in Hollywood to date, costing over four and a half million dollars, $200,000 more than *Gone With the Wind*—and almost no one went to see it. The film eventually bankrupted Wanger, and the footage was repossessed and recut by Security First National Bank. *Joan of Arc* was the *Heaven's Gate* of the late 1940s.

Despite heroic performances from Bergman and José Ferrer, it was too long, too dull, and too pious for the postwar cynicism of its audience. It was also said that Bergman's adulterous affair with Roberto Rossellini, all over the press by the time the film opened, made it hard for the public to accept her on the screen as a saint—though the beauty and sensitivity of Bergman's performance makes this hard to believe today.

RIGHT:

Karinska with Ingrid Bergman at Karinska's Malibu beach house.

OPPOSITE:

Ingrid Bergman in Joan of Arc, 1948, directed by Victor Fleming.

The main salon of Karinska's house in Domrémy-la-Pucelle, France, the birthplace of Joan of Arc. Her collection of Joan of Arc relics surpassed that of the local museum.

The shooting was plagued by the usual production problems, and the wardrobe department was not exempted from the general turmoil. Shortly after being hired Pène du Bois dropped out of the project, and Karinska was asked to take over the job with Dorothy Jeakins, a young sketch artist. Together, despite Karinska's daily firing and rehiring of Jeakins, the two made some of the most scrupulously genuine costumes ever produced for the screen.

Karinska insisted on clothing all the crowd scenes, right down to the extras, in authentic period dress—without cutting any of the customary corners in terms of quality. She also refused to use any of the bright, shiny colors and fabrics of the day, despite their impressive effect on film, insisting instead on using the muted colors of real medieval clothing that she had carefully researched in books and museums. Initially, according to Karinska, Bergman thought that little Joan should wear a red dress. "What peasant wears red chiffon?" asked Karinska in disbelief, and Joan wore no red. From Joan's simple peasant outfits to the magnificent fur-lined cape of the dauphin, the clothes were hand sewn and "cut and constructed exactly in the manner of the fifteenth century, set[ing] new standards for period-costume design for films."[62]

By the end of the filming, tensions between the director and producers had mounted to such an extent that Fleming walked off the set in protest, and Karinska loyally walked off with him. (When Fleming died, only a few weeks after the movie was released, his photograph was added to Karinska's altar of the special people in her life, which, by the time of her own death, include Louis Jouvet, George Balanchine, Tanaquil Le Clercq, and André Derain.) At this late stage, however, the costumes were already virtually completed, and Jeakins finished the few that were not. Moreover, this time Karinska's credit on the screen had been contractually guaranteed.

Despite the movie's many weaknesses, it was recognized by the film industry as a noble effort and was nominated for nine Academy Awards—although not Best Picture—and, as a kind of consolation prize, Wanger was given a special award for

Karinska (back row, second from left) and friends at her Malibu beach house in the 1940s; included are Raoul Pène du Bois (left of Karinska), Willa Kim (front center), and George Balanchine (right of Kim).

his contribution as a producer. And in this, the first year the Academy recognized costume design as a distinct category, Karinska and Jeakins were nominated for Best Costume Design for Color Film. (Through 1966 two costume awards were given, one for color and one for black-and-white film.)

Karinska happened to be in New York working with Balanchine and could not attend the awards ceremony, but a fellow nominee, Edith Head—who had done much lobbying to initiate the award for costume design—was there with high expectations for her sumptuous Austrian gowns in *The Emperor Waltz*.

There was no doubt in my mind that I would win that Oscar. I deserved it—for longevity if nothing else. I had been doing motion pictures before the Oscars even existed. And besides, my picture had the best costumes of any nominated picture. The serious competition was *Joan of Arc,* designed by Madame Karinska and Dorothy Jeakins. To my mind there was no way Ingrid Bergman's sackcloths and suits of armor could win over my Viennese finery. . . .

Elizabeth Taylor was only seventeen when she presented that first award for best costuming, and she was as beautiful as everyone had ever imagined her to be. . . . As she flounced up to the podium, I could feel my whole body get tense. She announced the nominees, then opened the envelope and named the winners.

Karinska and Jeakins for *Joan of Arc.*

It took a moment for me to realize that I had lost. Since I am not very emotional, no one knew that I was in shock. Bill squeezed my hand and we watched the remaining presentations, but I do not remember the rest of the evening.[63]

Meanwhile, Karinska, fast asleep in New York, was awakened by a phone call informing her she had won the Academy Award. The caller was none other than an excited George Balanchine, a fact that seemed to please Karinska as much as the award itself.

On April 12 Karinska wrote to Louis Jouvet:

I am still with my Joan of Arc—I love her deeply.

Nobody here recognizes me, they think I've had an operation on my face—they don't understand that the "lift" in my face is the "lift" in my soul that is shining on my face because I am so close to Joan, and every day, morning and evening, I kneel down before her picture and I ask her for "courage," for it is with her courage that she succeeded.

I received my Oscar not for the costumes, but for my suffering, for my loyalty to Joan. . . .[64]

It was during the course of her demanding research in preparation for costuming this film that Karinska began what would become a lifelong obsession with Joan of Arc. She started by collecting relics, statues, medallions, and images of the saint. And as a final gesture of worship she made a pilgrimage to Domrémy-la-Pucelle, the tiny town in Lorraine where Joan was born. There she surprised even herself when she impulsively made an offer on the only house for sale at the time.

A stone cottage near the local church, it was graced with a garden, soaring beamed ceilings, and much medieval charm, and Karinska knew she had to have it. It was, however, to be sold at auction, and Karinska was aware that the local butcher, much wealthier than Karinska at the time, was also going to bid for it. So she started a rumor that a wealthy American heiress was also planning to buy it—at any cost. Losing hope, the butcher withdrew from the auction, and the house was Karinska's. For the next two decades she visited this property every summer for several weeks at a time, restoring and preserving all its old charm and furnishing it with medieval antiques. Its central room eventually resembled a chapel to St. Joan.

By the mid-1960s Karinska owned more Joan of Arc relics than the local museum, and guided tours were rerouted through her house. Under the guidance of Père Donceur, a specialist on Joan of Arc who had been hired as a consultant for Wanger's film, Karinska also amassed a library of over 150 books on the saint, many very old and very rare, and in 1974 she donated them to the Centre Jeanne d'Arc in Orléans. The center's meeting room was renamed the "Salle Karinska" in honor of the gift.

While some of Karinska's acquaintances thought that her adoration of St. Joan went beyond worship to an extreme form of over-identification, she never appeared openly fanatical. But certainly her sentiment toward the saint ran deep, and it lasted until the end of her life. On occasion, at the debut of a favorite young ballerina, she would fasten her into her sparkling new tutu and tiara and then quietly slip into her hand an old medal featuring the young Joan astride a horse or being burned at the stake.

§

Despite Karinska's success in Hollywood, she was to make the dance costumes for only two more films after *Joan of Arc*—*Hans Christian Andersen,* starring Danny Kaye and Zizi Jeanmaire in 1952 (Balanchine was originally slated as choreographer, hence Karinska's involvement), and *Daddy Long Legs,* starring Fred Astaire and Leslie Caron

OPPOSITE:
Renée (Zizi) Jeanmaire and Danny Kaye in Hans Christian Andersen, *1952.*

in 1955. Not only was filmmaking, with its petty politics and compromises, unsuited to Karinska's imperial nature, but something far more interesting gave her a reason to settle for good in New York. She retrieved her Oscar, sold her Malibu house, and came back to New York to work for Balanchine. This time the collaboration would proceed without interruption for the remainder of her life.

Karinska's heart lay in the dance, and throughout her Hollywood years she had shuttled back and forth to New York, keeping her hand in the ballet world. She never closed her New York atelier, but had moved it from 56th Street to more spacious, but rather dusty, quarters on West 44th Street, in the middle of the theater district. There she continued to produce costumes for Broadway shows as well as the ballet. Her nephew, Lawrence Vlady, helped oversee the large operation, and his own masterful work as a maker of masks and other three-dimensional props became an integral and important addition to Karinska's business.

While walking around the Upper East Side one day, Karinska saw a town house she liked and, though her funds were by this time depleted, she used an informal loan arrangement she had with her accountant, and managed to put down a deposit on 17 East 63rd Street, a huge, wide, four-story mansion. Karinska lived on the top floor, which opened onto a large rooftop garden, and rented out the two middle floors to a law firm. Toussia Saylenoff, her assistant and shop manager, lived in the basement — as far from Madame as she could be.

Toussia, a tiny, seemingly frail Armenian woman, had been a dancer with one of the many small Russian companies that abounded in the post-Diaghilev era. When, because of a foot injury, she was forced to stop dancing, she applied for a job with Karinska and was hired — despite her lack of any real sewing abilities. She worked for Karinska for the rest of her life performing a variety of functions, including companion, secretary, bill keeper, servant, and resident costume-shop spy. At Karinska's funeral forty years later Toussia was to be found prostrate, face down, before the open casket, for longer than anyone cared to acknowledge. Theirs was a strange and incomprehensible relationship, although, as Natasha Molostwoff—a longtime Russian friend of Karinska's and senior administrator at the School of American Ballet—once pointed out, "Everybody wants a slave." Karinska was the czarina in her world, and Toussia upheld the hierarchy.

But she was a slave who wreaked havoc in Karinska's atelier, forever pitting the egos and affections of the workers against each other, probably in some ill-considered attempt to preserve Madame's attention and assert her own authority in Madame's absence. Some think Toussia believed she was Karinska; others, that she was just plain nasty. But whatever the truth behind this memorable little tyrant who lived on cigarettes, rice, and hot dogs, no one has ever disputed her deep and total devotion to Madame. In Karinska's old age, which lasted a very long time, Toussia was always there taking care of her employer, making phone calls, arranging fittings, and scribbling in her mysterious notebook. (This medium-sized loose-leaf journal was composed more of stapled swatches of fabric than of words and in its strange bulky way functioned as a kind of Rosetta Stone when the reconstruction of a given costume became necessary.)

OPPOSITE:
Leslie Caron in Daddy Long Legs, 1952.

Despite their constant bickering and Toussia's frequent outbursts of "I keet, I keet," she never quit—and as the two women reached their eighth decades Karinska bought Toussia a wide-screen color television on which she watched murder mysteries and Westerns while Karinska, on the other side of the salon, read with the aid of a magnifying glass. Over the mantel in this living room decorated with heavy antiques, embroidered chairs, lace lamps, and Flemish tapestries, two fifteenth-century carved wooden angels—each four feet tall and painted with gesso and gold leaf—held vigil. The two statues represented the fulfillment of a promise that Karinska had made. Years before, during her early and uncertain days in New York, she had been fond of dressing up and sitting in the Palm Court of the Plaza Hotel, dreaming of the day she could afford to take tea there. One afternoon, while walking down Third Avenue, she was smitten by two angel sculptures in a dusty antique shop. Gazing at them through the window, she promised them that if they would look out for her she would one day return for them. So strong was Karinska's faith and so fierce was her loyalty that when she later prospered in her work she indeed did go back for the angels. And they continued to look out for her: she now had not only a thriving business but also a substantial mortgage on a New York town house, the ultimate sign of success in her new homeland. Karinska was well aware of her financial responsibilities, and during the ensuing decades she took on enormous amounts of work.

Between 1951 and 1966 she costumed twenty-nine operas for the Metropolitan Opera, including *Il Barbiere di Siviglia, Don Giovanni* (a production that lasted thirty-two years) and *Otello*—all three designed by Eugene Berman; *Der Rosenkavalier,* designed by Rolf Gérard; *Macbeth,* designed by Rudoph Neher; *Martha,* designed by Motley; and *Falstaff,* designed by Franco Zeffirelli.

Herman Krawitz, technical administrator for the Metropolitan Opera, worked with Karinska throughout her tenure there and recalls his experience with a mixture of admiration and exasperation.

There were times when Karinska's schedule would cause me a certain amount of concern. . . . She refused to give me anything until it was right. It would drive me crazy! I mean we were having dress rehearsals and [general manager] Mr. [Rudolf] Bing would look at me: "Where's the costume for Roberta [Peters]?" I said, "Mr. Rudolf, you will not have any problem opening night." I was always gambling. But I never, never lost! It was close. But it was worth it.

I looked in London, I looked in Italy, I looked to satisfy the question, "Am I doing the right thing? Is she really the only one?" So I would be prepared for the attack, "Why do you pay for this woman?" . . . I took it that we were first and the only first. And Karinska was one of the reasons, at least in production. . . . We were king of the heap, and she put us there.[65]

Cecil Beaton insisted that Karinska execute his costume designs for two mammoth productions at the Metropolitan Opera. For *Turandot,* in 1961, the company's first presentation of Puccini's opera in over thirty years, there were no less than four hundred costumes. The colors dramatically intensified onstage, act by act, beginning with drab indigos, grays, and blacks (ruined in Beaton's estimation on the first night

Sketch by Eugene Berman for Bartola in Il Barbiere di Siviglia *and Caesare Valletti, Fernando Corena (as Bartola), and Margaret Roggero in costume, 1954.*

Sketch by Motley for Leonora in Il Trovatore *and Antonietta Stella being fitted in the costume by Karinska (second from right), 1959.*

OPPOSITE:

Cesare Siepi and Roberta Peters in Don Giovanni *at the Metropolitan Opera, 1957.*

88

Sketch by Cecil Beaton for Turandot *and the production onstage, 1961.*

Sketch by Franco Zeffirelli for Nanetta in Falstaff *and Judith Raskin in the costume; (below) Judith Raskin with Gabriella Tucci and Rosalind Elias in the production, 1964.*

Eleanor Steber being fitted for Arabella, *with Karinska and Rudolf Bing, general manager of the Metropolitan Opera, 1955.*

Karinska with the designer Rolf Gérard and Renata Tebaldi in her La Traviata *costume.*

Anna Moffo as Violetta in La Traviata, *1966. Cecil Beaton, the designer, described the costume as "a cruel red, with loops of fabric like great tear drops scattered on the skirt and an arrogant peacock train."*

by an extra creeping onstage in the wrong costume: "her orange bottom was the biggest and most prominent, a full sun that never set"[66]) and climaxing in the final scene composed of lush pinks, yellows, and oranges. In the center of all this glory stood Birgit Nilsson in a costume so huge and so well fortified that it was referred to as the "castle."

For Beaton's lavish production of *La Traviata* five years later he designed a yellow dress to be worn by Renata Tebaldi, and Karinska executed it as instructed. This time it was the diva who objected. During her fitting Tebaldi's translator declared, "Madame Tebaldi doesn't care for the costume." Great flattery and protestations followed, but Tebaldi could not be convinced. Finally the translator was asked, "Why does Madame Tebaldi not like the color?" "Well," it was explained, "Madame Tebaldi feels it looks like they have been throwing eggs at her." After further reassurances that this was not the case and that everyone thought the gown gorgeous, Tebaldi spoke for herself and said, "Well, let *them* sing!" The costume never made it onstage.[67]

§

Some of Karinska's least satisfying commissions during the late 1940s and early 1950s—undertaken more for the money than for love—were costumes for the Ice Capades, Ice Follies, and Sonja Henie's hugely popular extravaganza at the Center Theatre in New York.

Karinska's knowledge of the characteristics of various fabrics with regard to perspiration, gravity, and movement was unparalleled, but she had little sympathy for the properties of those same fabrics when subjected to the extreme humidity of an ice-skating rink. She refused to compromise quality by using "miracle net"—a pure nylon tulle that was impervious to humidity—and yet was miserable when she saw her beautiful, spry cotton-and-silk tutus flop and droop on the ice. She also objected to the use of bulky, unsightly zippers, so necessary for quick changes. (Ballet tutus are, instead, always fastened with hooks and eyes for a better fit, and to prevent

Jinx Clark and chorus men in Holiday on Ice, *Sioux City, Iowa, 1958.*

For "At the County Fair," an Ice Capades production, designer Miles White and Karinska collaborated on costumes for skating vegetables and barnyard animals. A detail of one of White's sketches and the finished chicken costume are shown here.

the possibility of pinched skin and unzipped zippers onstage.) On one occasion designer Miles White dressed some skaters as vegetables for a sequence; Karinska was horrified. "In the Midwest, they do not wish to see vegetables, they see vegetables every day. They wish to see girls."[68] She was also mystified by the use of skate covers. To Karinska the disguise was obvious, and their obstruction of the line of the leg and foot baffled her. She always had a ballet dancer's concern for purity of form and line.

CHAPTER FIVE

Alexandra Danilova in Gaîté Parisienne, *1944.*

etween 1941 and 1948 Karinska executed almost half of Ballet Theatre's forty-odd new productions, including such works as *Princess Aurora,* with fantastically elaborate designs by Léon Bakst; *Bluebeard,* designed by Marcel Vertés (for which Karinska herself crocheted Bluebeard's chain mail in silver wool); and *Waltz Academy,* a Balanchine ballet with sets designed by Oliver Smith, codirector, with Lucia Chase, of Ballet Theatre.

Karinska would later execute the costumes for many Broadway shows designed and produced by Smith, among them *Billion Dollar Baby, On the Town, Miss Liberty* (all staged by Jerome Robbins), and the 1954 revival of Balanchine's *On Your Toes.* "She was at that time *the* preeminent creator of costumes," said Smith. "They were a revelation to Americans because they were so sophisticated." As for her collaborative skills, Smith commented that "She was very kind to young designers, very encouraging, and knocked herself out just as much for them as for someone of enormous prestige." The respect was mutual. "I wouldn't dream of going to Karinska and telling her how to make a costume, it would be like an apprentice going to Michelangelo and telling him how to make a drawing."[69]

Over time Karinska and Smith became friends. He often was invited to her formal and ornate dinner parties, where shots of vodka were served in her large collection of silver "thimbles." The impeccable meals were always prepared by one of several Chinese chefs (all called "Lee" by Karinska) to whom she paid vast weekly salaries. Smith recalled Karinska as being a "warm, hospitable, gutsy, flirtatious, obsessive, very loquacious individual who used very strange, unexpected metaphors for things. . . . She could also be very scatterbrained, slightly hysterical, but in back of it all there was a mind of steel. She expressed enormous passion and if she didn't like something she was violent about it."[70]

Another successful but less amiable collaboration, enduring through three decades, was that of Karinska and Irene Sharaff. Smith, who often worked with the two, observed their relationship:

I think Sharaff learned a great deal from Karinska—they were very, very close, and Irene had an enormous admiration for her. . . . Sharaff invented a fantastic, wonderful, accordion type of tutu, but she wouldn't have been able to do it without having worked with Karinska. She wouldn't have figured it out herself.[71]

This particular pairing of dynamic, single-minded women did not, however, end in friendship, and few words passed between them in later years. It was clearly a case of the clashing of two iron wills. Sharaff recounts a lurid tale about the costuming of Leonard Bernstein's *Candide* in her memoir *Broadway and Hollywood.*

When Karinska was given the job of executing the costumes, I handed her at the end of the week a portfolio of about two hundred and fifty costume sketches, with memos on most of

Sketch by Cecil Beaton for Camille
and Alicia Markova in the costume, 1946.

97

Sketches by Esteban Francés of the Rooster and the Cat for Renard *and in costume: Lew Christensen, John Taras, Fred Danieli, and Todd Bolender; 1947.*

them pertaining to materials, colors, and other details, for her to look over during the weekend. We made a date to meet on the Monday to discuss the costumes and to start choosing materials. She turned up at my apartment on Sunday morning. Taking one look at her face, and hearing at the same time that she had just lit a candle at the church on the corner, I sensed disaster. I quickly led her to a chair and gave her a stiff brandy. As she revealed the sad tidings, it was necessary to pour her more support, for she had left the portfolio of sketches in a taxi. They were lost. She could not remember whether it had been a yellow cab, a green one, or another kind. I was stunned and for some minutes speechless. Then, as I started to ask her if she had telephoned the Lost and Found Departments of the cab companies, she suddenly pulled handkerchiefs out of her handbag and the scarf from around her neck and began to tie them on the legs of chairs and tables. Seeing her at this, I had a fleeting thought that one of us must be going mad. However, she in turn started to reassure me by explaining that that was what they used to do in Russia, at the same time fervently praying, to find something lost or mislaid. Absurd or not, in a few days, during which frantic efforts were made to trace the sketches, the portfolio was retrieved.[72]

Sharaff, prior to her death, reportedly refused to speak about Karinska, saying only, "I don't want to speak ill of the dead."

§

Throughout the early 1940s Balanchine worked on Broadway as well as with various ballet companies, and Karinska managed to work with him numerous times. For

Denham's Ballet Russe de Monte Carlo she executed twenty-five ballets between its founding in 1938 and 1946, and among these were six for Balanchine during his two-year tenure as ballet master of the company. These included Stravinsky's *Danses Concertantes,* for which Karinska produced Eugene Berman's snappy, short, and sophisticated "shrapnel punctured"[73] garments described by Edwin Denby as "brilliant as scarabs, if scarabs came in several colors"[74]; a new version of *Le Bourgeois Gentilhomme,* also with costumes by Berman; *Raymonda,* with costumes by Alexandre Benois; and *The Night Shadow* (later called *La Sonnambula*), with fabulous fantasy costumes by Dorothea Tanning.

Balanchine's freelancing came to an end in 1946 when he formed yet another company with Lincoln Kirstein, who had just returned home from service in World War II. Ballet Society was founded as a member-supported nonprofit organization, and its first performance—on November 20, 1946, at the Central High School of Needle Trades in New York City—featured a program consisting of Ravel's *The Spellbound Child* and the premiere of Hindemith's *The Four Temperaments.* Karinska prepared the costumes for both. Two years later, when Ballet Society became the New York City Ballet and gave its premiere performance—a program of *Orpheus, Concerto Barocco,* and *Symphony in C*—Karinska made all the costumes. Balanchine had found his final home in ballet, and Karinska was alongside for the next thirty years, reaching, in collaboration with him, the apotheosis of her work. Not only would she be involved in some of the most elaborate and beautiful productions of her life, but in the constancy of her presence, the vigilance of her standards, and the immaculate execution of her creations she would profoundly influence the way ballet appeared to its new American audience.

The streamlined look that she and Balanchine would pioneer was not especially evident in those first performances. *The Four Temperaments,* for example, was buried under the asymmetrical, layered designs of Kurt Seligmann, and *Concerto Barocco* was ensconced in Eugene Berman's synthetic rubber constructions. "He had no idea of how to build the structure to support his decorative schemes," says Kermit Love. "He depended on Karinska as a translator." These two ballets were quickly stripped of their magnificent but inhibitive costumes, and the now famous "leotard" ballets were born.[75] For Stravinsky's *Orpheus,* however, Karinska had magically translated the designs of Isamu Noguchi into the lightweight, portable, yet three-dimensional costumes that to this day remain stunning in their bizarre, erotic, and mythic effect.

§

In late 1949, at the age of sixty-three, Karinska embarked on a new phase of her career. Balanchine asked her to not only make but design the costumes for a new ballet entitled *Bourrée Fantasque,* set to music by Emmanuel Chabrier. She produced lovely, jaunty black tutus flecked with bright colors and accessorized—in keeping with the lighthearted spirit of the ballet—with fans, gloves, and headpieces. While the honor and freedom of designing costumes herself were important to her, Karinska really had been "designing" throughout her career, each time she translated a sketch into fabric. "I think anything you designed became Karinska's. Otherwise, it just didn't happen," explained one designer.[76] Karinska slipped into

Beatrice Tompkins and Herbert Bliss in Punch and the Child, *1947.*

Maria Tallchief and Nicholas Magallanes in Kurt Seligmann's costumes for The Four Temperaments, *1946.*

Isamu Noguchi's designs for Orpheus, *1948, with Maria Tallchief as Eurydice, Edward Bigelow as Pluto, and (below) Herbert Bliss as Apollo.*

Sketch by Karinska for Maria Tallchief's headdress for the second movement of Bourrée Fantasque.

OPPOSITE:

Tanaquil Le Clercq and Jerome Robbins in Bourrée Fantasque, *1949. Ballanchine asked Karinska to design as well as execute the costumes for this ballet, and thus, at the age of sixty-five, Karinska began a new phase of her career.*

this new role easily and enthusiastically, and over the next several decades she designed over thirty ballets. In them, one can detect not only her characteristic brilliance of style and detail, but something more of her personal taste.

Karinska's conception of feminine beauty echoed Balanchine's, and it was here, with the female dancers, that they created what were perhaps their most inspired and influential images. The Balanchine ballerina that Karinska dressed was a woman on a pedestal, untouchable yet soft and vibrant—not an imposing goddess or empress with hard edges and uplifted bosom, but a real woman inhabiting her own body, draped in silk chiffon or cotton tulle that conformed to her true shape. In Balanchine's hands her movements became metaphors for her character—recognizably American, but classic, too. She was long, lean, young, athletic, energetic, and powerful, but she was dressed for some mythical court life, not for the gym. She was the Young Girl at the ball dressed in white in *La Valse,* the spiky, sexy insect in *Metamorphoses,* the tightly bodiced Dewdrop in *The Nutcracker,* the hip-swinging saloon girl in *Western Symphony,* the cheerful cheerleader in *Stars and Stripes,* the peach-and-pearl-veiled fairy in *A Midsummer Night's Dream,* and the shy, sheerly clad geisha in *Bugaku.*

But, whatever her role, the ballerina's own physique was visible and available for adventure, and this freedom was one of Karinska's greatest contributions. The dancer was never merely a mannequin for Karinska's virtuosic display, but remained, as for Balanchine, the focus of the whole endeavor. This celebration of female form reached a new peak in 1950 when Karinska recostumed Balanchine's *Symphony in C.* Here, in the forty identical white tutus, the aptly named "Balanchine/Karinska tutu" or "powder-puff tutu," was born, forever changing the way a ballet dancer could look.

§

One of the great inventions of theatrical costuming of all time, the tutu—probably derived from the French child's word "tu-tu" or "cul-cul" meaning "bottom," and thus seeming to relate to the panties onto which the layers of tulle are attached—first appeared in Paris, in a long version, in 1832, on Marie Taglioni in *La Sylphide.* As dancing became more virtuosic and modesty less prevalent, the skirt was gradually shortened to show more leg—first the ankle, then the knee, then the thigh. Before Balanchine and Karinska put their minds to it, the standard existing tutu, and still the most common around the world except at the New York City Ballet, was the British or Russian "pancake," so-called because of its deep, wide, and very flat skirt, supported by a wire hoop at the outer edges. Karinska had been making this type of tutu herself until she met Balanchine, although she preferred not to use a hoop but rather spokes that radiated out from the waist like an umbrella.

This type of tutu, however, had many qualities unsuited to Balanchine's vision of the way his dancers should move. The hoop or umbrella skirt often takes on movement of its own, echoing that of the dancer several beats later, in a way that is not always musically appropriate. And if dancers move quickly and close together, as they do in Balanchine ballets, their hoops can collide and tip, adding unchoreographed elements to the proceedings. Finally, because the skirts are wide and weighty they

Merrill Ashley (foreground) with Sandra Jennings, Maria Calegari, and Garielle Whittle in Symphony in C, 1980.

Leslie Roy, in a Symphony in C tutu, with Madame Sophie Pourmel, the New York City Ballet wardrobe mistress, 1979.

often reach to the knees, whereas Balanchine wanted to see more, see the legs, their arabesques and penchés moving easily, naturally, and freely, not fighting to get out from under a hoop. He did not like the sudden revelations of posterior that an extended leg would sometimes produce under a tipped pancake tutu. In short, Balanchine wanted a smaller, shorter, softer, lighter, more natural and flattering tutu, and Karinska gave it to him.

Strictly speaking, this was not the first appearance of a short, fluffy tutu on the stage. Harriet Hoctor, the American toe dancer who performed on the vaudeville circuit during the 1930s, wore a similarly short tutu, with the obvious purpose of showing off her sensational legs. Curiously enough, though any direct influence is difficult to document, Balanchine may well have seen Hoctor dance when he arrived in America in 1933, and in 1936 he actually choreographed pieces for her to perform in the Ziegfeld Follies. Once again, as with *Star and Garter,* the vernacular, the popular, even the so-called vulgar may be seen to merge in Balanchine and Karinska's work. After all, Hoctor and Balanchine had the same motive in their costuming—to maximize the visual effect of the body.

The *Symphony in C* tutu, the prototype for the powder-puff tutu, had no hoop and only six or seven layers of gathered net (as opposed to the twelve or more used for the hoop tutu). The layers, each a half-inch longer than the previous one, were short, never precisely aligned, and tacked together loosely to give the skirt an unprecedented softness and fullness. The skirt fell in a natural, slightly downward slope over the hips to the tops of the thighs. But the skirt was only the most obvious of the changes and details that Karinska instituted. It was in her experiments with the bodice that Karinska really revolutionized the tutu.

Symphony in C *tutu, 1950. This is the original prototype of the Karinska/Balanchine "powder puff" tutu with its soft skirt, as distinguished from the "pancake tutu" with its flat, horizontal skirt shaped by a hoop at the outer edge.*

Made before the panties or skirt are attached, the bodice is the foundation of the costume. Karinska's experiments with the cut, shape, seaming, and decoration of the bodice had begun in 1932, when she made her first one for members of the Ballets Russes de Monte Carlo. Using anywhere from six to fifteen panels of fabric, Karinska was a pioneer in the practice of cutting on the bias (the diagonal of the fabric, as opposed to straight up and down or across), for a highly fitted garment. Cutting on the bias was a much-admired technique in the couture world of Paris in the 1930s, where Karinska no doubt came across the idea. But there the beauty of the bias cut was usually found in loose-fitting garments, where the diagonal created its own kind of shape and sexy cling. Karinska's tremendous innovation was in using the bias cut for a tightly fitted bodice, where the give and take of the cut could be used to accommodate the aerobic requirements of a dancer's—or opera singer's—rib cage. "No one else knew how to do a bodice like that or even knew why you should do a bodice like that," says Broadway and ballet designer Patricia Zipprodt. "Most of them were so clumsy, straight-up-and-down bodices with seams, seams, seams, but never any alteration in the fabric, until Karinska. Her costumes were danceable things, singable things."[77]

A typical Karinska bodice would be a mixture of panels, the back and center front usually cut the normal way, with various bias-cut panels in between, under, and around the ribs and diaphragm. Out of this extremely smooth and elegant-looking composition came another, less practical quality that epitomizes the sensual magic of Karinska's invention. She used only "living" fibers—ones made by plants or animals. These fabrics, unlike inert synthetics, give off an energy all their own, and, when complemented by stage lights, their various hidden qualities rise and shine. Thus, the

OVERLEAF, LEFT:
A Musical Joke *tutu, 1956.*

OVERLEAF, RIGHT:
Ballet Imperial *tutu, 1964.*

Susan Hendl and Joseph Duell in La Valse, *1979.*

ballerina's torso, wrapped in its straight and biased panels, would gleam as it moved around the stage, giving off alternately light and shadow, matte and sheen, like the facets of a precious stone. When ballerinas are described as glowing, or appearing chiseled like jewels, there is, therefore, real science behind the illusion.

Other Karinska touches can best be viewed by looking at examples—and there are many; Karinska made over nine thousand costumes for the New York City Ballet alone. In 1951 she designed the long tulle dresses for Balanchine's *La Valse,* and these mysterious, elongated, haunting ball gowns so perfectly complemented the eerie, pendulous tone of the ballet and Maurice Ravel's music that the ballet is unimaginable without them. Zipprodt attributes her own career decision to having once viewed these costumes.

I had just come to New York and I was trying to figure out what to do with my life. I was painting and waitressing at Schrafft's—the whole routine of starving young people with dreams. I used to spend a great deal of time with John Mealy who was doing a big color story for *Life* and he dragged me to the ballet. It was *La Valse* and in comes Tanaquil Le Clercq in this white dress. Bang. I went down to FIT [Fashion Institute of Technology] and beat on their doors and got a scholarship and went to school. I wanted to design for this company, for Balanchine. What Karinska had said with this dress changed my life.[78]

(The white satin and tulle gown Zipprodt saw was, interestingly, not really white but rather a luscious cream color. Karinska knew that a true white has an empty, flat appearance onstage.) Later in the ballet, during her courtship with Death, this bride of youth dons a cape of sheer, black gauze and a beaded, black choker and carries a bouquet of dried black roses, thereby succinctly transforming her innocence into a poignant image of impending doom. The layering of dark over light gave an intangible sensation of the sinister that accentuated the essence of the music itself.

Layering of colors, often very disparate ones, was one of Karinska's specialties, and it was never more apparent or used to better dramatic advantage than in the other women's costumes in *La Valse*. Attached to heavy, silver-gray halter-cut bodices with low-slung backs, the long skirts were composed of up to six layers of color—red, orange, purple, and pink—all topped by a single layer of translucent gray. Balanchine took advantage of this unusual depth of color in his choreography when he had the women lift the edges of their skirts and fling them in the air to release a cascade of colors, each not quite looking like itself because of its neighbor's omnipresent glow. For the headpieces Karinska employed contradiction to perfection, sewing large, black-rimmed rhinestones into the wiry weave of black horsehair. They, like the costumes and the ballet, were sprightly and elegant but tinged with death. It was truly haunting elegance.

The subtler effect of layering similar colors can be found throughout Karinska's work, beginning with *Cotillon,* in 1932. For the Snowflake costumes for Balanchine's *Nutcracker,* in 1954, she juxtaposed beige, pink, and blue tulle for an airy, pale, not-quite-there feel—the feel of snow. For the "Emeralds" section of *Jewels,* in 1967, she covered three layers of yellow-beige tulle with one of dark green and one of light green. For *Raymonda Variations* in 1961, the overwhelming color of the tutus is bright

Tanaquil Le Clercq in La Valse, *1951. The designer Patricia Zipprodt remarked, "What Karinska had said with this dress changed my life."*

Bodice of a Swan Lake *tutu from Rouben Ter-Arutunian's 1964 design.*

pink, although the top layer is, in fact, of a pale blue. According to Karinska's canon, a single solid color is a dead event under the lights, inside a proscenium, and it is only by juxtaposing and combining that one can suggest the real blue-white of snow, the green of an emerald, or even the pink of a pastel ballet.

A different type of layering effect is apparent in Karinska's costumes for Balanchine's *Serenade*. First choreographed in 1934, this ballet set to Tschaikovsky's yearning score was Balanchine's first in America, and it had withstood various costuming styles for almost twenty years. There were leotards and skirts, then short tunics, then decorated ones, but when Karinska designed the pale blue gowns in 1952 for the New York City Ballet's production it was as if this great ballet had been through a long genesis and was only now in full bloom. So simple as to seem inevitable, the long-waisted, plain blue bodices ended in low-slung, diagonally placed (a very flattering line on a woman's hips that Karinska used frequently), ankle-length skirts of finely woven tulle. Each skirt was made of just one, much-gathered layer— twenty yards of fabric in all. Otherwise blue all around, in front of each leg, from hip to ankle, Karinska placed a sheer panel of beige tulle through which the dancer's legs

OPPOSITE:

Brahms-Schoenberg Quartet *tutu for Violette Verdy in the First Movement, 1966.*

RIGHT:

Karin von Aroldingen and Adam Lüders in Serenade, *1983 (designed 1952).*

Tracy Bennett, Kyra Nichols, Maria Calegari, Peter Martins, Merrill Ashley, Stephanie Saland, Susan Hendl, and Victor Castelli in Divertimento No. 15, *1978 (designed 1966).*

would appear. The effect of this small detail is, like the ballet itself, subtle, yet exaggerated; sexy, yet demure. The overall effect of thirty-two of these windswept costumes on a moonlit stage, moving with Balanchine to Tschaikovsky, is one of the single most romantic atmospheres on any theatrical stage in this century.

Unlike many designers, who see a certain shade of color in their mind's eye and then proceed to stir the dye vats to reproduce it, Karinska disliked dyed colors. She knew that they were unstable and under the heat of the stage lights would inevitably change color and preferred to work within the "limitations" of what was available and what she could find on her numerous shopping trips to Paris. She would often buy hundreds of yards of a material she liked and put it on the shelf for a future ballet, and, with uncanny frequency, Balanchine would sooner or later come up with a ballet where she could indeed use it to perfection. To this day there remain drawers of new and antique lace, gold braid, silver roses, strings of bugle beads, and bolts of fabric that Karinska bought and never used. These treasures are kept in one of her old bureaus in the New York City Ballet costume shop, and sometimes, for a very special costume, a length of lace or a strand of beads will be carefully extracted from the stash. But mostly the bureau is kept under lock and key; what is in it is irreplaceable in today's manufacturing world. Ironically, the result of Karinska's insistence on using ready-made colors is a legacy of dyed ones. The browns and beiges and blues and pinks she used are no longer made and cannot be found at any price, so when the *Serenade* costumes need replacing, the vats of dye are filled and hundreds and hundreds of yards of tulle are plunged into the boiling liquid. Karinska would be horrified.

Dropped or diagonal waists were not the only figure-enhancing techniques Karinska used. While her famous *Symphony in C* tutu had a faceted bodice that reached to the hip, where the skirt began, many of her costumes—such as the beautifully tailored and somewhat more complex tutus for Balanchine's *Divertimento No. 15*—featured a yoke, an extra section of costume that reached from the skirt to the waist. The upper bodice section was shaped to meet the yoke at the waist on the sides and in a flattering V in the front. At the waistline, behind the joining of bodice and yoke, lies a series of invisible vertical elastics that together allow the dancer full movement from the waist and hips in all directions. The dancer does not feel them, and the audience does not see them; their presence is just one more detail that contributes to the overall fluid effect. Breaking a costume-making custom, Karinska often made the yoke in a different shade from the upper bodice, as in the 1966 ballet *Brahms-Schoenberg Quartet,* thereby recasting the appearance of the figure. The contrast, however subtle, creates depth, texture, and richness, qualities that correspond to and enhance the grandeur of Balanchine's ballet.

While these various details are of a visible and exterior nature, Karinska's innovations were not only for the audience but also for the dancer, and to peer inside one of her costumes is to view the matte side of luxury and the very loving dedication of this woman to the dancers she dressed. Made of cotton drill—a heavy, tightly woven fabric that gives shape and support to the satin it backs, and absorbency to the sweat and perfume of the human being it lays against—the bias-cut panels on the inside of a bodice are as beautifully cut, stitched, and finished as those on the outside. Seeing this, one can readily understand why a Karinska costume lasts three or four

Sketch by Rouben Ter-Arutunian for Melissa Hayden's tutu in Cortège Hongrois *and the tutu on a mannequin at Karinska's shop, 1973.*

times longer than most others. With its delicate weaves, intricate seaming, and hand-stitched edges, each costume is made with the precision, quality, and strength of a military uniform.

Karinska's fittings were conducted for multiple purposes, of which physical fit and aesthetic beauty were only the most obvious. Fittings were tests of her laboratory results, and Karinska was interested not only in the static visual aspect of her work—and here most other designers cease their interest—but in the physical performance of her creations. "She understood the velocity of fabric," says Suzanne Farrell, a ballerina she clothed for almost twenty years.[79] "Are you comfortable? Can you move?" she would ask, and if there was any hindrance, seen or felt, Karinska was known to tear out the entire garment on the spot and begin again. Her work attitude was notable for its extraordinary lack of ego, considering what a strong personality she did have. But her work was about the work, not about herself, and she would never insist on any feature or aspect of a costume just because she had designed it, or labored for days over it—especially if the dancer was restricted in any way or if Balanchine was not pleased.

§

A tutu under construction in Karinska's atelier, c. 1974.

A handmade decoration on a costume.

In all the dance world, elasticity is all—in dancer and apparel alike. While the invention itself was not Karinska's, her development of a two-piece vest for male ballet dancers released their arms and chest to move articulately and independently. Originally a tailoring stunt from the mid-eighteenth century—in which the sleeves of a jacket were attached to an underlining over which was fitted the sleeveless body of the jacket—and later used by Chanel and Dior in their fashion collections, it was Karinska who first put it on the ballet stage. By allowing a dancer to raise his arms above his head without his entire jacket drifting up his chest and bunching, the technique gave male dancers a previously impossible elegance. Kermit Love first remembers seeing such a costume on Igor Youskevitch in Balanchine's *Theme and Variations* in 1947. "I remember Youskevitch commenting on how free he felt, how liberating it was. But it wasn't only that he was free, but it had the look of freedom." This example illustrates one of the basic differences between Karinska and her competitors. Her work was haute couture for the stage, whereas large costume shops—including Brooks, originally a military tailor, and Eaves Costume Company—would deliver a costume made with only a minimum of time and effort. "You would say, 'This is the costume,'" says Love, "but you were not moved. It had an A-B-A look. They all invested money in the shows, so they wanted to keep their charges down on costs and labor. But with a costume from Karinska you would say, 'Ah! This is Raymonda, this is Prince Desirée, this is Princess Aurora.'"[80]

It was in the exploration of decoration—on a neckline, a waistline, a sleeve, a headpiece, or a skirt—that Karinska's work went beyond the relative simplicity of couture dressmaking to the theatrical, where exaggeration is imperative to elicit the maximum visual effect from a great distance. She was the kind of woman who made long-term investments—not in stocks and bonds, but in seam allowances. Karinska felt about antique lace the way most women feel about diamonds. She was a master of the unnecessary detail—the back twist of braid, the inset brocade flower, the hand-embroidered cuff closure, the beaded design in four shades of red. "She loved concealing things, which I thought was an elegance of hers," says Stanley Simmons, a designer who worked with Karinska. "There were ribbons under chiffon, or ribbons under the net, or rhinestones on the second layer of the net and not necessarily on the top. She would put an orange satin ribbon under a piece of gray and put mirrors on the satin ribbon for no reason at all—it was mystery."[81]

"She never stopped inventing," says Love, "whether it was with a crochet hook and a bit of ribbon, tacking it and twisting it and manipulating it. If she did it on one side she'd turn it over and look at the other side, 'Well maybe there's a possibility here.'"[82] Zipprodt comments that Karinska would "build up. Like Rembrandt used glazes. It's the same mentality. People didn't know how to think this way before she thought this way."[83]

The result of Karinska's indefatigable energy in this area is awesome to behold—up close. Yet, ironically, the vast majority of any audience viewing the costumes on a stage from their distant vantage point would never see the bejeweled green version of a ladybug hidden under a flap of silk on the waistline of the "Emeralds" costumes, or the exquisite variety of bodices and skirt backs on the *Midsummer Night's Dream* fairy dresses, every single one folded differently and woven with gold and pearl braids.

But while it is the rare audience member who might note the luxury of detail, every viewer receives the sensation of texture, depth, and richness. But Karinska made costumes not only to be seen but to be worn, and much of her care and detail was for the performers themselves, who, despite their preoccupying nerves, would certainly feel the security of being beautifully presented—from the smooth seams of the lining to the velvet black-tipped roses at their breasts.

Perhaps the ultimate example of a Karinska detail is to be found in the five Spanish girls' costumes in the second act of *The Nutcracker*. At the center of each of their low décolletages Karinska placed a small Victorian-style pendant. Inside the pendants belonging to the four corps de ballet girls was a tiny photograph of Balanchine, and inside the one belonging to the principal dancer was one of Lincoln Kirstein. Quite invisible to the audience, this affectionate and personal gesture pleased everyone backstage and provided the dancers with a special secret to carry onstage.

In the vast, barely seen underworld of petticoats and other ruffled undergarments, Karinska ruled supreme. For the *Liebeslieder Walzer* costumes there were different shades of beige, each with a differently decorated ruffle, one with a pale pink ribbon woven through the edge, one with a special piece of antique lace Karinska had found

Tanaquil Le Clercq and André Eglevsky in costumes designed by Eugene Berman for Roma, *1955.*

in Paris, and another with ruffles both over and under the petticoat. Others, like the Eugene Berman costumes for a ballet called *Roma* (reused for Balanchine's version of *Le Baiser de la Fée* in 1972), have short, soft, silk overskirts with a lining of ribbon-strung ruffles that continue right up to the waistline. These underlayers are almost entirely concealed during the performance, except when the dancer moves a certain way, lifts her leg in a certain direction, or falls into her partner's arms a certain way. Then, and only then, will a hint of the gorgeousness that lies hidden be revealed, and then, just as in Balanchine's choreography, there will be a moment of magic.

It might seem like an enormous expenditure of labor, time, and expense for such a small, intangible reward, but that is precisely why Karinska was a true artist in her trade and not simply an efficient costume maker. Nothing about her costumes was skimped on—financially or materially—and no amount of human labor was too much, even for something concealed. Karinska put it best herself in an interview about her magnificent costumes for the Metropolitan Opera's production of *La Traviata*. Here, even the hoops under the gowns were encircled in lace. "They ask me why when the lace doesn't show. It is for the soul, I say."[84]

CHAPTER SIX

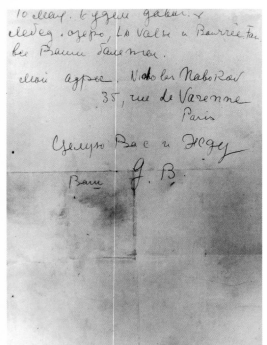

*Letter in Russian from George Balanchine
to Karinska, 1952.*

Though romantic liaisons were far from being the focus of Karinska's life, there were a few. While she often declared she had had enough of marriage, she was not without admirers; she simply had no interest in setting up house with anyone. André Derain is believed to have been a lover sometime during the mid-1930s, and she kept his pipe, a gift from his widow, throughout her life. She even telephoned Derain to talk about things long after his death in 1954. She was not without her superstitions and prone to making theatrical gestures.

It is a longstanding Karinska family legend that sometime in her youth, in Russia, Karinska had spoken with a clairvoyant who had told her that she would have a great love in her life but that it would not be romantically returned. And it became apparent to all, including the lady herself, that this was indeed the truth, and that the great love in question was George Balanchine. As she was eighteen years his elder, it is unlikely that there was ever any actual romance between Karinska and Balanchine, but over the course of their collaboration of more than forty years, something deeper than friendship arose. "She was," explained Oliver Smith, "in love with Balanchine, the concept of him."[85] This letter to Karinska from Balanchine, written in April of 1952 from Milan where he was staging some of his ballets, attests to one facet of their relationship.

Dear Varvara Andryevna,

How could you think that I forgot you? That will never happen. As far as I am concerned, you represent half our success; you give us an elegance that did not exist. . . .

Thank you for the sketch, which unfortunately I could not use. It arrived too late. I did a few things myself, thinking of you. But it did not turn out well, although infinitely better than anything done here. In your art you are unique in the world. . . . Next time, you and I will do a ballet here in Milan. I cannot begin to describe what they do here. The person in charge of the costumes is an amiable incompetent. Come to Paris for the opening of the opera on May 10th. We are doing *Swan Lake, La Valse,* and *Bourrée Fantasque*: all your ballets.

My address: c/o Nicholas Nabokov
                35 rue de Varenne, Paris

I kiss and wait for you.
    G. B.

True to his word, the following year Balanchine was again in Milan to stage *Le Baiser de la Fée* and *Symphony in C,* and he tried to convince the manager of La Scala, Dr. Antonio Ghiringhelli, to import Karinska, too.

I wish very much to have your permission to send Mme. Karinska to design the costumes and supervise their execution. Mme. Karinska is unsurpassed as an artist for theater costumes. . . . You will forgive me for saying, just between us, that at La Scala the costumes are not given top priority and they lack elegance. Whereas in ballets costumes are of primary importance and should really be of "haute couture" and therefore truly created on the dancers themselves. In addition, I have learned through experience that costumes designed by scenic artists rarely succeed, painters do not know enough about fashion design. I might mention that Mme. Karinska will not bother or annoy anyone and will not compete with your costumers. She will come as a designer and I am sure that she will leave behind her a heritage of good taste and elegance. While on the subject, I wish to know if there is in Italy a new fabric that is "tulle"—fluffy nylon? It can be found in all nuances, it is of great finesse, very solid and not expensive. If you do not have it we could bring you some if your government would permit it. Costumes of this fabric would last a very long time.

I have given you so many details because it seems to me that the presence of American dancers and of Mme. Karinska would contribute enormously to the quality of your finest productions.

By the 1950s and 1960s, Karinska and Balanchine were so experienced in their respective professions that their collaboration on a new ballet took on all the fanfare of sharing a cup of tea—literally. If Balanchine was about to begin a new ballet, or was even simply turning an idea over in his head, he would, unannounced, present himself at Karinska's atelier for afternoon tea. Sitting and sipping, Balanchine would tell her in vague, brief terms what his idea for the ballet was. For example, for *Liebeslieder Walzer* he might have told her it would be set to Brahms lieder, with four couples in two parts. Karinska would immediately respond by rolling out a bolt of silk she had been saving for just this project and begin to drape and pin it onto a mannequin. Balanchine might sip his tea and murmur, "Yes . . . and with red flowers," or he might say slowly and deliberately, "Could be . . . could be . . ."—meaning he hated it.

These informal discussions took the place of actual working sketches, a customary intermediary stage that Karinska, an unskilled draftsperson, rarely utilized. When she did produce sketches they were usually after the fact, and drawn using the finished costume as the model. "I work with color and material," she explained. "Never make a sketch without the material. Forget the drawings. They are nothing! My costumes move. The people are not sticks. They are alive. They have legs. One designer sent me sketches with pretty faces, carefully drawn, but no legs. I told him, 'Certainly some pretty faces will wear the costume, but not the pretty faces you have drawn. Make me the legs so she can move.'" Karinska was certainly more couturier than costume designer as the professions were defined by Chanel: "Costume designers work with a pencil: it is art. Couturiers with scissors and pins: it is a news item."[86]

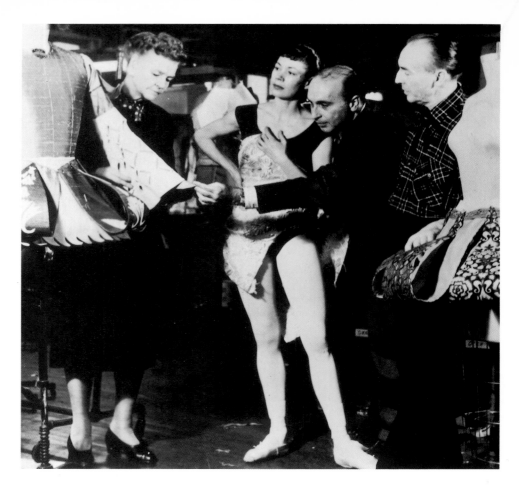

Karinska, Diana Adams, designer Esteban Francés, and George Balanchine at a fitting for Figure in the Carpet, *and (opposite) Mary Hinkson and Arthur Mitchell in the costumes, 1960.*

Not using sketches gave Karinska the freedom to change her mind all along the sewing process, and this suited Balanchine's needs perfectly.[87] She was so sure in her craft that, for her, flexibility was not an imposition but a release, just as it was for Balanchine when he choreographed a ballet. This spontaneity and confidence—so evident in the tale of a young dancer slipping and falling during a *Serenade* rehearsal and Balanchine's incorporating the mishap into the final ballet—has many echoes in Karinska's costume making. Things were often changed at any time, in any place, including in the wings between one entrance and another. Karinska was always ready to volley with Balanchine.

Another curious legacy—or rather the absence of one—has resulted from Karinska's disdain of sketches. There is nothing tangible to copyright, nothing two-dimensional to stamp with a name and date and put in a file for future reference or reproduction. Her designs exist only on the stage itself, each night when the curtain rises. The finished costumes are the blueprint, as transient as the dancer's entrances and exits, but as fixed as the image imprinted in the mind of a viewer.

§

Despite their great mutual respect, Karinska and Balanchine did not always agree. On occasion she would listen to his ideas about what he wanted for a ballet, and as soon as he climbed in the elevator to leave she would announce, "George doesn't know what he wants. I know what he wants. I'll give him what he wants"—and proceed to do so. Betty Cage, manager of the New York City Ballet for over thirty years, remembers Karinska, after some tiff, swearing on "the head of my dead father"

RIGHT:
Nicholas Magallanes and Nora Kaye
in The Cage, *1951.*

The Seven Deadly Sins *designed by Rouben*
Ter-Arutunian, 1958, and Allegra Kent
and Lotte Lenya in the production.

122

Tanaquil Le Clercq, Hugh Laing, Nora Kaye,
and Brooks Jackson in Antony Tudor's
Lilac Garden, *1951.*

that she would never speak to Balanchine again, and Balanchine likewise calling Karinska a "terrible, selfish woman" when she refused to will her gorgeous East Side town house to the New York City Ballet, wishing instead to leave it to her daughter, Irene. (He thought it would be the perfect setting for a club for his dancers, a place they could come after performances to relax, eat, and socialize.)[88]

But the fights were few and far between, and their reliance on each other was enormous. Leslie Copeland, manager of the men's wardrobe at the New York City Ballet since 1951, observed, "She loved beige and gold, and he loved pink and blue—how could they go wrong?"

§

Karinska also loved blue—on herself—and her single most notable physical trait in her later years was the color blue, an impressive topping of silver-blue hair echoed by her gray-blue eyes. The overall effect was one of supreme sophistication and total authority. If she was not being likened to a princess it was to an empress—but not only on account of her looks. Karinska's manner was imperious, extreme, emotional, and demanding, and working for her was not easy. Perfection was the goal, and human feelings were clearly secondary concerns when quality was at stake.

Karinska could always be found shouting and her tyrannical behavior in pursuit of beauty was legendary. For those who did not speak Russian there was added confusion. Designer Willa Kim recalls of her days in Hollywood as Karinska's apprentice at Paramount: "She was always screaming for something in Russian, which I didn't understand, and I was always running about trying to figure out what she wanted."[89] Max Litwin, a tailor who worked in Karinska's shop for years, wore a hearing device that he put to good use with Madame. If he heard her bracelets approaching, the warning signal for all, he would turn off his hearing aid until her verbal tirade was over and then calmly ask an onlooker, "What did she say?"

Not all her workers resorted to such passive-aggressive defenses. Once, just when Karinska had finished tearing out a week's work by Elsie, a master milliner, and began to walk away, an iron flew past her head and bounced off the wall. Karinska calmly turned her head and said only, "You missed," and stepped onto the elevator. One worker declared, "Madame, you are a female Rasputin!" On another occasion, Karinska went so far as to tear up her own daughter's work after Irene had come from Paris to oversee the shop during one of Karinska's illnesses. There was even a legal scandal of sorts when Karinska and her head cutter and draper went to war and Karinska told Balanchine, "Either she goes or I go." Within union rules the woman could not be fired and so some elaborate presentations had to be made to the union to enable what amounted to a temporary leave of absence.

"She could be absolutely awful without justification to people in the shop," says Edward Bigelow, longtime New York City Ballet manager, "but they stayed even when they were being insulted. There was not that much turnover." Compensating for Karinska's temper was an unswerving loyalty to her employees. She knew their value and did, on occasion, let them know with gifts and praise, and she would defend a worker she liked just as violently as she would condemn one she did not.

Salvucci, Karinska's men's tailor, Rouben Ter-Arutunian, Karinska, and Toussia Saylenoff with Ter-Arutunian's sketches for Swan Lake, *1964.*

Karinska with Shaun O'Brien, in his costume as the sorcerer von Rothbart in Swan Lake, *at her 57th Street shop, 1965. Karinska told the dancer, "O'Brien, this is my masterpiece." The wings of his cape were individually feathered in layers of gauze, metallic fabrics, and horsehair.*

125

Ollie Olsen, a cutter and draper, was also a drinker, and for a time Balanchine was insisting that he be fired. But Ollie could cut and sew silk satin like no one else and Karinska told Balanchine, "If he goes, I go." Ollie stayed, and it was arranged for him to work in the shop alone, late at night. "Karinska knew what someone could contribute," says Love. "She was not afraid to have good people around." And the loyalty was returned by her cutters, drapers, milliners, and sewers, demonstrating that unexpected but dependable law that functions in most artistic endeavors: namely that the pursuit of excellence has an even stronger instinctual draw than the need for emotional self-preservation.

§

Sometime in the mid-1950s Karinska purchased a big colonial-style house in Sandisfield, Massachusetts. On her property, rechristened St. Joan Hill, she indulged her love of roses — roses of all colors but yellow. Although she tailored many yellow costumes in her life, she hated the color and would ferociously pluck from her garden any flowers of the offending color that dared to raise their heads. At St. Joan Hill she also raised lambs, giving them names like "Frou-Frou" and "Tutu," and each year she would trim their wool, spin it, and weave blankets from it to give as gifts. The blankets were always accompanied by a card from the lamb.

Knowing the importance of her hands to her profession Karinska — with the discipline of a dancer — performed hand exercises every day, squeezing a small red rubber ball in her palms to retain strength and flexibility. And those hands, with painted but sometimes chewed nails, and laden with the ever-present dangling bracelets, were never still — as the needlepoint pillows, embroidered boxes, and tapestry blankets that filled her houses and those of her friends attest. For the bed Balanchine used when he visited St. Joan Hill she embroidered an entire coverlet depicting the legend of Joan of Arc. Like the artisans sewing the Bayeux Tapestry, Karinska could always be found, needle and thread in hand, stitching, stitching, stitching.

The 1950s saw one Karinska triumph after another on the City Center stage where the New York City Ballet performed. She re-dressed Antony Tudor's wistful *Lilac Garden* with costumes that he admitted were "divinely beautiful," although he complained that the New York City Ballet version of his ballet was too rich and too sumptuous and that "the people wearing [such costumes] could not have had the thoughts my people had. . . . It became a rich family. My ladies aren't rich."[90] Balanchine echoed the sentiment: "I like the ballet. But Tudor wanted it to be danced in simple dresses, middle-class English style. Here we wear beautiful, elegant gowns and tiaras — like kings and queens."[91]

For Balanchine's one-act *Swan Lake* Cecil Beaton designed such luxurious sets and costumes that Kirstein wrote, "It is the most beautiful thing we have ever achieved, and the house is sold out every time we do it. Karinska's tutus were applauded every time they arrived on stage. She even managed to find some real swan feathers."[92] For a later production designed by Rouben Ter-Arutunian, Balanchine and Karinska again pursued the eternal problem of suggesting wings without cluttering a dancer's

Tanaquil Le Clercq in Metamorphoses, *1952.*

Tanaquil Le Clercq and Jacques d'Amboise in Western Symphony, *1955. Critic B. H. Haggin thought Le Clercq's hat "to say nothing of the way she wore it — alone worth the price of admission."*

line with flapping attachments: "Costume wings that carry much conviction are a severe trial to fabricate," wrote Kirstein.[93] But for this production Karinska had some new ideas. She cut the tutu itself in a manner that emulated the image—short in front and longer in back. The dancer's body itself took flight in brilliant simplicity.

Wings, but of an insect nature—butterflies', fireflies', and a Kafkaesque beetle's—were again the challenge in Balanchine's 1952 ballet *Metamorphoses,* set to the music of Paul Hindemith. But Karinska had been studying these intricate constructions from the live models in her garden for years, and she was ready to reproduce them. John Martin, dance critic for *The New York Times,* wrote of the ballet:

Balanchine and Karinska have really gone to work and turned out an idiotic, visually gorgeous, richly humorous extravaganza. . . . Karinska has designed a basic costume, which, though perfectly decorous, has the intent of nudity, and upon this she has added in each movement some little bits of identifying regalia—minimal trunks for a company of circus acrobats, wee tutus, masks, antennae, and the like for a horde of Chinese insects; huge wings for a flock of mammoth birds. They are all perfectly beautiful. . . .[94]

Tragically, the costumes were later destroyed in a warehouse fire, and the ballet and its gossamer-winged underworld were returned to dust.

§

While ballets themselves are by nature as ephemeral as a live performance, Karinska's costumes were not always equally fragile. First performed in 1954 without scenery or costumes, *Western Symphony,* Balanchine's tribute to the cowboy lore of his adopted country, found its true voice when dressed by Karinska several months later. (That it took two enthusiastic Russians to produce a seminal American stage work was an irony often noted.) The glorious bushels of ruched ribbons and tulle that comprise the tutus are still used today, forty years later, though the bodices and internal workings of the costumes have been replaced and reworked numerous times. It is fortunate that these subtle, colorful, fluffy gatherings of Karinska's imagination were constructed on a foundation as solid as the Parthenon's, for they are virtually impossible to reproduce today both technically and financially. They are unquestionably one of Karinska's masterpieces and, as one writer observed, they "got reviews of their own."[95] Critic John Martin wrote:

It is a triumphant piece of interpretation, picking up Balanchine's style and humor at every turn, and making definite everything that was previously subject to question. The work is really a classic ballet, based on the legend of the old West more or less as it has been perpetuated in Hollywood. The girls do not really wear tutus, but their brief skirts are little masses of ruffles that strongly suggest the tutu, while at the same time they are whopped up at the sides like the sauciest kind of dresses of the Sixties. Their millinery is incredibly perky, their color schemes are marvelously daring, and the general effect is of the most elegant brassiness.[96]

Another critic, P. W. Manchester, wrote that the ballet "delights its audience even more now that it has a street background, complete with saloons, and costumes

Judith Fugate, Jay Jolley, Colleen Neary, Steven Caras, and Muriel Aason in Fanfare, 1977 *(designed 1953).*

Allegra Kent as the sleepwalker from La Sonnambula, 1979.

129

which make all the girls look like Marlene Dietrich in *Destry Rides Again* (and very nice, too) and all the boys look like Roy Rogers. The company continues to dance it for about ten times its worth. And of course there is Le Clercq's hat."[97]

Tanaquil Le Clercq, Balanchine's wife at the time, was one of Karinska's most beloved ballerinas, and she crowned her lanky elegance in the fourth movement of *Western Symphony* with a huge, curled, brimmed, and plumed hat made of wired black horsehair. In its immense, sexy transparent curves this hat epitomized the affectionate, raucous tone of the ballet itself and, ironically, made an appropriate reappearance over twenty years later as the Merry Widow's hat in Balanchine's rendition of the Franz Lehár waltz in his ballet *Vienna Waltzes*.

It was also for Le Clercq that Karinska designed what she admitted was her favorite costume. Having its genesis in both the corsetry of her Parisian days and in the boned bodices for Gypsy Rose Lee, the tiny, tight, pearly-pink Dewdrop costume for Balanchine's 1954 production of *The Nutcracker* is indeed the delight and envy of every female dancer. The bodice is composed of fifteen boned seams connected by translucent, dew-colored net. An extra layer across the bosom enhances mystery while preserving modesty. (This bodice would reappear in the pink and black costumes for the girl in *Slaughter on Tenth Avenue,* only then the skirt was sexy fringe, not ballerina net.) The skirt of the tutu has taken on various lengths over the years, depending on the individual ballerina's physique. For Le Clercq, the Dewdrop skirt was a short, spontaneous sprout of tulle reaching to just below the hips and revealing her gorgeous long legs in both front and back. Balanchine requested this briefest of versions again twenty-six years later for the teenaged Darci Kistler, whose dynamism and precision of leg closely echoed that of Le Clercq's. Upon this costume of so little visible substance Karinska dripped rhinestone dewdrops around the neck and hip. And with the same drops, in all shapes and sizes, she devised a headpiece of the most exquisite glitter and delicacy. The costume was a vision of liquid beauty.

The Nutcracker, a full-length work in two acts, provided Karinska with her largest full-scale original project for Balanchine yet, and to this day the ballet is an almost overwhelming showcase for her designs and workmanship. For the Victorian Party Scene in Act I she made lush gowns, bustles, and petticoats in subtle shades of mauves and browns—each one different, each decorated with antique lace and handmade crocheted ornaments. For the Mouse Scene Karinska's nephew, Lawrence Vlady, created the masterful, humorous heads and bouncing bodies of the oversized mice, while she outfitted the pint-size soldiers in military regalia of blue, black, and yellow.

In Act II the dense, brown richness of the Spanish Hot Chocolate costumes was lifted by layer after layer of thick blue, pink, orange, and purple ruffles. The Arabian Coffee dancer, in a prime example of Karinska's clever juxtapositions, wore the color and texture of royalty while revealing herself like a harem seductress. She wore a gold-and-blue velvet bikini with a revealing skirt of bias-cut, blood-red matte Indian silk weighted with gold brocade. The Marzipan Shepherdesses' wired tutus bursting with marzipan fruits were inspired by a candy box from Schrafft's. And surrounding the glistening Dewdrop were the Flowers, whose simple pale silk bodices were hung with pleated deep pink petal layers punctuated by an occasional cheeky green leaf.

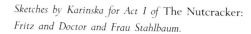

The Party Scene in Act 1 of The Nutcracker.

BELOW:
Angels in the dressing room, 1976.

OVERLEAF, LEFT:
Scenes from Act 1 of The Nutcracker *(clockwise, from top left): Jessica Lynn Cohen as Marie, Macaulay Culkin as the Prince, and Bart Robinson Cook as Drosselmeyer in the Party Scene; Jessica Lynn Cohen as Marie, nursing the wounded Nutcracker; Macaulay Culkin as the Nutcracker Prince; the Snowflakes; The Bunny, Robert Lyon as the Mouse King, and The Nutcracker Prince.*

OVERLEAF, RIGHT:
Scenes from Act II (clockwise, from top left): Nilas Martins and Lourdes Lopez as "Hot Chocolate"; Katrina Killian, Isabel Kimmel, Jennifer Tinsley, and Samantha Allen as the "Marzipan Shepherdesses"; Darci Kistler and Damian Woetzel in the Pas de Deux; Monique Meunier as "Coffee."

Michael Byars, Jennie Somogyi, and Elizabeth Walker as "Tea."

Polichinelles with William Otto as Mother Ginger.

Arch Higgins as the "Candy Cane."

LEFT:

Kyra Nichols as "Dewdrop" with the "Flowers."

The Finale, with Diana White, Miriam Mahdaviani, Alexander Ritter, Darci Kistler, Kyra Nichols, Philip Neal, Nilas Martins, Monique Meunier, Elizabeth Walker, Michael Byars, and Immaculada Velez.

Kirstein compared the onstage effect of costume and choreography to "a revolving bed of Fabergé enamel roses,"[98] while Kermit Love describes them as "pure couture. You could accept them from Patou or Balenciaga or any design house in Paris because they have that look. That's what makes it glorious. It was as though she said, 'This is my glory piece.'"[99]

True to form, all this glory was not quite ready on the day of the February premiere, and a half-hour before the performance both Balanchine and Jerome Robbins could be found backstage, needle and thread in hand, patiently sewing seams alongside an hysterical Karinska and her frantic stitching ladies.[100] On a few unannounced occasions during the next decade Balanchine and Karinska themselves participated in the ballet. In the Party Scene, the two hobbled around nimbly as the Grandfather and Grandmother of the Stahlbaum family, both elegantly decked out in Karinska's finery.

Wendy Whelan and Arch Higgins in Jerome Robbins's Dances at a Gathering, *featuring Joe Eula's designs of 1969.*

Diana White, Evelyn Carton, and Helene Alexopoulos in costumes from Stars and Stripes, *1979 (designed 1958).*

For Balanchine's 1956 *Allegro Brillante,* a concise, extended exercise in the speed, clarity, and possibility of the classical ballet vocabulary, Karinska devised some very simple—so simple that they were uncredited in the program—yet very revolutionary costumes for the women. When the curtain rose on a whirling circle of dancers dressed in soft, slim, knee-length blue and pink chiffon dresses, it was probably the first time audiences had seen a style of dress that has since become as standard a style of classical costume as the tutu.[101] This dress, with its thin, blouse-like chiffon top, radiates femininity, allows total freedom of movement (it is far less restricting to both back and legs than the much more highly constructed tutu), and punctuates that movement with a barely perceptible flair of flying silk.

As a basic style Karinska's chiffon costume has enjoyed more reincarnations in more ballets than could ever be traced. Perhaps its most romantic and lovely occurred in 1969, when Karinska executed Joe Eula's designs for Jerome Robbins's masterwork, *Dances at a Gathering.* The five principal female dancers were dressed in pale pink, lavender, olive green, light blue, and mustard yellow, respectively, each dress with a slightly different neckline, sleeve line, and waistline, thus underscoring the subtle yearning differences that the choreography suggested.

Just as Karinska had epitomized the flavor of the Old West in *Western Symphony,* she did the same for the "Red, White, and Blue" in the 1958 ballet *Stars and Stripes,* in costumes of military precision and happy exaggeration. Displaying bodices of royal blue and red velvet interlaid with heavy red silk, woven gold braid, and fringed epaulets, the two regiments of women exerted the charm and allure so often missing from real-life patriotic celebrations. The regiment of men was dressed in slim navy uniforms decorated with gold buttons and braid. All the dancers wore tall caps, brims edging forward, each topped by a red or blue ostrich feather, its vertical stance vibrating with all the energy and cocky wit of Balanchine's choreography.

In 1959 Karinska designed her first and only costumes for Martha Graham, the queen of modern dance, who was Balanchine's guest in his theater that season. Graham and Balanchine each choreographed separate sections of the orchestral works of Anton Webern for a ballet called *Episodes,* and while Balanchine's section was performed in simple leotards and tights, Graham's section, based on the story of Queen Elizabeth I and Mary, Queen of Scots, was elaborately outfitted. Graham describes working with Karinska in her memoir *Blood Memory.*

Mr. Balanchine was so wonderful to work with, considerate and concerned—a joy to be with. It was equally exciting to work with Karinska, the Russian couturier, who designed the costumes and spoke in a wonderfully pronounced English. I asked for a dress that would be like the dress I'd had Isamu Noguchi design for Medea in *Cave of the Heart.* My idea was to have a dress that Mary would wear onstage and then step out of so that she became a woman and the dress would stand onstage as a symbol of her as the queen.

Karinska took us to her room, which was filled with boxes overflowing with fabrics and feathers. All her acolytes surrounded her. She would say to one of them, "Bring me the box with the feathers. No, the other feathers. And the beading. Yes, the black beading."[102]

Graham declared simply, "In my . . . black dress, with its abstraction of the ruched collar, I had the security of feeling beautiful every time I appeared in it on stage."[103]

LEFT:

Suzanne Farrell and Peter Martins in Allegro Brillante *during the late 1970s. It was in this ballet in 1956 that Karinska first introduced this style of soft, chiffon dress that was to become as much a standard ballerina's costume as the tutu.*

Nicholas Magallanes and Violette Verdy; Jonathan Watts and Melissa Hayden; Bill Carter and Diana Adams; and Conrad Ludlow and Jillana in Liebeslieder Walzer, *1960.*

Arthur Mitchell as Puck in Midsummer Night's Dream, *1962.*

OPPOSITE:

(Top right) Sketch by Croquill of an insect used by Karinska for the child fairies in the Overture, (top left) the 1962 sketch by Karinska for those characters, (middle left) the child fairies onstage, and (below right) Julie Michael as a child fairy.

This is not a security that theatrical performers take for granted. Indeed it is far more rare than the viewing public might expect.

The following year Balanchine and Karinska embarked together on what was for both one of the grandest and most moving works of their long and prolific careers. In *Liebeslieder Walzer,* a fifty-minute ballet for four couples, two pianists, and four singers set to the love songs of Johannes Brahms, the quality and tone of the choreographer's and the designer's work were seamlessly matched on a new level. The ballet, lacking a formal outline, is the story of the human heart in the arena of love—a distant and yet much-frequented place. This was only one of the muted contradictions in this ballet that holds the swell of emotion on this side of sentimentality, rendering its romantic yearning, quiet resignation, and desperate silences all the more moving.

Karinska's gowns were not only exquisite objects of art by themselves, but they gave off an almost eerie perfume, as if they had already known and lived and worn the passions of the ballet in some previous life. Their previous life, of course, had been as endless uncut yards of Parisian silk, and yet, in passing through Karinska's hands, they not only took on the shape and decoration of period gowns and waistcoats but also somehow, in some way, a soul had been stitched into the bodice along with the lace.

The waltzes were set in two sections, indicating the public face of love and the private one. The ankle-length satin gowns of the first section were a mass of elegant enigmas. While all appeared to be in the same color family of creamy, silvery beige, each glowed with a discrete radiance—and, indeed, Karinska had found four different satins of the same basic hue, each warming to a different tone under the stage lights. The effect is soothing yet disconcerting, mirroring love's axiom that nothing is ever quite what it seems. While conveying the sensation of great lushness, the dresses in fact were made of only three layers. The two petticoats were decorated with the most unusual details, including a ruffle of pink chiffon sewn not on the outside but on the inside, facing the dancer's legs, and an outward ruffle threaded with peach silk ribbon. For the décolletages Karinska delved into her box of antique lace and designed a different neck and shoulder line for each gown, each full and radiant. The surprising effect was one of vivid color in a neutral scheme and sumptuous depth in few layers.

In the second section of the ballet, the ceiling of the ballroom is lifted to reveal the starry night sky, and the shimmering silk of the ballroom costumes gives way to translucent tulle—signifying the less-veiled intimacy of lovers when left to themselves. Here Karinska's blending of colors and layers soared to new heights, with a boldness only an artist possessing her wealth of experience would dare—blues, greens, yellows, grays, and pinks, none a clear representative of its hue. Costumes made of love's nature if ever such apparel existed, they were the colors of bared passions and souls now freed from the confines of social behavior.[104]

The following year Karinska designed over one hundred costumes for Balanchine's rendition of *A Midsummer Night's Dream,* the first full-length original American ballet. Upon announcing the production Balanchine said to Karinska, "Mendelssohn will help me and Botticelli will help you, and we will not fail."[105] And they did not. The ballet was an enormous public and critical success for the New York City Ballet, and

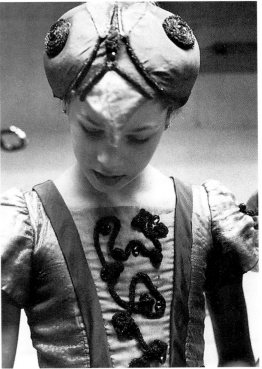

LEFT:

Kipling Houston, Catherine Morris, and Helene Alexopoulos as Lysander, Hermia, and Helena.

A 1962 sketch by Karinska for Titania,
her cavalier, and her retinue.

Suzanne Farrell and Helgi Tomasson as Titania
and Oberon in the 1970s.

Kay Mazzo as Titania with Bottom in the 1970s.
Bottom's head was made by Lawrence Vlady, Karinska's
nephew.

Jacques d'Amboise in the Divertissement from Act II of the 1967 film of the ballet. This photo clearly illustrates Karinska's use of the two-part vest which allowed the dancer to move his arms freely without the entire costume riding up his chest.

Victoria Hall, Cornell Crabtree, and courtiers in Act II.

Edward Villella as Oberon, Karinska, and conductor Robert Irving, opening night in 1962.

in the re-creation of Shakespeare's magical forest Karinska's love of whimsical detail took full flight.

There were glimmering child-bugs (based on drawings by Croquill given to Karinska by Kirstein); diaphanous peach silk and pearl-encrusted forest fairies; their queen, Titania, a Botticelli grace on the half-shell; winged butterflies; silk jersey–swathed mortal lovers; and a royal court of gold-brocaded courtiers. Bottom, the donkey whose "eye cannot hear" and "ear cannot see," received a lovable and poignant depiction thanks to Balanchine's unerring sympathy for the true hero and Lawrence Vlady's genius for giving animal faces a human touch.

Karinska's next commission for Balanchine could not have differed more completely from Shakespeare's comedy. Inspired by gagaku, ancient Japanese court music, *Bugaku* was a small ballet for five couples set to a sinewy, twisty score commissioned from Toshiro Mayuzumi. Erotic in the extreme, the dance depicts public and private sexual rites, and Karinska's dressing of it balances Balanchine's daring with delicacy and irony. For the opening dance the women, in black Japanese wigs, wear tutus of extraordinary invention—the lead in pink, the others in white. Karinska, modeling the skirts on chrysanthemums, placed hundreds of overlapping silk petals on a thin tutu supported by a hoop. In the bodice seams she inserted a quarter-inch of gold brocade between each pair of satin panels, an exquisite and time-consuming touch that remains barely visible to the audience yet imparts to the dancer and the ballet itself the appropriate extravagance and flourish. In the second half of the ballet the lead female dancer is at first covered with a magnificent long, white cape rimmed with translucent horsehair. But the cape is soon shed to reveal a tiny white bikini decorated with strategically placed white daisies, a throwback to Karinska's Folies-Bergère days. The effect, suggestive of places and acts that lie beyond theatrical limits and yet contained and ritualized, once again provides an unerring context for Balanchine's choreography.

Bugaku, featuring (opposite) Suzanne Farrell and Edward Villella, and (below) Allegra Kent and the corps de ballet.

CHAPTER SEVEN

New York Times *dance critic John Martin and Karinska at the 1962 Capezio Dance Award ceremony, and (below) Karinska's citation.*

I n 1963 the life of the New York City Ballet and the School of American Ballet took on a new kind of temporal permanence when the Ford Foundation put into Balanchine and Kirstein's hands the largest single financial endowment ever given to one dance organization in American history: an award totaling over $7 million—to be dispensed between the School of American Ballet and the New York City Ballet in timely increments. Balanchine's wish was to at long last secure the talents of Karinska exclusively for his company. Not only would such an arrangement allow him greater time and freedom to work with Karinska on any given production, but the financial security would provide a haven for the seventy-seven-year-old queen of costuming.[106]

After a long and arduous search—Karinska was very particular about her surroundings—she found a new atelier on West 57th Street near Fifth Avenue. With its large picture windows above Henri Bendel, Bergdorf Goodman, and Tiffany's, the elegant shop pleased her enormously, and she would often cut a conversation short by saying, "Come, let's go stand by the window," where she would imperiously survey the bustling street below. She had begun east of Fifth Avenue and now she was back on the other side of it almost twenty-five years later. The shop was now part of the financial responsibility of the New York City Ballet; thus, Karinska, for the first time in her life, could afford to work solely on ballet costumes, and she promptly and happily relinquished all her Broadway and opera commissions.[107] Until this point Karinska had carried a perpetually enormous workload, not only to pay her own rather steep bills, professional and personal, but to be able to afford to work for Balanchine cheaply. Beginning with her first original designs for *Bourrée Fantasque* in 1949, which she donated to the company, she had never refused Balanchine's requests, even though the company was not always able to reimburse her for her usually high costs.[108] Agnes de Mille no doubt was speaking for Karinska's other clients as well when she said, dryly, "We always had the feeling she charged us more so that she could make costumes for George Balanchine for nothing."[109]

Part of the original Ford Foundation plan had been to set up an apprentice

Sketch by Rouben Ter-Arutunian for Harlequinade, 1965, and Patricia McBride and Helgi Tomasson in the ballet.

program in which Karinska could pass on her knowledge to young costume designers. But Karinska resisted the idea. She offered to teach embroidery to anyone who wished; however, when it came to novices slowing down her daily operations, she had little patience. Being entirely self-taught Karinska did not imagine that she could pass on to others what she knew. She believed it was a question of love and of having the feelings in the hands. And both of these, she was convinced, were God-given.

In 1964 the company moved from the City Center of Music and Drama on West 55th Street to Lincoln Center and into their sumptuous new quarters at the New York State Theater. Designed by architect Philip Johnson especially for Balanchine and Kirstein, the theater virtually doubled the space in which the dancers were accustomed to performing. Balanchine immediately began to restage old ballets and to create new ones that were in keeping with the capacious grandeur of the new site. Naturally, the costumes followed suit, and the ensuing decade saw one huge production after another.

That first year Balanchine restaged his 1941 *Ballet Imperial* on a regal scale, and Karinska dressed this second version in stiff tutus, sashes, and glittering, stylized *kokochniks* of royal blue and gold. The following year there were two lavish evening-length ballets: *Harlequinade* and *Don Quixote*. The first, a colorful commedia dell'arte extravaganza, was designed by Rouben Ter-Arutunian, a brilliant Armenian designer whom Balanchine favored in the last decades of his life. Though Karinska would execute Ter-Arutunian's costumes with great success for many large ballets—*Swan Lake* in 1964, *Cortège Hongrois* in 1973, *Coppelia* in 1974, and *Union Jack* in 1976—their collaboration was rarely without conflict and often entailed extreme disagreements in the great Russian tradition, attended by showy silent standoffs and dramatic hand-throwing. Nevertheless, the costumes always made it onstage eventually.

Don Quixote was one of Balanchine's most ambitious projects to date—a three-act

George Balanchine, Karinska, and Esteban Francés looking over Francés's sketches for Don Quixote; Edward Bigelow is in the background.

Balanchine and Karinska fitting Suzanne Farrell for Don Quixote, 1965.

Costumes designed by Esteban Francés from Act II
of Don Quixote, and (below) Teena McConnell
as the Duchess and Francisco Moncion
as Don Quixote onstage.

version of Cervantes's novel set to music commissioned from Nicolas Nabokov. In hiring the Spanish painter Esteban Francés as designer for both scenery and costumes Balanchine hoped to achieve some of the weighty visual effects of seventeenth-century Spanish culture, and the results were magnificent. The ballet as a whole, however, received mixed reviews. For Balanchine's new muse, Suzanne Farrell, who was to dance the role of Dulcinea, Karinska created several costumes from Francés's designs, but perhaps the most charming was the silver-blue tutu made for Dulcinea's reincarnation as Marcella the shepherdess, in mourning for the death of the Poet. With a pale, pleated, blousy top, corseted waist, and a short, round, pumpkin-shaped skirt, the costume was the essence of feminine youth and grace and epitomized Balanchine's great dancer. This ballet was the public declaration of Balanchine's great love for Farrell. Four years later, when Farrell decided to marry a young dancer in the company and not Balanchine, Karinska, in a cool and quiet gesture of strength and defiance, insisted upon making Farrell's wedding gown. Although Balanchine, in his highly emotional state, viewed the action as one of betrayal, Karinska was one of the few around him who dared to declare her contrary opinion about the whole affair. She, like Balanchine, admired Farrell deeply and, aware of the dancer's spirituality, sometimes gave her one of her treasured Joan of Arc medallions wrapped in a length of antique lace in a heartfelt gesture of feminine solidarity.

§

In 1966 Balanchine choreographed a new ballet to Arnold Schoenberg's orchestrations of Johannes Brahms. *Brahms-Schoenberg Quartet,* set in four sections, while

Sketches by Raoul Pène du Bois for John Taras's ballet Jeux, *and Allegra Kent and Melissa Hayden onstage, 1966.*

Bart Cook and Jacques d'Amboise in costumes from Brahms-Schoenberg Quartet, 1979 (designed 1966).

essentially plotless, exuded the rich atmosphere of nineteenth-century life under the Hapsburgs. Once again Karinska outdid herself—in the lush detailing of satin bodices inlaid with embroidery and rhinestones; in the subtle, three-dimensional motifs of military uniforms, swords, and daggers; and in the occasional floral flourish, all set in "autumnal reds and browns, dusty rose, silvery pink and maroon."[110] The Allegro first movement exhibited knee-length tulle skirts topped with shaded yokes; the skirts of the Intermezzo, the second movement, were romantically edged in black satin; the Andante third movement featured blue satin bodices bordering petal-shaped peachy pink, stiff tulle skirts, each rimmed with solid satin; and the Rondo fourth movement, a gypsy celebration of a courtly though daredevil nature, had skirts of pink organza topped by black tulle and long velvet ribbons flashing in red and orange. The back of each of the black bodices on the tutus for the last movement flaunted the requisite Karinska touch; a tiny inset of pink satin that forms a flattering triangular shape when the bodice is fastened. From the audience it could hardly be seen but there it was, something luxurious, something extra.

Luxury was the byword for Balanchine's next production. *Jewels,* the first three-act "plotless" ballet, was set to music by Fauré, Stravinsky, and Tschaikovsky. Its sole conceit was to create an aural and visual feast. Starting from the simple but multifaceted settings of "Emeralds," "Rubies," and "Diamonds," Karinska went to work on what became her most glittering exposition ever.

In his history of the New York City Ballet, *Thirty Years,* Lincoln Kirstein talks about the technical strategies employed and the "problem of creating glitter without wiping out face and form." Pearls were rejected as being "too close to flesh color and nonreflective."

Karinska's taste and ingenuity robed it [*Jewels*] in a sightly cohesion appropriate to its flashing pretexts. Dresses and tailoring were fitted and blazoned with lapidary skill. Some cost-conscious carpers questioned the need for consummate attention to needlework which is so

George Balanchine with his ballerinas from Jewels: "Emeralds," Mimi Paul and Violette Verdy; "Rubies," Patricia McBride; and "Diamonds," Suzanne Farrell; 1967.

Suzanne Farrell in the "Diamonds" costume. For this photograph she wore her headpiece backwards.

delicate between the fingers that the detail is bound to be lost on the far side of the footlights. But Karinska declared: "I sew for girls and boys who make my costumes dance; their bodies deserve my clothes."[111]

In late 1969 Balanchine decided to revive his 1949 production of Stravinsky's *Firebird* and to showcase the seventeen-year-old prodigy Gelsey Kirkland in the central role. In 1945, at the instigation of Oliver Smith, Marc Chagall had executed designs for a production of this ballet for Ballet Theatre, and four years later the New York City Ballet had acquired the sets and costumes from impresario Sol Hurok for the nominal fee of $4,250. When Balanchine's production was mounted in 1949, with Maria Tallchief as the Firebird, it became the newly formed company's first box-office hit. By 1969 the ballet had been out of the repertory for years and the production had become so tattered that Chagall asked to have his name removed from the credits.

In 1945 Karinska had been approached by Smith to execute the painter's sketches for Ballet Theatre, but because of other obligations — not to mention her abhorrence of the plan to literally paint the artist's designs onto the costumes — she did not participate in the project. But in 1969 she would have her way. The costumes were to be rendered in three-dimensional, textured appliqués with minimal use of a paintbrush. Chagall's hundred or so sketches were obtained from the artist's personal collection and installed in Karinska's atelier on 57th Street in specially constructed velvet-lined trunks with large padlocks.

Karinska began by collecting a varied assortment of materials, fabric itself being only the most mundane. Wire, papier-mâché, plastics, beads, feathers, sequins, and endless yards of horsehair were employed as she turned Chagall's designs into tangible, workable shapes for the human body. Her method was directly descended from the early chiffon "paintings" that she had exhibited back in Russia before she had ever made a costume. The *Firebird* project was enormous, and the shop was awash in the reds, turquoises, yellows, blues, and oranges of Chagall's watercolors. At one point during the process the painter himself visited Karinska's shop and was pleased with the physical translations of his whimsical work.

The extravagance and expense was unprecedented: the Prince's purple silk vest and hat were trimmed with real mink; and the Princess's final wedding gown, on view only in the ballet's final tableau, was fashioned from as many as fifteen different shades and textures of red, including silk, velvet, organza, tulle, and satin. Karinska was unstoppable. The monster costumes were so huge, padded, wired, and wonderful that Jerome Robbins, who choreographed their scene, said simply, "I choreographed on the costumes."[112]

For the Firebird herself there were at least three versions of the costume. Kirkland wore the one that is the most similar to Chagall's original idea — a light and flickering red, yellow, and blue paneled tutu. Later, an enormous white-and-gold lamé silken, winged version by Kermit Love, based on Chagall's front curtain design, was made for Karin von Aroldingen, but the costume was so voluminous that Balanchine had to rechoreograph the role around the mammoth sculpture, its tall wings, and its train of shimmery silk. Later still, a more manageable costume — a compromise of the

A 1945 sketch by Chagall for the Firebird and the costume by Karinska, 1970.

OPPOSITE:

Gelsey Kirkland and Jacques d'Amboise in the 1970 production of The Firebird.

A full-size sketch by Karinska of the Princess's
headdress, based on the traditional kokochnik.

Gloria Govrin as the Princess in white, 1970.

previous two—was used, and the choreography was again changed accordingly. While the ballet to this day retains a place in the repertory, it is more for its startling aural and visual display—thanks to Stravinsky, Chagall, and Karinska—than for its dancing or dramatic content. Balanchine knew how much the project meant to the eighty-four-year-old Karinska, and after its premiere he approached her backstage, bowed his head, and asked her, "Are you happy?" She nodded.

§

Around this time, there was a great deal of work being done by Balanchine and Karinska on another ballet with a bird motif, the famously unrealized *The Birds of America*. Based on the life of John James Audubon, the famous American ornithologist and artist, with the stories of the lost French Dauphin, Pocahontas, and John Smith thrown in for good measure, the ballet was on Balanchine's calendar for decades, during which time Karinska performed enormous amounts of research on how to turn apples and strawberries into tutus and a swallowtail into a tailcoat. The ballet never materialized, and the prototypes were relegated to a rusty rack.

The 1970s continued with more big ballets, and Karinska's pace never slackened. She continued to meet Balanchine's challenge despite her impressive age—she was approaching ninety. She maintained her defiant energy, strong hands, and whirring mind. Her only loss, albeit a devastating one, was her eyesight. While never going completely blind, she developed severe glaucoma, and her ability to identify people and distinguish details was vastly impaired. She mourned her loss but never entirely gave up hope, writing to Alain François, her grandson, "I am so unhappy to not have [my eyes] anymore, but I have confidence that my new doctor can give them back to me. I go three times a week." Despite the obvious need in her profession for good eyesight, Karinska was by now so knowledgeable about form, fabric, and color that seeing it in her mind was tantamount to the real thing, and her taste and technique never faltered.

For Balanchine's 1970 ballet *Who Cares?*, set to George Gershwin's romantic tunes against a backdrop of New York City's skyline, she fashioned soft and sexy ballet versions of Ginger Rogers and Fred Astaire designs. For *Scherzo à la Russe*, conceived for the 1972 Stravinsky Festival, she simplified and perfected the pale organza tunic and pearlized *kokochniks* of her native culture so that the young women looked as young and fresh and feminine as they in fact were; it is a rarity for a designer to enhance and not obscure the natural effervescence of his or her subjects. For *Pulcinella* Karinska once again worked with her old friend Eugene Berman, bringing to life his colorful designs reminiscent of Venetian Carnevale imagery. In the 1976 production of *Chaconne* Karinska, always ready for innovation, used stretch fabric for entire costumes, men's and women's, for the first time and, far from being critical of this modern invention, she rejoiced in the very apparent opportunities for function and fit that it offered.

In 1977, at the age of ninety, Karinska gave a magnificent farewell performance with her extravagant and intensely beautiful costumes for Balanchine's last full company celebration, *Vienna Waltzes*. That her last production was her most glam-

Karinska, Lincoln Kirstein, and George Balanchine with dancer Susan Hendl in Who Cares? *costume, 1970.*

RIGHT:

Kay Mazzo and the corps de ballet in Scherzo à la Russe, *1972. This ballet represented the last appearance of the pearl-encrusted Russian* kokochniks *that Karinska had been making all her life.*

BELOW, LEFT AND RIGHT:

Sketch by Patricia Zipprodt for the corps men in The Dybbuk *and Patricia McBride with the men onstage, 1974.*

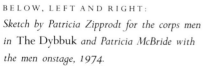

Curtain call after the premiere of Pulcinella.
Front, from left: George Balanchine (in costume),
Eugene Berman, Violette Verdy, Edward Villella,
and Jerome Robbins (in costume); 1972.
Balanchine and Robbins performed the roles
of beggars for the premiere.

Suzanne Farrell and Peter Martins in Chaconne,
1976.

Karin von Aroldingen in costume for the "Tales of the Vienna Woods" from Vienna Waltzes.

Sara Leland and Bart Cook with the corps in the "Explosion Polka" from Vienna Waltzes.

158

Stephanie Saland in "Der Rosenkavalier" waltz.

orous, resplendent, and sensual was a fitting finale. *Vienna Waltzes,* a fifty-minute ballet set to various Viennese waltzes, had five movements and required over sixty gowns and as many velvet-and-brocade waistcoats and vests. With every inch imported from Paris, each costume cost over five hundred dollars, and once again budget-minded associates queried, "Why silk?" "Because it moves," Balanchine replied, never tiring of explaining. "It's natural, made by worms. Nylon doesn't move, it's made by machines."

This ballet marked the crowning achievement of Balanchine's rule. It was a celebration of pure joy and beauty and languid waltzing on a scale never before seen in his theater. That Karinska was still there to dress this ballet seems only natural and yet some kind of final miracle.

The Finale in
"Der Rosenkavalier"
waltz from
Vienna Waltzes.

Shortly before the premiere, as the final touches of the ballet were being masterminded in rehearsal and in the costume shop, Karinska attended her last fitting with Balanchine. Forty-five years had passed since that first fitting in Paris for *Cotillon,* when she covered up her nerves and inexperience with terrified dignity while Bérard and Balanchine ran tulle through their fingers and discussed colors and fabrics. She was now old and physically frail, walking with a cane, her eyes failing, but her hair still shone blue, her Chanel suit and white blouse were neatly fastened, and her wrists were draped with the trademark bracelets. And her iron will remained. She was unveiling for Balanchine her latest, and her last, creations—the creamy white ball gowns for the last waltz, the "Rosenkavalier Waltz," each with a differently cut neckline, low-slung back, dropped waist, and full, lush skirts and train that were, and are, an exaltation of bias-cut silk satin. The gowns practically danced alone, and Balanchine was thrilled.

A short time later Toussia found Madame unconscious on the floor in her apartment. Karinska had suffered a massive stroke. Her grandson, Alain François, is convinced that her mind had literally exploded with joy at Balanchine's happiness with her dresses. To please him had been the greatest wish and the greatest triumph of Karinska's life.

Underneath Suzanne Farrell's *Vienna Waltzes* gown, nestled in the soft ruffles, was a small gold rose. It was there ostensibly to indicate where the ballerina should hold her train while she waltzed, but really it was there for no reason at all. It was there for Balanchine and Farrell and Karinska to know it was there.

§

In 1986, three years after the deaths of both Balanchine and Karinska (Karinska tenaciously held on to life in a nursing home for six years after her stroke, never regaining speech or memory), *Liebeslieder Walzer* was restaged by the New York City Ballet, and the re-creation of the original costumes proved almost impossible; the satin and lace simply could not be precisely reproduced in color, quality, or texture. While the final results in the new production were beautiful they were different.

Just beneath the stage of the New York State Theater lies the pit room, a huge, crowded, cool space where all the costumes of the New York City Ballet are stored when not in use. There, in a dark corner, lies the costume graveyard. There are only two skeletal members of this elite, two gowns from the 1960 production of *Liebeslieder Walzer,* slung over wire hangers that droop under the weight of their loads—some thirty yards of fabric. They are the only surviving blueprints for Karinska's *Liebeslieder* creations and, as such, have been mutilated in the loving and necessary attempt to reproduce them. With eight-inch squares cut out of their skirts to use as fabric samples, and lace cut from their shoulders, they carry an aura of heroic tragedy, wounded satin soldiers. In their torn glory and indestructible dignity, they are, perhaps, the most revealing witnesses to Karinska's art, her rendering of the human soul in silk.

WHAT *(WHO?)* IS A FIRE (?) BIRD (?)?

Lincoln Kirstein

What does a FIREBIRD (Jar Ptitza: Rus.) look like? Is it (she?) a phoenix, a flaming moth or an incandescent sphinx? Are its (her) feathers pheasant, quetzal, peacock or hummingbird? If you design a dancer as a Fire (?) bird, can you alchemize your fantasy of flame into man-made material? When an artist imagines a winged beast as human metaphor, how far does energy in ingenuity propel him toward manufacture? Is he just doodling, or does he, to some degree, analyze the technical steps by which possibility or ultimate achievement are contrived?

When draftsmen indicate lines on paper, with pen or pencil, and wash these with color, there are three possibilities. Either the intent is concrete and conscious, vague or accidental, or their combination. In a painting which finally stands, abandoned or complete, something fixed and unalterable, whatever its intention, the effect is frozen, to be judged for competence or pleasure. Nothing further can happen but frame it and hang it. When an artist, (in this case, Marc Chagall, an easel-painter), makes sketches to be used for theater, the problem—not for him, but for his costumer—is complex. Granted his work and fame over the last sixty years, his familiar repertory of Russo-Jewish folk formulae, nevertheless, indications on his costume-sketches are, to say the most: sketchy. It is impossible to know how far he imagines these hints as cut, sewn, embroidered. Naturally, he wished them to be "perfect" but to the executant dressmaker, this is hardly a rule of thumb. As a busy painter, Chagall needn't trouble overmuch with scissors, needles or fittings. He provided rough maps, sketches in fact, entrusting realization to advanced skills of professional seamstress or tailor.

Famous painters over the last three centuries have seldom worked in theaters, although great Renaissance or Baroque artists and architects did not disdain days spent on occasional pageantry. In the 18th century, François Boucher was something of an exception. By then, official management had established an institutional bureaucracy at once conservative and self-serving, exclusive. In the 19th century, Delacroix had a glancing interest for theater, mostly in costume. At the end of the century advance-guard Parisians and Muscovites—Lautrec, Vuillard, Maurice Denis, Korovin, Golovin—did work on individual shows, which only much later generally affected a theatrical climate. But when, in 1917, Diaghilev found Picasso, through the enthusiasm of Cocteau, the role of easel-painter as stage designer took on, briefly, something of the nature of a *metier.*

But those easel-painters who offered their sketches to be used by Diaghilev for his last dozen seasons, with the possible exception of André Derain, Pavel Tchelitchew (later Christian Bérard, who was only prevented by Diaghilev's death from designing)

ABOVE, LEFT AND RIGHT:
Chagall's sketch of a Flower Maiden and Karinska's full-scale sketch of the bodice.

RIGHT AND BELOW:
Karinska, Jerome Robbins, George Balanchine, and dancers in costume, *1970, and the finished costume.*

Flower maidens, Beriozka maidens, and youths onstage.

were more intrigued by the atmosphere of theatrical performance and attendant publicity than they were involved with dancing as such. There is separation in kind and quality between costume-*designs* by Alexandre Benois and Léon Bakst and costume-*sketches* by Braque, Miró, or Chagall. Bakst and Benois left nothing to chance, or rather, to the taste, interpretation or competence of tailors or dress-makers. The more famous *easel*-artists left everything. This "everything" included among other capital factors: proportions of fields of color, choice of texture and material, cut of bodices, length of skirts, make-up, hair-do. Bakst and Benois may have first thought of themselves as easel-painters, but when they abdicated from the ambition of independent painterly prestige, surrendering themselves to theater and its transitory glories, they became peak professionals. They drew well. Any falsification in stylish formulae of rendering was eschewed in their working-drawings, although Bakst's best water-colors are beautiful in their own right. Both were so correct, museum-conscious and pedantic that they bored Diaghilev into repudiating them with unseemly abruptness. They were saturated in the past, unable to keep up with his present while Diaghilev kept dowsing for a future. Now slight scraps from Bakst or Benois bring ridiculous prices. Sacred objects, they are splinters from the True Cross of St. Sergius the Great. We can read from their marginal notes the minutiae of their intent — how minds, hands, eyes worked — what they wish to have expressed, how exactly this was to be effective and effected.

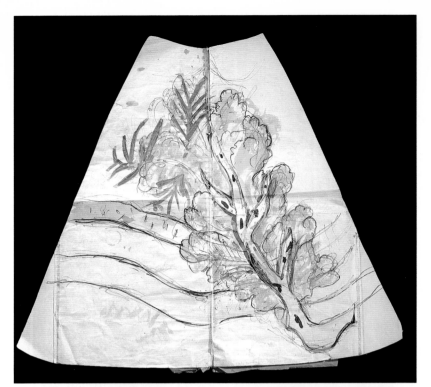

Chagall's sketch for the Beriozka maiden
and (above, right) a full-scale sketch of the skirt
by Karinska.

RIGHT AND OPPOSITE:
A sample of the skirt design in fabric and the costume.

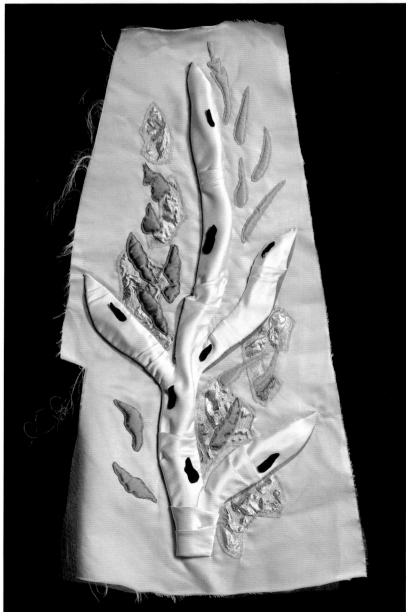

Chagall's sketch for the Princess in the red wedding dress, and Gloria Govrin and Peter Martins in the final tableau of the ballet.

Jerome Robbins and Karinska in the rehearsal hall at the New York State Theater for a dress parade of The Firebird, 1970.

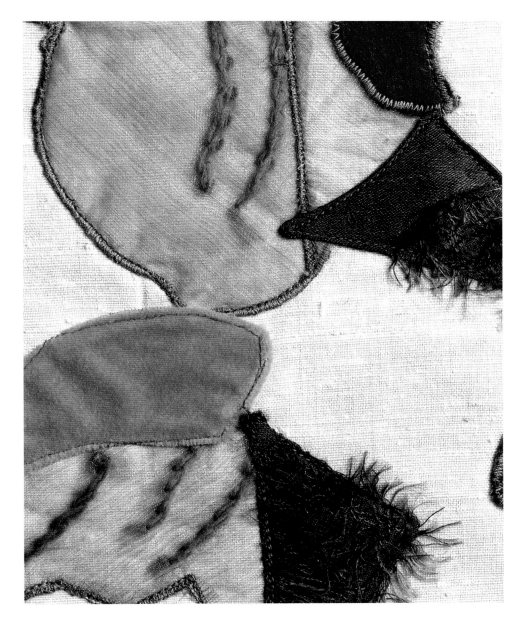

Chagall's sketch for the Youth with pitcher and a sample of material appliquéd by Karinska for the costume of the same character.

The First World War, the Russian Revolution, separation from Imperial theaters and ballet-schools, robbed Diaghilev from 1914 until 1924 of the kind of chances for dancing and choreography which first unleashed the staggering impact of his Paris seasons from 1909 through 1913. After that, for his next decade, with an astounding flair as catalyst and survivor, he substituted novelty in music and painting for what had been before revelations of dancers and dancing. To a large degree, although he neither invented nor discovered the School of Paris, he promulgated it. However, due to discoveries in his last decade, we tend to forget his first. Then, he used neither Nabi, Post-Impressionist, Fauve or Cubist painters. When he came to use them, they were past the apogee of Fauvism and Cubism. With the Sur-realists he got in on the ground floor; although in contact with their circles, he was unattracted by Bonnard, Vuillard, Van Dongen, or Modigliani. He confused Munich and Berlin with Vienna and had no eyes for Klimt, Schiele or Kokoschka. His earliest enthusiasms for an advance-guard were English: Frank Brangwyn, Aubrey Beardsley. He talked to Gordon Craig and Count Kessler about a ballet but he saw Craig was no use for repertory. Nor was Adolph Appia. Diaghilev needed cloths, not architectural screens or vast flights of steps. Diaghilev's visual interests were secondary; his real passion was for music. His personal taste as a collector ran to rare books and icons. He used modern painting as poster-art, his famous cloths as one-man shows. His poster-artists served him well. The painters, of whom Rouault with his "Prodigal Son" (1929) is a fair example, were not averse to being borrowed but they rarely worked hard. Rouault's costume sketches were actually non-existent. They were extracted from piles of sketches, and constructed "*in the style* of Rouault" by a dressmaker. Easel-painters provided notions, not maps. If Diaghilev's artists triumphed, it was as much his choice of their genius (among many forgotten failures: he was not infallible) as it was the skill, indeed genius of Prince Schervachidze's scenic-painting in the Russian manner—canvas worked on the floor with pooled color, rather than attacked neatly on the French perpendicular paint-frame.

Chagall's designs for FIREBIRD are in the (post-) Diaghilev manner, executed charmingly, light-heartedly, hastily—in water color. Anyone glancing at them would guess they issued from the hand of this world-famous painter. But what they might mean in terms of woven fabric, in balance of proportions for a particular dancer's body, or even exact tones of iridescent or blunt color—there is a slight indication. They were done in full confidence that somebody else, across the Atlantic, would edit, interpret, and execute them, while Chagall got back to more important business, his canvases. Chagall's notions have his idiosyncratic charm, but his drawings for FIREBIRD are neither explicable for texture nor clear as to scale. We cannot be sure whether he intended this monster to be five feet tall or that one, ten. We can't know whether his Firebird sports real plumes or the fruit of a loom. Nor can we learn whether Chagall himself knew or cared.

He was supremely fortunate in being certain that Madame Karinska always cared and would, eventually, come to know. She studied Chagall's sketches as if they were written in Welsh, Olmec or Linear B. Innumerable choices lay before her. Her shelves are loaded with the loot of Seventh Avenue's wholesale fabric supply-houses—plastics, foils, sequins, braids, passementerie, fake jewels. Given a whisper from Chagall, she managed to trumpet echoing visual arias, cadenzas, cabalettas, whole choirs of resonant color and rich tactile sonorities. Her costumes glow exactly as Stravinsky's orchestration shimmers. Naturally Chagall trusted Karinska; friends, they had long worked together. But now it was some thirty years after his original FIREBIRD; first impulses were suggestive, but any explication or reinterpretation of his designs might take valuable time from his easel. However, he gave Karinska enough, quite enough for her to worry herself sick—whether she could please him or not. What would he really want, if only he were here to ask? What would he prefer, between two, three or six overlays of net, horsehair or tarletan? Would changeable-silk be better? Do you add or suppress sequins as accents; do you indicate highlights in paint or foil? So, finally, his and her costumes were created. They became creations, variations on themes by a painter, but focused, final, frozen in three dimensions—sturdy against sweat, violent motion, repertory storage: work-able, achieved.

Inspecting at close range these masterworks of spidercraft, one naturally wonders: why such emphatic attention to detail? Why could not far coarser (and cheaper) means have contrived the same, or roughly similar effect? These are only stage-dresses, not sacerdotal vestments. The only answers to such eminently pragmatic, sensible and insensitive questions are metaphysical.

If you equate Balanchine's ballet-dancing or ballet-dancers with any other entertainment or entertainers, Karinska's costumes (simply?) don't make sense. She seems to be making them for herself, rather than for someone to make money out of their being worn. This is almost true. But also, she makes them for particular dancers she has long known and admired, not alone for them to move or work in, but to *be* in. It is possible that the actual facture—handiwork, cutting, sewing—is lost on the gross public. Stages are far from an audience's eyes. Dancers move constantly, fast or slow. Few people are trained to use their eyes more than to catch a general blur. But dancers are different in kind from many in their audience. Like doctors, soldiers or cooks, they are in service, and not primarily for themselves. They serve an ancient traditional craft whose wide historic frame locates their current identity and present employment. They are in uniform; so are chameleons. The chameleon's skin is very well-tailored although he is nude. Costumes for the ballet-dancers' service-company—are his or her uniform, or multiform. If we take Wellington's description of a battlefield resembling a ballroom, Karinska may well be the greatest military tailor of all time. Apart from any economic or institutional survival, ballet-dancing is a constant personal battle against both artistic imperfection and physical hazard. Karinska's reckoned recklessness is a parallel to the endless struggle on a metaphysical and physical level of ballet's impermanent permanence. Dancers who have been fitted to Karinska's armor are better equipped for the fight. This they deeply sense, sewn into her glowing satin, supported by the security of her corseting, the buoyancy of her skirts, glorified by the lavish plumage of her preposterous luxury.

Ballet began by being, and remains, a court art with a High Style. If America has become, as Russia has been for centuries, an imperial power, so the uninterrupted tradition of academic stage-dancing, is imperial. It is dependent on central authority, designated by apostolic succession, on a rigid discipline in early schooling. It is by no accident that the empires of Great Britain, the Soviet Union, the United States maintain ballet as national assets. The Court of St. James, Kremlin, and White House maintain their numinous magnetism, no matter who staffs these castles. No revolution or confrontation, neither the French upheavals of 1789 or 1848, the industrial revolutions of Manchester and Birmingham, the Russian of 1905 or 1917, in any serious way interrupted the descent of virtuoso dancing in state-supported opera-houses. Why has the classic dance in America, whether offered by the Kirov, Bolshoi, the Royals, Danish or British, as well as our native companies, attracted a public now rivaling in size and enthusiasm that of ball-games? Why is Prince Charles so fervently, nay, so frantically, welcomed by our middle-class, up-tight White House? Why do we read Karinska's clothes as concrete proof of the realism in fairy-tales? If Firebirds aren't real, what are?

For more than half a century, Karinska has been the veritable fairy god-mother of loom and spindle, attending the births, coming-of-ages and unions of performing artists. One big reason Balanchine's dancers have developed into a corps, a body of ladies-in-waiting, a *corps des pages,* indeed a *corps de ballet,* is because Karinska has dressed them as they have come to think they deserve. — 1970

NOTES

1. Letter from George Balanchine to Antonio Ghiringhelli, January 16, 1953.

2. Quoted in article by Victoria Huckenpahler, *Dance Magazine,* January 1978, 45.

3. John Braden, interview with author, January 30, 1992.

4. Quoted in article by Barbara Varro in the *Philadelphia Inquirer,* October 16, 1968.

5. Boris Kochno, interview with Holly Brubach, July 6, 1990.

6. Coton, p. 76.

7. Rosette Rony, interview with author, November 30, 1991.

8. Kochno interview.

9. Stokes, 185.

10. Haskell, 192.

11. Agnes de Mille, interview with author, April 6, 1992.

12. Parker, 364.

13. Diana Menuhin, *Journal of the Society for Dance Research* (VI:2), Autumn 1988, 68.

14. Kirstein, *Ballet,* p. 177.

15. Phelps, 141.

16. Jean Cocteau, from the program for *La Machine Infernale,* Comédie des Champs-Élysées, 1934.

17. See Appendix I for a translation of the correspondence.

18. Cochran had been presenting a great deal of ballet since Diaghilev's death, filling the void, pleasing audiences, and providing jobs to out-of-work dancers and choreographers. Karinska and Balanchine probably first met in London in 1930 or 1931 while both were working on such a revue, he choreographing and she helping, uncredited, by sewing costumes.

19. Quoted in Beaton, 43–44.

20. While this cannot be confirmed, it is possible that Karinska made something for Pavlova sometime before her death in 1931. Beaton may well have heard this from Karinska herself.

21. Beaton, 43–44.

22. Vickers, 188.

23. Beaton, 58–59.

24. Ibid., 46–47.

25. Osato, 108.

26. Vickers, 309.

27. Markova, *Markova Remembers,* 76.

28. Osato, 110–11.

29. *Harper's Bazaar,* April 1936.

30. *Vogue,* March 1937, 104.

31. In 1936 René Blum split with De Basil and, with Serge Denham, formed another company, the Ballet Russe de Monte Carlo. For further explanation see the chronology.

32. Anderson, 36–37.

33. Ibid., 36.

34. Edward Downes in Anderson, 38.

35. Lawford, 94.

36. Philip Dyer letter to author, May 27, 1992.

37. *Harper's Bazaar,* January 1940.

38. Ibid., August 1940.

39. Ibid., February 1940.

40. Ibid., October 1940.

41. The music did receive a complete reincarnation in 1972 in *Violin Concerto* and was hailed as a masterpiece, an opinion which Balanchine seconded in a rare admission,

saying, "It is very well made."

42. Walker, 103–4.

43. Irving Kolodine in Walker, 104.

44. Denby, 205–06.

45. Todd, 76.

46. Sharaff, 37.

47. Kermit Love, interview with Edward Bigelow, November 3, 1989.

48. Ibid.

49. Ibid.

50. De Mille, *Dance to the Piper,* 300–01.

51. Quoted in Perlmutter, 155–56.

52. Newspaper article by Ellen Scott.

53. Head, *Hollywood,* 60–61.

54. Love interview, November 3, 1989.

55. Ray Milland letter, October 20, 1944.

56. Maeder, 14–15.

57. Agee, 120.

58. Chierichetti, 32.

59. Agee, 378–79.

60. Higham, 290.

61. Minnelli, 178–79.

62. La Vine, 110.

63. Head, *Hollywood,* 73–74. Head went on to win eight Oscars during the following years, which no doubt lessened the sting of losing that first one.

64. See Appendix I for complete letter.

65. Herman Krawitz, interview with Edward Bigelow, September 14, 1989.

66. Quoted in Vickers, 424.

67. Alvin Colt, interview with Edward Bigelow, September 1, 1989.

68. Quoted in article by Joan Alleman Rubin, *Dance Magazine,* June 1967, 50.

69. Oliver Smith, interview with the author, March 11, 1992.

70. Ibid.

71. Ibid.

72. Sharaff, 101–02.

73. Levy, x.

74. Denby, 83.

75. Altering a designer's inventions was not always met with equanimity. When Balanchine saw Seligmann's costumes for *The Four Temperaments* he exclaimed, "We see nothing! We see nothing! We don't see Mary Ellen [Moylan, a dancer in the ballet]." He suggested cutting the costumes and Seligmann protested, "Nothing can be cut! Where, then, is Seligmann?" Mary Ellen Moylan in the Anne Belle film *Dancing for Mr. B: Six Balanchine Ballerinas,* 1989.

76. Love, interview with author, January 30, 1992.

77. Patricia Zipprodt, interview with Edward Bigelow, September 26, 1989.

78. Ibid.

79. Suzanne Farrell, interview with the author, February 13, 1992.

80. Love, interview, January 30, 1992.

81. Stanley Simmons, interview with Edward Bigelow, September 21, 1989.

82. Love interview, November 3, 1989.

83. Zipprodt interview.

84. *Washington Star,* Washington, D.C., April 17, 1966.

85. Smith interview.

86. Charles-Roux, 237.

87. Contrary to what might be expected, Balanchine did not always get what he wanted from a designer. Referring to the sets produced for the 1967 *Glinkiana,* Kermit Love recalls Balanchine exclaiming, "All I asked for was a little bit of muslin and a little bit of paint, and they built me a house! Can I live in it? No. Can I rent it? No. I can't even sell it. To get rid of it, I have to burn it!" Love interview, January 30, 1992.

88. Betty Cage, interview with the author, March 13, 1992.

89. Willa Kim, interview with Edward Bigelow, February 15, 1990. One of Kim's first tests with Karinska involved her closing her eyes and opening her mouth, into which Karinska popped a lump of raw bacon fat—a delicacy in Revolutionary Russia—which Kim dutifully swallowed.

90. Quoted in Perlmutter, 213.

91. Ibid., 213–14.

92. Quoted in Vickers, 349.

93. Kirstein, *Thirty Years,* 131.

94. Martin, *New York Times,* November 26, 1952.

95. Reynolds, 163.

96. Martin, *New York Times,* 1955.

97. Quoted in Reynolds, *Dance News,* April 1955, 163.

98. Kirstein, *Thirty Years,* 133.

99. Love interview, January 30, 1992.

100. It became legend in Karinska's later years that she only began making the costumes for a ballet when the choreographer got in the elevator to come up to her shop to view them.

101. This is very difficult to substantiate given the endless number of ballets and costumes that have come and gone unrecorded over the years. *Allegro Brillante* does serve as the landmark production to have used this chiffon costume from its premiere until today.

102. Graham, 235.

103. De Mille, *Martha,* photo caption.

104. Karinska's designs for *Liebeslieder Walzer* became so inseparable from the ballet as a whole that the Balanchine Estate, despite the inevitable cost to a ballet company, requires their reproduction for any new staging of the ballet. The costumes for *Serenade, La Valse,* and *Stars and Stripes* are required for the same reasons. Barbara Horgan, interview with the author, January, 29, 1992.

105. Quoted in *Newsweek,* January 29, 1962.

106. The New York City Ballet became the first, and remains to this day, the only American ballet company to have its own costume shop, elsewhere a luxury afforded only to state-subsidized companies.

107. There were to be two exceptions to this rule, both for the Metropolitan Opera. In 1964 she executed for Franco Zefferelli his designs for *Falstaff* and in 1966 she executed for Cecil Beaton a new production of *La Traviata.*

108. Cage interview.

109. De Mille interview.

110. Kirstein, *Thirty Years,* 189.

111. Ibid., 192.

112. Jerome Robbins, interview with author, April 7, 1992.

Agee, James. *Agee on Film.* New York: McDowell, Obolensky, 1958.

Anderson, Jack. *The One and Only: The Ballet Russe de Monte Carlo.* New York: Dance Horizons, 1981.

Beaton, Cecil. *Ballet.* Garden City, N.Y.: Doubleday and Co., 1951.

Cassini, Oleg. *In My Own Fashion.* New York: Simon and Schuster, 1987.

Castle, Charles. *Oliver Messel.* London: Thames and Hudson, 1986.

Charles-Roux, Edmonde. *Chanel and Her World.* New York: Vendome Press, 1981.

Chierichetti, David. *Hollywood Costume Design.* New York: Harmony Books, 1976.

Chujoy, Anatole. *The New York City Ballet.* New York: Alfred A. Knopf, 1953.

————, and P. W. Manchester. *The Dance Encyclopedia.* New York: Simon and Schuster, 1967.

Coton, A. V. *A Prejudice for Ballet.* London: Methuen & Co., 1938.

De Mille, Agnes. *Dance to the Piper.* Boston: Atlantic Monthly Press/Little, Brown and Co., 1951.

————. *Martha.* New York: Random House, 1991.

Denby, Edwin. *Looking at the Dance.* New York: Popular Library, 1968.

Dietrich, Marlene. *Marlene.* Trans. Salvator Attanasio. New York: Grove-Weidenfeld, 1989.

Engelmeier, Regine, and Peter W. Engelmeier, eds. *Fashion in Film.* New York: TeNeues Publishing Co./Prestel, 1990.

Garcia-Marquez, Vincente. *The Ballet Russes.* New York: Alfred A. Knopf, 1990.

Graham, Martha. *Blood Memory.* New York: Doubleday, 1991.

Haggin, B. H. *Ballet Chronicle.* New York: Horizon, 1970.

Harding, James. *Cochran.* London: Methuen, 1988.

Haskell, Arnold. *Balletomania, Then and Now.* New York: Alfred A. Knopf, 1977.

Head, Edith, and Jane Kesner Ardmore. *The Dress Doctor.* Boston: Little, Brown and Co., 1959.

————, and Paddy Calistro, with a Foreword by Bette Davis. *Edith Head's Hollywood.* New York: E. P. Dutton Inc., 1983.

Higham, Charles. *Cecil B. DeMille.* New York: Da Capo Press, 1973.

Katz, Leslie George, Harvey Simmonds, and Nancy Lassalle, proj. dirs. *Choreography by George Balanchine.* New York: The Eakins Press Foundation/Viking Penguin, 1984.

Kchessinska, Mathilda. *Dancing in St. Petersburg.* Trans. Arnold Haskell. London and New York: Victor Gollancz, 1960.

Kirstein, Lincoln. *Ballet: Bias and Belief.* New York: Dance Horizons, 1983.

————. *Firebird: Chagall/Karinska. An Exhibition of Ballet Costumes at the Library and Museum of the Performing Arts, The New York Public Library at Lincoln Center.* New York: The Library, 1970.

————. *Thirty Years.* New York: Alfred A. Knopf, 1978.

Knapp, Bettina Liebowitz. *Louis Jouvet, Man of the Theater.* New York: Columbia University Press, 1957.

Kochno, Boris. *Christian Bérard.* London: Thames and Hudson, 1988.

La Vine, W. Robert. *In a Glamourous Fashion: The Fabulous Years of Hollywood Costume Design.* New York: Charles Scribner's and Sons, 1980.

Lassaigne, Jacques, and Marc Chagall. *Drawing and Watercolors for the Ballet.* New York: Tudor Publishing, 1969.

Lawford, Valentine. *Horst: His Work and His World.* New York: Alfred A. Knopf, 1984.

Leese, Elizabeth. *Costume Design in the Movies.* New York: Frederick Ungar Pub. Co., 1977.

Levy, Julian. *Eugene Berman.* American Studio Books, n.d.

Leymarie, Jean. *Chanel.* New York: Rizzoli, 1987.

Lifar, Serge. *Ma Vie.* New York and Cleveland: World Publishing Co., 1970.

Madsen, Axel. *Chanel: A Woman of Her Own.* New York: Holt & Co., 1990.

Maeder, Edward. *Hollywood and History: Costume Design in Film.* New York: Thames and Hudson, 1987.

Markova, Alicia. *Giselle and I.* London: Barrie and Rockliff, 1960.

————. *Markova Remembers.* Boston: Little, Brown and Co., 1986.

Martin, John. *Modern Ballet.* New York and Cleveland: World Publishing Co., 1952.

McConathy, Dale, with Diana Vreeland. *Hollywood Costumes: Glamour, Glitter, Romance.* New York: Harry N. Abrams, Inc., 1976.

Minnelli, Vincente, with Hector Arce. *I Remember It Well.* Garden City, N.Y.: Doubleday and Co., 1974.

Osato, Sono. *Distant Dances.* New York: Alfred A. Knopf, 1980.

Parker, Tyler. *The Divine Comedy of Pavel Tchelitchew.* New York: Fleet Publishing Corp., 1967.

Perlmutter, Donna. *Shadowplay: The Life of Antony Tudor.* New York: Viking, 1991.

Phelps, Robert. *Professional Secrets: An Autobiography of Jean Cocteau.* Trans. Richard Howard. New York: Farrar, Straus & Giroux, 1970.

Preminger, Eric Lee. *Gypsy and Me.* New York: Ballantine Books, 1984.

Prichard, Susan Pezez. *Film Costume: An Annotated Bibliography.* Metuchen, N.J.: Scarecrow Press Inc., 1981.

Rewald, Sabine. *Balthus.* New York: Harry N. Abrams, Inc., 1984.

Reynolds, Nancy. *Repertory in Review.* New York: The Dial Press, 1977.

Sharaff, Irene. *Broadway and Hollywood: Costumes Designed by Irene Sharaff.* Cincinnati: Van Nostrand Reinhold Co., 1976.

Stokes, Adrian. *Russian Ballets.* New York: E. P. Dutton and Co., 1936.

Todd, Michael, Jr., and Susan McCarthy Todd. *A Valuable Property: The Life Story of Michael Todd.* New York: Arbor House, 1983.

Vickers, Hugo. *Beaton.* Boston: Little, Brown and Co., 1985.

Walker, Katherine Sorely. *De Basil's Ballet Russe.* New York: Atheneum, 1983.

APPENDIX I: CORRESPONDENCE, 1949
MADAME KARINSKA AND LOUIS JOUVET

Paris, 25 February 1949

Madame KARINSKA
72 Malibu Beach
Pacific Palisades
California, USA

My dear Varia,

When this dreadful thing [the sudden death on February 12 of Christian Bérard, "Bébé"] happened I wanted to send you a telegram on board ship, but then I didn't do it because I didn't know how to tell you the news. Irene [Karinska's daughter] told me she had written you right away about the circumstances by which we lost our dear Bébé.

I write today not to tell you of my suffering, as I can guess it is the same as you feel because I know what I felt and still feel myself. You must have seen in the newspapers what a moving ceremony all of Paris organized for our Bébé, and the sadness of the numerous friends he had.

Today I am writing because I am also in a real predicament concerning the *Tartuffe* we were supposed to do together, [Bébé] having told me the evening before his death that he had finally found the way in which he would do the play.

He was thrilled with the picture of the costume that Irene made for *Les Fourberies de Scapin,* and he was thinking of doing all the costumes for the play in the same way, with painted fabric; the only exception would be Tartuffe, who'd be dressed in black. We were supposed to start working as soon as *Les Fourberies* was finished.

So here I am at a standstill and quite confused and anxious to know with whom I'm going to be doing this play. Irene thought that [André] Derain would be the only man who could do anything worthwhile. We spoke for a long time about the project and she said, quite rightly, that, since you were coming back here to France for vacation, it would be better to wait for your return before approaching Derain.

I'm writing today to ask your opinion on the subject, for I must absolutely put the play on at the beginning of the next season. Would you give this some thought and write to me about your feelings? I believe you are the only one who can make Derain decide. I shall do nothing without your opinion on the matter. You remember the problems we had getting him to decide to do *L'Ecole des Femmes*!! [Bérard eventually designed the production, not Derain.]

Your advice is of the greatest importance to me. I won't say anything more about it for now and I apologize for dictating this letter but I don't have a moment's free time, as I am shooting [a film] all day long, and I want you to be able to think about this problem.

I was very happy to see you sparkling again. I send you kisses from the bottom of my heart.

Your Louis

Friday, 11 March 1949

Madame VARIA KARINSKA
23 East 53th Av.
New York C. (USA)

My dear Varia,

I have just received your letter of 1 March which must have crossed with mine. You have the same idea as I about TAR-TUFFE. I'm happy that you told me you want to do the play with me.

This is a very big thing for me, and of tremendous importance. The play has never been done *honestly*. I hope with all my heart that DERAIN will accept, but should I go and see him first? Wouldn't it be better that you ask him yourself, by telling him that we have the same thought but that I don't dare to incur his refusal? If not Derain, then I really don't see who could do this, and it causes me great anguish.

When do you expect to be back in Paris?

I am still receiving many letters from friends every day, or from people unknown to me who tell me of their sadness about BÉRARD's death and the loss that his departure means to the Theater. It is most upsetting.

I sense that you are in a very good state of mind and I envy you. Don't forget me in your thoughts. My whole heart is with you.

Please, I beg of you, write me . . . I kiss you with all my soul.

Your Louis

Louis Jouvet

P.S. There is in NEW YORK at the present moment a Monsieur Jacques GAUME who is the representative of the Maison Pierre FREY, [a firm that] makes quite lovely fabrics and he would be happy if you would see him. He will undoubtedly introduce himself to you as having been sent by me. Welcome him, I beg you, and advise him. His address is: 820 Third Av. NEW YORK CITY

Les Fourberies de Scapin goes well and earns much.

---

17 East 63 St.
New York.
13 March [1949]

My very dear Louis,

I received your letter [of February 25] two weeks late because it had been sent to Malibu Beach.

Mark the change of address!

In the meantime, I am sure you will have received my letter in which I tell you about Derain. I'll do everything to make him do it [*Tartuffe*]. I'll start by sending him coffee every month.

It seems to me that Eugene Berman could do *Tartuffe*. He arrives in New York on the 23rd of March. I can talk to him about it *if* you authorize me to do so. Let me know.

Yesterday, I saw the manager of *La Folle de Chaillot*. [The play was being presented on Broadway at the time with costumes executed by Karinska.] The play is still doing very well. He told me they were coming to Paris to make the movie of *La Folle de Chaillot*, but with you. And they want me to do the costumes. It would help *Tartuffe* a great deal if I could help Irene do the costumes for you.

New York is quite dead at this time. Business is very poor here and everyone is complaining. You wrote that dear Bébé wanted to do the *Tartuffe* costumes with painted fabric, but I don't see it. Send me *Tartuffe* by air mail so I can read it, I've forgotten it already—and I'll speak to Gene Berman.

I kiss you as I love you. I will help you.

Varia

Paris, 25 March 1949

Madame KARINSKA
17 East 63 Street
New York, N.Y., USA

My dear Varia,

I am a little late in answering your letter of 13 March, which made me happy. I have been very busy lately and a little tired.

I did indeed receive your letter in which you told me about Derain, and also about Eugene Berman. As I think about it, I have some misgivings about both Derain and Berman. I don't believe at all that Berman could do *Tartuffe*. He is an architect before anything else. Maybe he'd be able to do the sets, but surely not design the costumes.

As for Derain, I fear that the way he'd design the play, with its set and costumes, would already be an *interpretation* and a *performance* of the play, before it is even played. Do you understand what I mean? Derain would create a *Tartuffe* that is not objective.

I would like to stage this play as a likable and honest comedy. When *Tartuffe* is performed, it is always Tartuffe's hypocrisy or Orgon's stupidity that is played. They always want to teach a lesson to someone, sometimes with Tartuffe as an obscene lecher, sometimes dressed as a priest. I would like the play to remain pleasant and to become instructive only upon reflection, after the performance.

You must have received a package about Tartuffe by now. With this letter, I am now sending you the drawings that were made when the play was first performed by Molière. On the one hand, there is an engraving by Chauveau, the first engraving in the first edition of Molière; you'll see Tartuffe as a young man, elegant, and not at all a character who rolls his eyes and looks like a pharisee.

There are also four drawings on a kind of fan that were drawn by Le Pautre and represent several scenes from *Tartuffe*. Finally, there is a Le Pautre drawing giving an idea of the set and the characters that I like a lot.

Bébé was much inspired by these documents. When he told me he wanted to do the *Tartuffe* costumes painted, I understood that he rightly wanted the play to be done within a likable, elegant, and pleasant convention. He saw the set as a large room seen from the back, with huge bay windows on each side, and stage-front, two doors on the right and left of the stage, one of which was the entrance to the house and the other [leading to] the small secret room where Damis hides in the third act.

I'm also making you a little sketch of this set, following Bébé's indications, and I send you this with two other sketches, based on Bébé's designs, in which he was working out the set-up.

Now I am wondering whether a man such as [Georges] Braque wouldn't be more appropriate for doing *Tartuffe*. Braque—I hope you remember the *Fâcheux* he did for Diaghilev—has a poetry and a charm that seem to me to be more fitting and that would better serve the play than Derain would, because of the violence and the force he'd put into his sketches, and into his conception.

Think about that, my very dear Varia, and tell me what you think. This is an important thing for me, and there must not be any errors made in the production of this play. I trust you, your instinct, your sensitivity, *your spirituality*.

I await your answer and kiss you with all my heart.

Your Louis.

Louis Jouvet

P.S. Madame Talon, who was in charge of *La Folle de Chaillot* here, passed through Paris and told me that there is, indeed, a possibility of making a movie of *La Folle de Chaillot* in Paris. I'd be very happy if you were to come here to work on that project, so that I could then work on *Tartuffe* with you at the same time.

---

12 April [1949]

My very dear Louis,

I received your two letters, but I left for Hollywood again to supervise an "Ice Show," and at the same time I received the "Oscar" as designer for the costumes in color for *Joan of Arc*. The golden statue stands before me, and it seems to me that I owe you a large part of my success. For with you and with Bébé my glory has bloomed. I kiss you and I love you very much.

As for *Tartuffe*, it is an extraordinary play and I agree with you, having read it, that Braque would be very very good.

I see the costumes like the old engravings. I am weary of so much frivolity in Louis XIV costumes. It is one of the most beautiful periods. I see the shades of the costumes very balmy, very lush, but retouched and soothed by those black lines—as you see on the engravings, as if it were an *engraver* who had made them.

I see the shades, they'll be so beautiful, accentuated by these little black lines. Oh, I see them all finished—and of an extraordinary beauty. Alas, the engravings you sent me are so beautiful—and the sets are so simple—and the costumes will have such power and such exquisite elegance. Tartuffe has to be elegant, I don't see him as a priest or a vulgar man. I see him in black, as Bébé did. . . .

Oh! Louis, I would like to create another *Ecole des Femmes* for you! And I am *sure* that I am on the *right* track. If you could send me Louis XIV engravings of the women and men.

I've made a few sketches for myself, to convince myself that I'm right with my black lines. If you look at a flower, you always see that a red rose has this red-black reflection that I want to succeed in having in the costumes.

I am still with my Joan of Arc—I love her deeply.

Nobody here recognizes me, they think I've had an operation on my face—they don't understand that the "lift" in my face is the "lift" in my soul that is shining on my face because I am so close to Joan, and every day, morning and evening, I kneel down before her picture and I ask her for "courage," for it is with her courage that she succeeded. You are so close to me Louis, and I love you so much. We have remained two, and two have left us, and we will never see them again. But we must, you and I, hold on to their tradition and be loyal and true to all that is beautiful, no "compromise" with beauty!

I received my Oscar not for the costumes, but for my suffering, for my loyalty to Joan . . . I was sleeping when they phoned me—I didn't know the movie had been entered into the competition. I am ending my letter. I am sure you'll find time to read it.

I kiss you, my soul has embarked on the "strange love of absence," . . . how I would like to go and have supper with you today and talk about the costumes.

Your Varia

Paris, 21 May 1949

My dear Varia,

For two weeks now, we have been doing *Ondine* again, Irene must have written you about that, and the play is going well. I didn't answer your long letter, which hasn't left me since I received it, because I have still been thinking about the problem of *Tartuffe*.

Decidedly, I do not think that Braque would be very useful to us in doing the set and costumes. It would be difficult to replace him, but he doesn't have the great love of theater that Bébé had and that you yourself have; and I think that the simplest would be to find someone who might make the set according to the indications that Bébé left behind, and that you, yourself, do the costumes.

As for the set, do you think that Emilio Terry could do it? If not he, then I know a young architect, Louis Gillet's son, whom I could approach. In any case, the way in which you speak about the costumes reassures me entirely about that problem.

I have started to have people look for engravings of the period at the Bibliothèque Nationale and, when the choice is made, I'll have the documents photographed and I'll send them to you so you can think about them and advise me. The comparison you make with the rose, and that black-red fringe that surrounds the flower when you look at it attentively, seems to me to be a true discovery.

There is only one question that comes up, my dear Varia: Could you come back to France to do these costumes, and when would you be able to return?

I think of you almost every day with affection and tender feelings, which devoutly include Joan [of Arc] and Molière. I kiss you, my Varia, with all my heart.

Your Louis Jouvet

6 Sept. [1949]

My very dear Louis,

I haven't heard from you in quite a long time. How is your *Tartuffe* going? Who is doing the sets? Irene wrote me that you had *someone to do your costumes?* Are they good? I dream of nothing but *Tartuffe,* for I have decided to come on *November 1st* to do them for you; I have made sketches, models, I have some very interesting ideas for the women, . . . different colors as in painting. I'm going to the country on Saturday, and there I shall dream and work like a madwoman for you, if you still want me to do them. Write me quickly, for I want them to be a masterpiece, to have Bébé, Giraudoux, Joan, and Molière be my judges. And then, too, dear, to work with you, to be, talk, think together appeals to all of my soul, which here feels—a drama of emptiness, and I am afraid of that. You promised to send me *engravings from that period.* Do it soon, I have many books, but I'd like to receive yours. Irene has written me "Mama absolutely wants to do your *Tartuffe,* but you'll need to give [her] 100 dollars pocket money, and I'll work it out with her cashier." Well, dear Louis, that's the order given by my dear daughter whom I love so much. So work it out regarding my pocket money, dear one. Do you want the women to be dressed differently in each act? Write me *who is going to play the parts.* If you could send me the *women's measurements* I will be able to make the patterns here. How happy I am to be able to do this for you. I'll have the chance to go and see Joan, whom I love still more. My heart is a bit tired and I must make something beautiful to give me some self-assurance. Write me soon. I love you forever and I admire you. Send the documents quickly, do you have some scenes in color? That would be fantastic—I'll get them back to you.

Your Varia who adores you

Paris, 20 September 1949

Madame Varia KARINSKA
New York, USA

Very dear Varia,

Your letter of 6 September pleased me enormously. I sent you a telegram to tell you I was sending you the documents; they'll still be late, I don't think we'll have the photographs until tomorrow or the day after; be patient.

I am so thrilled with your letter announcing your arrival and assuring me of your friendship, which I need so very much under the circumstances. Everything you said about Bébé, about Giraudoux, about Molière, and about Joan made my eyes well up with tears.

I saw Irene, we spoke together. There is no question of money between us and Irene will ask what she wants from the cashier. You shall have your hundred dollars to play "the young girl" when you arrive.

Did you have a visit from a decorator, Mr. Esteban Francés? Pavlic Tchelitchew mentioned him to me for the sets. He told me he was sending me a model, but I haven't received it yet and I

asked him to go and see you to show you what he did. I am uncertain, for Pavlic said he is a very gifted and capable man, but I don't know if he will really have the spirit for Molière.

In any case, Pavlic has promised to help me regarding the set, in the event that I have no one, or to help me find someone. He is in Venice at the moment and will come to Paris at the end of the month. I am going to write Esteban myself as soon as I receive his model to tell him what I think and, in any case, to inform him *that you will be doing the costumes.*

With the promised documents, I'll send you the cast list as well as the measurements of the women and the men. I'll have Irene take them. I shall also send you photographs of each one, if you want me to. The delay in getting these documents has also caused me to delay writing to you, I beg you to forgive me.

We have been performing *Ondine* again with success. I'm shooting all day long and am a bit tired; I also need to pay some attention to my heart.

Write soon, as soon as you have some news for me and have received the first documents.

I kiss you with all my heart, which loves you and admires you—tenderly

Your Louis Jouvet

14 October 1949

My dear, you are before me in the role you play in *La Folle de Chaillot,* behind me in your portrait in Don Juan, on the left—simply Jouvet Louis—the adored one!

It's so quiet in my very lovely apartment, full of green plants, with my two canaries who are sleeping now.

If you only knew how hard I've been working, from 7 in the morning until the evening. I'm very tired, for I'm doing a big Ice Show for Sonja Henie, and the whole tableau has been designed by me and with success. . . .

I have just spoken with my dear friend Esteban, who read me your letter which he received from Pavlic, he is very tired of the uncertainty. I have seen the photo you sent me, unfortunately I've not seen the model, but I sense that it must be beautiful, magnificent, impressive; there are things to be changed but I believe he is the only one who'll make your *Tartuffe* honestly, for he loves the play and he has a great deal of purity and truth, which many people lack.

To play it, the 18th century must be forgotten, maybe the 18th century can be forgotten—but not the 17th century—that's a different thing. I know one thing we could ask him to do for you, which is to make you a performance worthy of the people whom we love.

How I wish I were near you, to talk with you, to be there, to advise you, for one thing is true . . . I love you very much, I would like to be of help to you, you are alone, very much alone, and you don't make decisions very quickly. Since he [Francés] admires you he would like to come to Paris, then everything would be very easy, but he has no money to pay for his trip—when do you want to go on? In his letter, Pavlic writes that Mlle. Marthe and Leon are very impressed with the model, the most important thing is that *Leon likes it,* for he knows about these things . . . more than many others do. Esteban does not agree with Pavlic at all that something grotesque is needed. . . .

I've received all the documents and the book I have here. The finest engraving is the large one of Tartuffe, the large one. The play "must" be played in this spirit.

I have the many engravings you sent me, but they don't have the French feeling, they are rather more Flemish, *I don't like them* for the play. The suggestion for Tartuffe is fine, but the engraving of Madame Pernelle won't do, for if we dress her like that she'll look like a priest and that's not it, it should be done much better.

Louis Jouvet as Dom Juan. The dedication reads "To Varia Karinska—with the gratitude of the French theater and the admiration of Louis Jouvet, Paris, 1948."

You have given me much to worry about, for while working on the Ice Show I am constantly thinking about *Tartuffe,* which I love.

In Esteban's set I find the motifs on the door too much, and then the small motif above it is too much, but the front, the two decorations on both sides I find splendid and very impressive; and with the shades of the costumes in colors of grey, raw silk in mauve and chestnut—all the shades of the costumes are covered as in the engravings . . . with a dusty yellowish and grey, there are no sharp shades . . . only [lines] in black and then the very beautiful ribbons in colors. If you look at Leonardo da Vinci's Assumption—the angel's sleeve with its ribbons and the very subtle shirt—Oh, that will be beautiful, Esteban must do it—I feel that it must be like that.

Forgive this letter, I kiss you as much as I love you, I am as always your Varia who loves you and who wishes you would finally make up your mind.

Varia

Paris, 24 October 1949

Varia my dear,

I received your letter after our phone call and since then I haven't written, for I was waiting to see Stanislas Lépri first from whom I had asked for a model.

Yesterday he brought me this model; it isn't perfect but quite acceptable. I asked him to revise and correct it, and he is supposed to come back soon to show it to me. I believe—if he is successful in his corrections—I'll do the set with him. As far as the costumes go, I told him you were doing those, and so he won't be involved with them.

I absolutely had to decide, and I am almost obliged to take Lépri's model considering how little time I have left. As soon as he has brought it to me, I'll have it photographed and will send you a copy.

I made a futile attempt to contact Georges Braque, which received no response. I really don't see anyone else to whom I could direct myself. Anyway, you'll see, the model that Stanislas Lépri made is, I repeat, quite acceptable.

If Esteban had stayed in Paris, I am sure—as you say—I could have finished the project with him; but at this point in time I really cannot have him come here; his trip would cost a lot and it is too late to start collaborating with him. I didn't expect that, since we had begun to work together, he would secretly leave for New York again, and so quickly at that.

I agree with you about Pavlic's letter, of which Esteban sent me a copy. It must have hurt him, but the spirit in which Pavlic wrote it is not offensive at all. To some extent it even praises Esteban highly. I am going to write Esteban myself to tell him so and to express my regrets that, this time, we weren't able to work together.

My very dear Varia, what I need to ask you in this letter is, on the one hand, to tell me exactly when you expect to arrive in Paris (for we're already at the end of October and we should be able to go on around 15 December), and, on the other, to hurry with your work on the costumes.

Everything you tell me on that subject pleases and enchants me. I agree with you about the Flemish character of some of the costumes which are not right for the play. But you yourself have the sense of what should be done, you have that sense admirably so, and I have complete confidence in you.

The document I sent you for Mme. Pernelle pleases me a lot. You object that if we dress Mme. Pernelle that way, she'll look like a priest. That wouldn't displease me (it was a very common dress among old ladies in the seventeenth century); but if you have something different in mind I leave it up to you.

The greys, the raw silks, the mauves, the chestnuts about which you speak are exactly what I wish, with perhaps a bit of yellow in there, which you mention anyway, when you say that these costumes should be covered with yellowish and grey dust and that there should be no sharp shades. Finally, the color black is essential for the costumes of Tartuffe and Orgon.

Where are you with your Ice Show? When does it go on? Write me soon, my dear, to tell me when you are arriving. Besides, I am not the only one awaiting you, Irene and the little children are just as impatient.

I rehearsed all day today, from nine in the morning until seven in the evening, and I'm dictating this letter in haste to send you my news and to tell you about my meeting with Lépri.

Forgive me if I leave it at this. I am a little tired, but very eager to hear from you. I thank you for your loyalty and your friendship under these circumstances.

And I kiss you very affectionately and tenderly with all my heart,

Your Louis Jouvet

27 October [1949]

My very dear Louis, have you finally found the painter who will do Tartuffe for you? When will you open? Please write me. Maybe the painter who does the set will also do the costumes? Maybe the things I did won't please you? Do as you want to, my dear, . . . and write me, I'll do what you want me to. Maybe my shades won't go at all with the new set designer? I'm waiting for news from you. I kiss you with all my heart,

Your Varia

6 November [1949]

My very dear Louis, I have to leave for Chicago today to deliver my show. If I don't leave I'll be in big trouble. According to Irene's letter I thought you were going to open in January, therefore I wanted to come in December, but now I don't know what to do, for I have obligations here which I cannot abandon. I'll die if I can't be of use to you. I am sending Irene some models, they're not all that well drawn, but if you like the shades and the line their execution will be perfect, for I have spent a lot of time working on this subject. I send you Mme. Pernelle,

Marianne, Elmire, and the women servants. I can sense them so well, and once made, they'll be of great value. I have many others you can choose from, but I need to know whether you like them and if you really are opening on 15 December, as you say. I am leaving for Chicago for ten days—I can't do anything else. I kiss you.

Varia   Write me soon

Paris, 17 November 1949

My very dear Varia,

I received your letters of 27 October and 6 November and today, the 17th, I still haven't answered you; forgive me, I am leading an impossible life. But I want to tell you right away what joy it gave me, last Saturday, to have Irene visit me and bring me the models you made for the play.

The ones for Elmire are marvelous and I asked Irene to leave them with me. They are in front of me now, where they enchant and reassure me. I also like the model for Marianne very much. And the choice of color and line and style in the specifications you gave for the men's costumes is very beautiful.

But among those, you didn't design the costumes for Orgon and Tartuffe, which are very important. Those costumes must be dark, and rather Louis XIII.

The one for Mme. Pernelle is much too much the grand lady; she must look like a little old woman, slovenly, cantankerous, disagreeable, unkempt.

Finally, the role of Dorine is not really that of a servant but of a lady companion. It is a woman in the tradition of Molière; she is dressed almost like Elmire, with as much elegance and care, but she wears a very large apron to show her status. If you consult the engravings I sent you, you'll see that in Le Pautre's drawings, the roles of Elmire and Dorine resemble each other.

Irene must have written you already; consequently, I will not be telling you anything new if I mention that I'm waiting for an answer from Georges Braque. If I didn't write you earlier, it's because I wanted to have heard from him to let you know.

Not knowing what to do about the set, after the failures with Esteban Francés and Lépri, I went searching for Braque more than two weeks ago. At that time he was still at his country house in Dieppe. He didn't refuse to collaborate with me, but since then I haven't heard from him. He is due back in Paris any time and I think I'll be able to tell you his definitive response as soon as he gets back, in about two or three days.

We cannot open 15 December. Irene is overburdened with work and tells me it's impossible for her to make the costumes before 10 January. So I have postponed the date for Tartuffe until then. Besides, I myself have to finish a film which will still take me several days in the beginning of December.

So all is working out very well, I think, for us to be able to do this Molière together. If Braque refuses to collaborate, you will do the costumes and I'll get [Georges] Wakevitch for the sets.

I'm dictating this letter in haste, as usual, as I'm counting on you and am awaiting you most impatiently. . . . I have hardly any time. But rest assured, my very dear Varia. I'm thrilled with your models and like them very much.

Write to tell me how you are and when you expect to come to Paris. I'll write you soon again. We must stay in touch in order to succeed with this play.

Forgive me this rambling letter and try to find all my tenderness, and all the confidence and hope I have in you among these messy sentences.

Thank you, with deep affection,
    with all my heart,
    your Louis Jouvet

Paris, 24 November 1949

My very dear Varia,

I have just phoned Irene to tell her that Georges Braque had agreed to do the sets and costumes for Tartuffe for us. She found that to be an excellent solution. In the confusion we were in, I must confess that Georges Braque's acceptance reassures me. I am certain that you, too, will approve of this decision.

The work you have done and the heart you have poured into it shall not be used for Molière this time around. But I am sure that these will be used for the next play we'll be putting on. Please do not regret any of it; I am certain that this first attempt shall allow us to stage another fine seventeenth-century work.

I'm writing you as well to let you know that I will need you for these [Braque's] costumes and I beg you to let me know when you'll be able to come to preside over their execution.

Besides, Irene and her children are sure of the joy it shall give me to see and kiss you.

Answer me on that point as soon as you can. I'm dictating this letter to you in all haste, without even having the time to measure my words. But surely you will read between the lines everything I am not saying.

I kiss you with all my heart,
    Your Louis Jouvet

3 December [1949]

My very dear Louis, I'm very happy that Braque is doing your Tartuffe. I am so happy because he'll create a miracle, as what he has done is so beautiful, and furthermore you'll be much more at ease. I am happy that it has worked out this way because I cannot come [to Paris] and since you have a great master now, I don't feel badly that I'm not coming. I'm leaving for Hollywood for five months on the 30th of this month, and on the 15th of June I'm leaving for three months in France, and then toward the end of the year I shall leave for Italy and Spain; I still want to see a good deal before dying, and especially with Alain [her grandson] whom I adore. I am deeply touched that you liked my models. I think they will be beautiful once they're made, but that will wait for another time.

I've just made Bourré Fantasque, a ballet with George Balanchine [it premiered on December 1], all the newspapers are talking about it as a triumph. . . .

Translation from the French by Marjolijn de Jager

Note: The play opened in Paris on January 27, 1950, with Jouvet as Tartuffe. The final credits list Braque as scenic designer only, and Irene Karinska as costume designer. Photographs from the production indicate that many of Karinska's ideas were employed, including those "little black lines" that suggested an engraving and the dark rim of a rose.

Portrait of Karinska in her blue Chanel suit, painted in 1974 by her friend, the designer John Braden.

This chronology includes only those productions for which Madame Barbara Karinska's participation has been confirmed. It should be noted that the "Karinska" credit was also used by Karinska's daughter Irene, who designed and executed costumes for European theater, ballet, film, and opera productions from 1940 through the 1970s.

Particular effort has been made to differentiate the two principal "Ballets Russes" companies that performed after the death of Serge Diaghilev in 1929. Their names were similar and changed several times. In the following entries, the appropriate names of the companies are given and superscript numbers are used to distinguish them.

A [1] indicates the company formed by Réne Blum and Colonel Wassily de Basil in 1929 as the "Ballets Russes de Monte Carlo." After 1936 it remained under the sole direction of de Basil. From 1939 until 1952 it was called the "Original Ballet Russe."

A [2] indicates the company formed by Blum in 1936 as "Ballets de Monte Carlo" and later under the direction of Serge Denham. From 1938 until 1962 it was called the "Ballet Russe de Monte Carlo."

All works are premieres unless otherwise stated.

1927

CASANOVA *(Film)*
Date   Released in 1927, Paris (rereleased in Paris, 1987)
Director   Noé Bloch
Costumes   Boris Bilinsky. Executed by Karinska (uncredited)

1928

SCHÉHÉRAZADE *(Film)*
Date   Released in 1928 by the Universum Film Aktien Gesellschaft (UFA-Film), Berlin
Director   Alexandre Volkoff
Costumes   Boris Bilinsky. Executed by Karinska (uncredited)

1930

LA NUIT D'AMOUR *(Operetta)*
Date   c. 1930, Opéra Russe à Paris
Music   Antoine A. Banès
Notes   On the basis of her work with Opéra Russe, Karinska was asked to execute the costumes for Ballets Russes's *Cotillon* (1932).

MANON *(Opera)*
Date   c. 1930, Teatro Colón, Buenos Aires
Music   Jules Massenet
Choreography   Boris Romanov
Costumes   Executed by Karinska

1932

COTILLON *(Ballet)*
Date   April 12, 1932, Ballets Russes de Monte Carlo[1], Opéra de Monte Carlo
Music   Emmanuel Chabrier
Choreography   George Balanchine
Costumes   Christian Bérard. Executed by Karinska (women's costumes)

LA CONCURRENCE *(Ballet)*
Date   April 12, 1932, Ballets Russes de Monte Carlo[1], Opéra de Monte Carlo
Music Georges Auric
Choreography   George Balanchine
Costumes   André Derain. Executed by Karinska

JEUX D'ENFANTS *(Ballet)*
Date   April 14, 1932, Ballets Russes de Monte Carlo[1], Opéra de Monte Carlo
Music   Georges Bizet
Choreography   Léonide Massine
Costumes   Joan Miró. Executed by Karinska

LE BOURGEOIS GENTILHOMME *(Ballet)*
Date   May 3, 1932, Ballets Russes de Monte Carlo[1], Opéra de Monte Carlo
Music   Richard Strauss
Choreography   George Balanchine
Costumes   Alexandre Benois. Executed by Karinska

MISCELLANEOUS, 1932
Karinska remade an orange and yellow tutu for Agnes de Mille's Paris debut in a solo concert on October 30, 1932. The costume, for a piece called *Stagefright,* had originally been made by de Mille's mother based on paintings by Degas.

1933

LES PRÉSAGES *(Ballet)*
Date   April 13, 1933, Ballets Russes de Monte Carlo[1], Opéra de Monte Carlo
Music   Peter Ilyitch Tschaikovsky
Choreography   Léonide Massine
Costumes   André Masson. Executed by Karinska

BEACH *(Ballet)*
Date   April 18, 1933, Ballets Russes de Monte Carlo[1], Opéra de Monte Carlo
Music   Jean Françaix
Choreography   Léonide Massine
Costumes   Raoul Dufy, Jeanne Lanvin. Executed by Lanvin, Lidvall, Karinska

SCUOLA DI BALLO *(Ballet)*
Date   April 25, 1933, Ballets Russes de Monte Carlo[1], Opéra de Monte Carlo
Music   Luigi Boccherini
Choreography   Léonide Massine
Costumes   Etienne de Beaumont. Executed by Karinska

LES SEPT PÉCHÉS CAPITAUX *(Ballet)*
Date   June 7, 1933, Les Ballets 1933, Théâtre des Champs-Élysées, Paris
Music and Lyrics   Kurt Weill, Bertolt Brecht
Choreography   George Balanchine
Costumes   Caspar Rudolph Neher. Executed by Karinska

LES SONGES *(Ballet)*
Date   June 7, 1933, Les Ballets 1933, Théâtre des Champs-Élysées, Paris
Music   Darius Milhaud
Choreography   George Balanchine
Costumes   André Derain. Executed by Karinska

MOZARTIANA *(Ballet)*
Date   June 7, 1933, Les Ballets 1933, Théâtre des Champs-Élysées, Paris
Music   Peter Ilyitch Tschaikovsky
Choreography   George Balanchine
Costumes   Christian Bérard. Executed by Karinska
Notes   Costumes were also used for the 1952 ballet *Caracole,* choreographed by George Balanchine to music by Wolfgang Amadeus Mozart

FASTES *(Ballet)*
Date   June 10, 1933, Les Ballets 1933, Théâtre des Champs-Élysées, Paris
Music   Henri Sauguet
Libretto   André Derain
Choreography   George Balanchine
Costumes   André Derain. Executed by Karinska

L'ERRANTE *(Ballet)*
Date   June 10, 1933, Les Ballets 1933, Théâtre des Champs-Élysées, Paris
Music   Franz Schubert
Libretto   Pavel Tchelitchew
Choreography   George Balanchine
Costumes   Pavel Tchelitchew. Executed by Karinska, Molyneux (Tilly Losch's dress)

LES VALSES DE BEETHOVEN *(Ballet)*
Date   June 19, 1933, Les Ballets 1933, Théâtre des Champs-Élysées, Paris
Music   Ludwig van Beethoven
Choreography   George Balanchine
Costumes   Emilio Terry. Executed by Karinska

1934

LA MACHINE INFERNALE *(Drama)*
Date   April 11, 1934, Comédie des Champs-Élysées, Paris
Director   Louis Jouvet
Script   Jean Cocteau
Costumes   Christian Bérard. Executed by Karinska

LES IMAGINAIRES *(Ballet)*
Date   June 11, 1934, Ballets Russes de Col. W. de Basil[1], Théâtre des Champs-Élysées, Paris
Music   Georges Auric
Choreography   David Lichine
Costumes   Etienne de Beaumont. Executed by Karinska

AMPHITRYON 38 *(Drama)*
Date   (Revival) October 8, 1934, Théâtre Athénée Louis Jouvet, Paris
Director   Louis Jouvet
Script   Jean Giraudoux
Costumes   A. M. Cassandre. Executed by Karinska

TESSA (THE CONSTANT NYMPH) *(Drama)*
Date   November 14, 1934, Théâtre Athénée Louis Jouvet, Paris
Director   Louis Jouvet
Script   Margaret Kennedy and Basil Dean, adapted by Jean Giraudoux
Costumes   Dimitri Bouchène. Executed by Karinska

1935

DREAMS (Ballet)
Date March 5, 1935, American Ballet, Adelphi Theatre, New York
Music George Antheil
Libretto André Derain
Choreography George Balanchine
Costumes André Derain. Executed by Karinska
Notes Costumes from Les Songes (1933)

LES CENCI (Drama)
Date May 6, 1935, Théâtre aux Folies Wagram, Paris
Director Antonin Artaud
Script Antonin Artaud
Costumes Balthus. Executed by Karinska
Notes Karinska made modified copies of Lady Iya Abdy's banquet scene gown and of a black gown with a white ruff for women of Parisian high society.

LES CENT BAISERS (Ballet)
Date July 18, 1935, Ballets Russes de Col. W. de Basil[1], Royal Opera House, Covent Garden, London
Music Baron Frédéric d'Erlanger
Libretto Boris Kochno after Hans Christian Andersen
Choreography Bronislava Nijinska
Costumes Jean Hugo. Executed by Karinska

CARNAVAL (Ballet)
Date (New production) July 30, 1935, Ballets de Léon Woizikowsky, Théâtre Trocadero, Paris
Music Robert Schumann
Choreography Léon Woizikowsky after Michel Fokine
Costumes Georges Annenkoff. Executed by Karinska

L'AMOUR SORCIER (Ballet)
Date September 10, 1935, Ballets de Léon Woizikowsky, London Coliseum
Music Manuel de Falla
Choreography Léon Woizikowsky
Costumes Natalia Gontcharova. Executed by Karinska

PETROUCHKA (Ballet)
Date (New production) September 10, 1935, Ballets de Léon Woizikowsky, London Coliseum
Music Igor Stravinsky
Choreography Léon Woizikowsky after Michel Fokine
Costumes Alexandre Benois. Executed by Karinska

MARGOT (Comedy)
Date November 26, 1935, Théâtre Marigny, Paris
Director Pierre Fresnay
Script Edouard Bourdet, adapted by Pierre Fresnay
Music Georges Auric, Francis Poulenc
Costumes Christian Bérard. Executed by Karinska, Lanvin (for Yvonne Printemps)

THE FIRST SHOOT, A TRAGEDY (Ballet)
Date December, 1935, A ballet in C. B. Cochran's revue "Follow the Sun," Manchester, England
Music William Walton
Libretto Osbert Sitwell
Choreography Frederick Ashton
Costumes Cecil Beaton. Executed by Karinska

MISCELLANEOUS, 1935
Karinska was one of the "famous costumers" who made costumes based on works of art for the Comtesse de Beaumont's "Bal" in Paris.

1936

APPARITIONS (Ballet)
Date February 11, 1936, Vic-Wells Ballet, Sadler's Wells Theatre, London
Music Franz Liszt

Libretto Constant Lambert
Choreography Frederick Ashton
Costumes Cecil Beaton. Executed by Karinska

MAYERLING (Film)
Date Released February 19, 1936, Nero Film, Paris
Director Anatole Litvak
Screenplay Joseph Kessel, Mme. V. Cube (based on novel Idyll's End by Claude Anet)
Costumes Georges Annenkoff. Executed by Karinska

L'EPREUVE D'AMOUR (Ballet)
Date (Revival) April 4, 1936, Ballets de Monte Carlo[2], Opéra de Monte Carlo
Music Wolfgang Amadeus Mozart
Choreography Michel Fokine
Costumes André Derain. Executed by Karinska

LES SYLPHIDES (Ballet)
Date (Revival) April 4, 1936, Ballets de Monte Carlo[2], Opéra de Monte Carlo
Music Frédéric Chopin
Choreography Michel Fokine
Costumes Karinska after designs by Alexandre Benois

PETROUCHKA (Ballet)
Date (Revival) April 4, 1936, Ballets de Monte Carlo[2], Opéra de Monte Carlo
Music Igor Stravinsky
Choreography Michel Fokine
Costumes Karinska after designs by Alexandre Benois

COPPELIA (Ballet)
Date (New production) April 7, 1936, Ballets de Monte Carlo[2], Opéra de Monte Carlo
Music Léo Delibes
Choreography Nicolas Zverev after Arthur Saint-Léon
Costumes Mstislav Doboujinsky. Executed by Karinska

LE LAC DES CYGNES (SWAN LAKE) (Ballet)
Date (Revival) April 9, 1936, Ballets de Monte Carlo[2], Opéra de Monte Carlo
Music Peter Ilyitch Tschaikovsky
Choreography Nicolas Zverev after Marius Petipa
Costumes Karinska

AUBADE (Ballet)
Date (Revival) April 11, 1936, Ballets de Monte Carlo[2], Opéra de Monte Carlo
Music Francis Poulenc
Choreography George Balanchine
Costumes A. M. Cassandre. Executed by Karinska

CARNAVAL (Ballet)
Date (Revival) April 16, 1936, Ballets de Monte Carlo[2], Opéra de Monte Carlo
Music Robert Schumann
Choreography Michel Fokine
Costumes Léon Bakst. Executed by Karinska

LA CASSE-NOISETTE (THE NUTCRACKER) (Ballet)
Date (Revival) April 25, 1936, Ballets de Monte Carlo[2], Opéra de Monte Carlo
Music Peter Ilyitch Tschaikovsky
Choreography Boris Romanov
Costumes A. Alexiev. Executed by Karinska

L'ECOLE DES FEMMES (Comedy)
Date (New production) May 9, 1936, Théâtre Athénée Louis Jouvet, Paris
Director Louis Jouvet
Script Jean-Baptiste Molière
Music Vittorio Rieti
Costumes Christian Bérard. Executed by Karinska, Lelong (M. Ozeray's gown)

LA BOUTIQUE FANTASQUE (Ballet)
Date (New production) June 15, 1936, Ballets Russes de Col. W. de Basil[1], Covent Garden, London
Music Gioacchino Rossini
Choreography Léonide Massine
Costumes André Derain. Executed by Karinska

LE BEAU DANUBE (Ballet)
Date (New production) June 16, 1936, Ballets Russes de Col. W. de Basil[1], Covent Garden, London
Music Johann Strauss the Younger, Joseph Lanner
Choreography Léonide Massine
Costumes Etienne de Beaumont. Executed by Karinska

L'APRÈS-MIDI D'UN FAUNE (Ballet)
Date (New production) June 19, 1936, Ballets Russes de Col. W. de Basil[1], Covent Garden, London
Music Claude Debussy
Choreography After Bronislava Nijinska
Costumes After Léon Bakst. Executed by Karinska

SCHÉHÉRAZADE (Ballet)
Date (New production) June 22, 1936, Ballets Russes de Col. W. de Basil[1], Covent Garden, London
Music Nikolay Rimsky-Korsakov
Choreography Michel Fokine
Costumes Léon Bakst. Executed by Karinska

DON JUAN (Ballet)
Date (Revival) June 25, 1936, Ballets de Monte Carlo[2], Alhambra Theatre, London
Music Christoph Willibald von Gluck
Choreography Michel Fokine
Costumes Mariano Andreù. Executed by Karinska

SYMPHONIE FANTASTIQUE (Ballet)
Date July 24, 1936, Ballets Russes de Col. W. de Basil[1], Covent Garden, London
Music Hector Berlioz
Choreography Léonide Massine
Costumes Christian Bérard. Executed by Karinska (Movements II, III, IV), Olga Larose (Movements I, V)

LE PAVILLON (Ballet)
Date August 11, 1936, Ballets Russes de Col. W. de Basil[1], Covent Garden, London
Music Alexander Borodin
Libretto Boris Kochno
Choreography David Lichine
Costumes Cecil Beaton. Executed by Karinska

CLÉOPÂTRE (Ballet)
Date (Revival) November 10, 1936, Ballets Russes de Col. W. de Basil[1], Academy of Music, Philadelphia
Music Various Russian composers
Choreography Michel Fokine
Costumes Léon Bakst, Sonia Delaunay. Executed by Karinska

MISCELLANEOUS, 1936
Karinska designed and executed the sarafan (traditional Russian dress) and kokochnik (headdress) worn by Mathilda Kchessinska at a Covent Garden gala, July 24, 1936.

1937

HARLEQUIN IN THE STREET (Ballet)
Date February 8, 1937, Arts Theatre, Cambridge, England
Music François Couperin
Choreography Frederick Ashton
Costumes André Derain. Executed by Karinska

THE MISANTHROPE (Comedy)
Date (New production) February 8, 1937, Arts Theatre, Cambridge, England
Director Robert Atkins

Script Jean-Baptiste Molière
Music Rameau, Lully, Gossac, Gretry
Costumes André Derain. Executed by Karinska

L'ILLUSION COMIQUE *(Comedy)*
Date (New production) February 15, 1937, Comédie
  Française, Paris
Director Louis Jouvet
Script Pierre Corneille
Music Vittorio Rieti
Costumes Christian Bérard. Executed by Karinska

FIRE OVER ENGLAND *(Film)*
Date Released February 25, 1937, London Film
  Productions, Ltd.
Director William K. Howard
Screenplay Clemence Dane, Sergei Nolbandov
Costumes René Hubert. Executed by Karinska

LES ELFES *(Ballet)*
Date (Revival) April 24, 1937, Ballets de Monte Carlo²,
  Opéra de Monte Carlo
Music Felix Mendelssohn
Choreography Michel Fokine
Costumes Christian Bérard assisted by Guillaume Monin.
  Executed by Karinska

THE BELOVED ONE (LA BIEN-AIMÉE) *(Ballet)*
Date (Revival) May 10, 1937, Markova-Dolin Ballet, King's
  Theatre, Hammersmith, London
Music Franz Schubert, Franz Liszt
Choreography Bronislava Nijinska
Costumes George Kirsta. Executed by Karinska, except
  those for Alicia Markova and Anton Dolin

ELECTRE *(Drama)*
Date May 13, 1937, Théâtre Athénée Louis Jouvet, Paris
Director Louis Jouvet
Script Jean Giraudoux
Music Vittorio Rieti
Costumes Dimitri Bouchène. Executed by Karinska

ARAGONESA *(Ballet)*
Date (Revival) June 17, 1937, Ballets de Monte Carlo²,
  London Coliseum, London
Music Mikhail Glinka
Choreography Michel Fokine
Costumes Mariano Andreù. Executed by Karinska

ORPHÉE ET EURIDICE *(Opera)*
Date (New production) June 17, 1937, Ballets Russes de
  Col. W. de Basil¹, Covent Garden, London
Music Christoph Willibald von Gluck
Choreography Lizzi Maudrik, David Lichine (Act 2, Scene 2:
  "The Temple of Love")
Costumes Karinska (Act 2, Scene 2 only)

LES ELEMENTS *(Ballet)*
Date (Revival) June 24, 1937, Ballets de Monte Carlo²,
  London Coliseum, London
Music Johann Sebastian Bach
Choreography Michel Fokine
Costumes Dimitri Bouchène. Executed by Karinska

KNIGHT WITHOUT ARMOR *(Film)*
Date Released July 9, 1937, London Film Productions, Ltd.
Director Jacques Feyder
Screenplay Lajos Biro, Frances Marion, Arthur Wimperis
  (based on novel *Without Armor* by James Hilton)
Costumes Georges Benda. Executed by Karinska

FRANCESCA DA RIMINI *(Ballet)*
Date July 15, 1937, Ballets Russes de Col. W. de Basil¹,
  Covent Garden, London
Music Peter Ilyitch Tschaikovsky
Choreography David Lichine
Costumes Oliver Messel. Executed by Karinska

LE COQ D'OR *(Ballet)*
Date (New production) September 23, 1937, Ballets Russes
  de Col. W. de Basil¹, Covent Garden, London
Music Nikolay Rimsky-Korsakov
Choreography Michel Fokine
Costumes Natalia Gontcharova. Executed by Karinska

LE LION AMOUREUX *(Ballet)*
Date October 6, 1937, Ballets Russes de Col. W. de Basil¹,
  Covent Garden, London
Music Karol Rathaus
Choreography David Lichine
Costumes Pierre Roy. Executed by Karinska

HOME AND BEAUTY *(Musical Revue)*
Date 1937 season, Adelphi Theatre, London
Producer Charles B. Cochran
Director John Murray Anderson
Music Nikolaus Brodszky
Choreography Frederick Ashton
Costumes Raoul Pêne du Bois, Thomas Becher. Executed
  by Karinska. ("At the Music Room Window," "Julika
  Kadar's Bedroom," "The Tapestry Room," except for
  Gitta Alpar's costumes)

MISCELLANEOUS, 1937
Karinska worked on costumes for the unfinished film
I, Claudius, starring Charles Laughton and Merle Oberon. In
the summer of 1937 Karinska made party dresses for a *fête
champêtre* given by Cecil Beaton and Michael Duff at
Beaton's country house at Ashcombe.

1938

GAÎETÉ PARISIENNE *(Ballet)*
Date April 5, 1938, Ballet Russe de Monte Carlo²,
  Opéra de Monte Carlo
Music Jacques Offenbach
Choreography Léonide Massine
Costumes Etienne de Beaumont. Executed by Karinska

LA SEPTIÈME SYMPHONIE *(Ballet)*
Date May 5, 1938, Ballet Russe de Monte Carlo²,
  Opéra de Monte Carlo
Music Ludwig van Beethoven
Choreography Léonide Massine
Costumes Christian Bérard. Executed by Karinska

PROTÉE *(Ballet)*
Date July 5, 1938, Russian Ballet¹, Covent Garden, London
Music Claude Debussy
Choreography David Lichine
Costumes Giorgio de Chirico. Executed by Karinska

CENDRILLON *(Ballet)*
Date July 19, 1938, Russian Ballet¹, Covent Garden,
  London
Music Baron Frédéric d'Erlanger
Choreography Michel Fokine
Costumes Natalia Gontcharova. Executed by Karinska

COPPELIA *(Ballet)*
Date (New production) September 20, 1938, Ballet Russe
  de Monte Carlo², Covent Garden, London
Music Léo Delibes
Choreography Reconstructed by Nicolas Sergeyev, additional
  dances by Léonide Massine
Costumes Pierre Roy. Executed by Karinska

EVE IN THE PARK *(Musical Revue)*
Date 1938–39 Season, Suppertime Show at the Trocadero
  Grillroom, London
Producer/Director Charles B. Cochran
Music and Lyrics George Frank Rubens, Cecil Landeau
Choreography Carl Randall

Costumes George Kirsta ("Eve Prepares in the Park").
  Karinska ("Champagne Taste"). Executed by Karinska

GOING TO TOWN *(Musical Revue)*
Date 1938–39 Season, Suppertime Show at the Trocadero
  Grillroom, London
Producer/Director Charles B. Cochran
Choreography Buddy Bradley
Costumes Doris Zinkeisen ("Going to Town" gown for
  Eileen Moore, "Peckin' and Posin'," "Beauty—Adorned
  or Unadorned," "The Hold Up"), Alexandre Vevern
  ("Champagne & Confetti"). Executed by Karinska

NIGHT LIGHTS *(Musical Revue)*
Date 1938–39 Season, Suppertime Show at the Trocadero
  Grillroom, London
Producer/Director Charles B. Cochran
Music Elsie April, Lorraine
Choreography Buddy Bradley, Antony Tudor
Costumes Doris Zinkeisen. Executed by Karinska
  ("A Fragonard Picture," except for singers' costumes;
  bustle costumes for "The Argyll Room, 1850–1878")

ROUND AND ROUND *(Musical Revue)*
Date 1938–39 Season, Suppertime Show at the Trocadero
  Grillroom, London
Producer/Director Charles B. Cochran
Music and Lyrics Annette Mills
Choreography Buddy Bradley
Costumes Karinska ("Ballroom Blues," "The Greeks Had a
  Word for It"). Executed by Madame Hayward

1939

CAPRICCIO ESPAGNOL *(Ballet)*
Date May 4, 1939, Ballet Russe de Monte Carlo², Opéra de
  Monte Carlo
Music Nikolay Rimsky-Korsakov
Choreography Léonide Massine, Argentinita
Costumes Mariano Andreù. Executed by Karinska, Mlle.
  Truchi

TOO MANY GIRLS *(Musical)*
Date October 18, 1939, Imperial Theatre, New York
Producer/Director George Abbott
Music and Lyrics Richard Rodgers, Lorenz Hart
Choreography Robert Alton
Costumes Raoul Pêne du Bois. Executed by Karinska, others

BACCHANALE *(Ballet)*
Date November 9, 1939, Ballet Russe de Monte Carlo²,
  Metropolitan Opera House, New York
Music Richard Wagner
Choreography Léonide Massine
Costumes Salvador Dalí. Executed by Karinska

GHOST TOWN *(Ballet)*
Date November 12, 1939, Ballet Russe de Monte Carlo²,
  Metropolitan Opera, New York
Music Richard Rodgers
Choreography Marc Platoff
Costumes Raoul Pêne du Bois. Executed by Karinska

MISCELLANEOUS, 1930s
During the 1930s Karinska was assisted, in Paris, by her
daughter, Irene. In 1939 Karinska made a 60-foot dragon of
rubber balls stuffed into a suede body and covered with
scales for Salvador Dalí's "Dream of Venus" exhibit at the
New York World's Fair.

1940

LOUISIANA PURCHASE *(Musical)*
Date May 28, 1940, Imperial Theatre, New York
Producer B. G. De Sylva

Director   Edgar MacGregor
Music and Lyrics   Irving Berlin
Choreography   George Balanchine, Carl Randall
Costumes   Tom Lee. Executed by Karinska (uncredited), others

A THOUSAND TIMES NEIGH (Ballet)
Date   Summer 1940, New York World's Fair, Ford Motor
   Show
Music   Tom Bennett
Libretto   Lincoln Kirstein
Choreography   William Dollar
Costumes   Alvin Colt. Executed by Karinska

VIENNA — 1814 (Ballet)
Date   October 14, 1940, Ballet Russe de Monte Carlo²,
   Fifty-first Street Theatre, New York
Music   Carl Maria von Weber
Choreography   Léonide Massine
Costumes   Stewart Chaney. Executed by Karinska

THE NUTCRACKER (Ballet)
Date   (Revival) October 17, 1940, Ballet Russe de Monte
   Carlo², Fifty-first Street Theatre, New York
Music   Peter Ilyitch Tschaikovsky
Choreography   Lev Ivanov, Marius Petipa, revived by
   Alexandra Federova
Costumes   Alexandre Benois. Executed by Karinska

CABIN IN THE SKY (Musical)
Date   October 25, 1940, Martin Beck Theatre, New York
Producers   Albert Lewis, Vinton Freedley
Music and Lyrics   Vernon Duke, John Latouche
Choreography   George Balanchine, Katherine Dunham
Costumes   Boris Aronson. Executed by Karinska, John Pratt
   (Katherine Dunham's costumes)

CAPRICCIOSO (Ballet)
Date   November 3, 1940, Ballet Theatre, Civic Opera
   House, Chicago
Music   Domenico Cimarosa
Choreography   Anton Dolin
Costumes   Nicolas de Molas. Executed by Karinska

TWELFTH NIGHT (Comedy)
Date   (New Production) November 10, 1940, St. James
   Theatre, New York
Producer   Gilbert Miller
Director   Margaret Webster
Script   William Shakespeare
Music   Paul Bowles
Costumes   Stewart Chaney. Executed by Karinska

MISCELLANEOUS, 1940
Karinska opened a high-fashion dress shop called "Karinska,
Inc." at 23 E. 56th Street in New York with Baron Nicolas
de Gunzburg and Natasha Paley.

1941

BALUSTRADE (Ballet)
Date   January 22, 1941, Original Ballet Russe¹, Fifty-first
   Street Theatre, New York
Music   Igor Stravinsky
Choreography   George Balanchine
Costumes   Pavel Tchelitchew. Executed by Karinska

GALA PERFORMANCE (Ballet)
Date   February 11, 1941, Ballet Theatre, Majestic Theatre,
   New York
Music   Sergei Prokofiev
Choreography   Antony Tudor
Costumes   Nicolas de Molas. Executed by Karinska

THREE VIRGINS AND A DEVIL (Ballet)
Date   February 11, 1941, Ballet Theatre, Majestic Theatre,
   New York
Music   Ottorino Respighi

Libretto   Ramon Reed after Boccaccio
Choreography   Agnes de Mille
Costumes   Motley. Executed by Karinska

DIVERTIMENTO (Ballet)
Date   June 27, 1941, American Ballet Caravan, Teatro
   Municipal, Rio de Janeiro
Music   Gioacchino Rossini
Choreography   George Balanchine
Costumes   André Derain. Executed by Karinska
Notes   Costumes from Les Songes (Les Ballets 1933)

ANNE OF ENGLAND (Drama)
Date   October 7, 1941, St. James Theatre, New York
Producer/Director   Gilbert Miller
Script   Mary Cass Canfield, Ethel Bordon
Costumes   Mstislav Doboujinsky. Executed by Karinska

LABYRINTH (Ballet)
Date   October 8, 1941, Ballet Russe de Monte Carlo²,
   Metropolitan Opera House, New York
Music   Franz Schubert
Choreography   Léonide Massine
Costumes   Salvador Dalí. Executed by Karinska

PRINCESS AURORA (Ballet)
Date   October 23, 1941, Ballet Theatre, Palacio de Bellas
   Artes, Mexico City
Music   Peter Ilyitch Tschaikovsky
Choreography   Anton Dolin after Marius Petipa
Costumes   After Léon Bakst. Executed by Karinska

SLAVONIKA (Ballet)
Date   October 24, 1941, Ballet Theatre, Palacio de Bella
   Artes, Mexico City
Music   Antonín Dvořák
Choreography   Vania Psota
Costumes   Alvin Colt. Executed by Karinska

BLUEBEARD (Ballet)
Date   October 27, 1941, Ballet Theatre, Palacio de Bellas
   Artes, Mexico City
Music   Jacques Offenbach
Choreography   Michel Fokine
Costumes   Marcel Vertès. Executed by Karinska

1942

THE LADY COMES ACROSS (Musical)
Date   January 9, 1942, Forty-fourth Street Theatre, New
   York
Producers   George Hale, Charles R. Rogers, Nelson Seabra
Director   Romney Brent
Music and Lyrics   Vernon Duke, John Latouche
Choreography   George Balanchine
Costumes   Stewart Chaney. Executed by Karinska, others

RUSSIAN SOLDIER (Ballet)
Date   January 23, 1942, Ballet Theatre, Opera House,
   Boston
Music   Sergei Prokofiev
Choreography   Michel Fokine
Costumes   Mstislav Doboujinsky. Executed by Karinska

PILLAR OF FIRE (Ballet)
Date   April 8, 1942, Ballet Theatre, Metropolitan Opera
   House, New York
Music   Arnold Schoenberg
Choreography   Antony Tudor
Costumes   Jo Mielziner. Executed by Karinska

STAR AND GARTER (Musical Revue)
Date   June 24, 1942, The Music Box, New York
Producer   Michael Todd
Director   Hassard Short
Music and Lyrics   Various

Choreography   Al White, Jr., Albertina Rasch
Costumes   Irene Sharaff. Executed by Karinska

THE SNOW MAIDEN (Ballet)
Date   October 12, 1942, Ballet Russe de Monte Carlo²,
   Metropolitan Opera House, New York
Music   Alexander Glazounov
Choreography   Bronislava Nijinska
Costumes   Boris Aronson. Executed by Karinska

RODEO (Ballet)
Date   October 16, 1942, Ballet Russe de Monte Carlo²,
   Metropolitan Opera House, New York
Music   Aaron Copland
Choreography   Agnes de Mille
Costumes   Kermit Love. Executed by Karinska

THE ROMANTIC AGE (Ballet)
Date   October 23, 1942, Ballet Theatre, Metropolitan
   Opera House, New York
Music   Vincenzo Bellini
Choreography   Anton Dolin
Costumes   Carlos Merida. Executed by Karinska

THE PIRATE (Comedy)
Date   November 25, 1942, Martin Beck Theatre, New York
Producers   Playwrights' Company, Theatre Guild, Alfred
   Lunt, Lynn Fontanne
Directors   Alfred Lunt, John C. Wilson
Script   S. N. Behrman
Costumes   Miles White. Executed by Karinska, others

HELEN OF TROY (Ballet)
Date   November 29, 1942, Ballet Theatre, Masonic
   Auditorium, Detroit, Michigan
Music   Jacques Offenbach
Choreography   David Lichine
Costumes   Marcel Vertès, Karinska. Executed by Karinska,
   Mme. Berthe

1943

SOMETHING FOR THE BOYS (Musical)
Date   January 7, 1943, Alvin Theatre, New York
Producer   Michael Todd
Directors   Herbert Fields, Hassard Short
Music   Cole Porter
Choreography   Jack Cole
Costumes   Billy Livingston, assisted by Grace Houston.
   Executed by Karinska, others

ROMEO AND JULIET (Ballet)
Date   April 6, 1943, Ballet Theatre, Metropolitan Opera
   House, New York
Music   Frederick Delius
Choreography   Antony Tudor
Costumes   Eugene Berman. Executed by Karinska

APOLLO (Ballet)
Date   (New production) April 25, 1943, Ballet Theatre,
   Metropolitan Opera House, New York
Music   Igor Stravinsky
Choreography   George Balanchine
Costumes   Karinska

1944

LADY IN THE DARK (Film)
Date   Released February 23, 1944, Paramount Pictures
Director   Mitchell Leisen
Screenplay   Frances Goodrich, Albert Hackett (Moss Hart)
Costumes   Raoul Pêne du Bois, Karinska, Edith Head,
   Mitchell Leisen. Executed by Karinska, others

GASLIGHT (Film)
Date   Released May 5, 1944, Metro-Goldwyn-Mayer
Director   George Cukor
Screenplay   John van Druten, John Balderston, Walter
    Reisch, based on play by Patrick Hamilton
Costumes   Irene Lentz Gibbons, Karinska (uncredited).
    Executed by Karinska

DREAM WITH MUSIC (Musical)
Date   May 18, 1944, Majestic Theatre, New York
Producer/Director   Richard Kollmar
Music   Clay Warnick
Choreography   George Balanchine, Henry Le Tang
Costumes   Miles White. Executed by Karinska, others

KISMET (Film)
Date   Released August 22, 1944, Metro-Goldwyn-Mayer
Director   William Dieterle
Screenplay   John Meehan
Costumes   Irene Lentz Gibbons, assisted by Karinska
    (uncredited). Executed by Karinska

DANSES CONCERTANTES (Ballet)
Date   September 10, 1944, Ballet Russe de Monte Carlo²,
    City Center, New York
Music   Igor Stravinsky
Choreography   George Balanchine
Costumes   Eugene Berman. Executed by Karinska

FRENCHMAN'S CREEK (Film)
Date   Released September 21, 1944, Paramount Pictures
Director   Mitchell Leisen
Screenplay   Talbot Jennings based on Daphne du Maurier's
    novel
Costumes   Raoul Pêne du Bois. Executed by Karinska

LE BOURGEOIS GENTILHOMME (Ballet)
Date   (New production) September 23, 1944, Ballet Russe
    de Monte Carlo², City Center, New York
Music   Richard Strauss
Choreography   George Balanchine
Costumes   Eugene Berman. Executed by Karinska

WALTZ ACADEMY (Ballet)
Date   October 5, 1944, Ballet Theatre, Opera House,
    Boston
Music   Vittorio Rieti
Choreography   George Balanchine
Costumes   Alvin Colt. Executed by Karinska

GRAND PAS DE DEUX FROM DON
QUIXOTE (Ballet)
Date   (Revival) October 25, 1944, Ballet Theatre,
    Metropolitan Opera House, New York
Music   Léon Minkus
Choreography   Anatole Oboukhoff after Marius Petipa
Costumes   Karinska

SENTIMENTAL COLLOQUY (Ballet)
Date   October 30, 1944, Ballet International, International
    Theatre, New York
Music   Paul Bowles
Choreography   George Balanchine, credited to André
    Eglevsky
Costumes   Salvador Dalí. Executed by Karinska

ON THE TOWN (Musical)
Date   December 28, 1944, Adelphi Theatre, New York
Producers   Paul Feigay, Oliver Smith
Director   George Abbott
Book and Lyrics   Betty Comden, Adolph Green
Music   Leonard Bernstein
Choreography   Jerome Robbins
Costumes   Alvin Colt. Principal actresses' costumes
    executed by Karinska

SONJA HENIE WITH HER 1945
HOLLYWOOD ICE REVUE (Ice Show)
Date   Fall 1944
Producer   Arthur M. Wirtz
Choreography   Catherine Littlefield
Costumes   Billy Livingston. Executed by Karinska (Russe
    Carnival costumes), Lawrence Vlady (animals), others

1945

ICE CAPADES OF 1946 (Ice Show)
Date   September 1945
Producer   John H. Harris
Choreography   Chester Hale
Costumes   Marco Montedoro. Executed by Karinska, others

INTERPLAY (Ballet)
Date   (New production) October 17, 1945, Ballet Theatre,
    Metropolitan Opera House, New York
Music   Morton Gould
Choreography   Jerome Robbins
Costumes   Irene Sharaff. Executed by Karinska

BILLION DOLLAR BABY (Musical)
Date   December 21, 1945, Alvin Theatre, New York
Producers   Paul Feigay, Oliver Smith
Director   George Abbott
Book and Lyrics   Betty Comden, Adolph Green
Music   Morton Gould
Choreography   Jerome Robbins
Costumes   Irene Sharaff. Executed by Karinska

1946

THE WOULD-BE GENTLEMAN (Comedy)
Date   (New Production) January 9, 1946, Booth Theatre,
    New York
Producer   Michael Todd
Script   Adapted from Jean-Baptiste Molière
Music   Jerome Moross, adapted from Jean-Baptiste Lully
Costumes   Irene Sharaff. Executed by Karinska

ANTIGONE (Drama)
Date   (New Production) February 18, 1946, Cort Theatre,
    New York
Producers   Katharine Cornell, Gilbert Miller
Director   Guthrie McClintic
Script   Louis Anouilh after Sophocles
Costumes   Valentina, Karinska (uncredited)

THE NIGHT SHADOW (LATER LA
SONNAMBULA) (Ballet)
Date   February 27, 1946, Ballet Russe de Monte Carlo²,
    City Center, New York
Music   Vittorio Rieti on themes of Vincenzo Bellini
Choreography   George Balanchine
Costumes   Dorothea Tanning. Executed by Karinska

RAYMONDA (Ballet)
Date   (New production) March 12, 1946, Ballet Russe de
    Monte Carlo², City Center, New York
Music   Alexander Glazounov
Choreography   George Balanchine and Alexandra Danilova
    after Marius Petipa
Costumes   Alexandre Benois. Executed by Karinska

KITTY (Film)
Date   Released March 31, 1946, Paramount Pictures
Director   Mitchell Leisen
Screenplay   Darrel Ware, Karl Tunberg
Costumes   Raoul Pêne du Bois, Karinska (uncredited).
    Executed by Karinska

ICETIME (Ice Show)
Date   June 20, 1946, Center Theatre, Rockefeller Center,
    New York
Producers   Sonja Henie, Arthur M. Wirtz
Choreography   Catherine Littlefield, Dorothie Littlefield
Costumes   Lou Eisele, Billy Livingston. Executed by
    Karinska, others

ICE CAPADES OF 1947 (Ice Show)
Date   September 4, 1946, The Gardens, Pittsburgh
Producer   John H. Harris
Choreography   Chester Hale. Assisted by Fred Kelly
Costumes   Marco Montedoro, Lou Eisele. Executed by
    Karinska, others

CAMILLE (Ballet)
Date   October 1, 1946, Original Ballet Russe¹, Metropolitan
    Opera House, New York
Music   Franz Schubert arranged by Vittorio Rieti
Choreography   John Taras
Costumes   Cecil Beaton. Executed by Karinska

LES PATINEURS (Ballet)
Date   (New production) October 2, 1946, Ballet Theatre,
    Broadway Theatre, New York
Music   Giacomo Meyerbeer
Choreography   Frederick Ashton
Costumes   Cecil Beaton. Executed by Karinska

BLUE SKIES (Film)
Date   Released October 16, 1946, Paramount Pictures
Director   Stuart Heisler
Screenplay   Arthur Sheekman
Choreography   Fred Astaire, Hermes Pan
Costumes   Edith Head (gowns), Waldo Angelo. Executed by
    Karinska

THE SPELLBOUND CHILD (Lyric Fantasy)
Date   (New production) November 20, 1946, Ballet Society,
    Central High School of Needle Trades, New York
Music   Maurice Ravel
Libretto   Colette (translated by Lincoln Kirstein, Jane
    Barzin)
Choreography   George Balanchine
Costumes   Aline Bernstein. Executed by Karinska

THE FOUR TEMPERAMENTS (Ballet)
Date   November 20, 1946, Ballet Society, Central High
    School of Needle Trades, New York
Music   Paul Hindemith
Choreography   George Balanchine
Costumes   Kurt Seligmann. Executed by Karinska

1947

RENARD (Ballet)
Date   January 13, 1947, Ballet Society, Hunter College
    Playhouse, New York
Music   Igor Stravinsky
Choreography   George Balanchine
Costumes   Esteban Francés. Executed by Karinska

PASTORELA (Ballet)
Date   (Revival) January 15, 1947, Ballet Society, Hunter
    College Playhouse, New York
Music   Paul Bowles
Libretto   José Martinez
Choreography   Lew Christensen, José Fernandez
Costumes   Alvin Colt. Executed by Karinska

BAREFOOT BOY WITH CHEEK (Musical)
Date   April 3, 1947, Martin Beck Theatre, New York
Producer/Director   George Abbott

Music and Lyrics Sidney Lippman, Sylvia Dee
Choreography Richard Barstow
Costumes Alvin Colt. Executed by Karinska

ICETIME OF 1948 *(Ice Show)*
Date May 28, 1947, Center Theatre, Rockefeller Center, New York
Producers Sonja Henie, Arthur M. Wirtz
Choreography Catherine Littlefield, Dorothie Littlefield
Costumes Lou Eisele, Billy Livingston, Kathryn Kuhn. Executed by Karinska, others

ICE CAPADES OF 1948 *(Ice Show)*
Date September 1947
Producer John H. Harris
Choreography Chester Hale
Costumes Freddy Wittop. Executed by Karinska, others

UNCONQUERED *(Film)*
Date Released October 11, 1947, Paramount Pictures
Producer/Director Cecil B. de Mille
Screenplay Charles Bennett, Frederic Frank, Jesse Lasky, Jr.
Costumes Karinska, Gwen Wakeling

PUNCH AND THE CHILD *(Ballet)*
Date November 12, 1947, Ballet Society, City Center, New York
Music Richard Arnell
Choreography Fred Danieli
Costumes Horace Armistead. Executed by Karinska

EASTWARD IN EDEN *(Drama)*
Date November 18, 1947, Royale Theatre, New York
Producer Nancy Stern
Director Ellen Van Volkenburg
Script Dorothy Gardner (based on the life of Emily Dickinson)
Costumes Donald Oenslager. Executed by Karinska

THEME AND VARIATIONS *(Ballet)*
Date November 26, 1947, Ballet Theatre, City Center, New York
Music Peter Ilyitch Tschaikovsky
Choreography George Balanchine
Costumes Woodman Thompson. Executed by Karinska
Notes A new production by New York City Ballet in 1960 used Karinska's costumes from *Symphony in C*

SONJA HENIE WITH HER 1948 HOLLYWOOD ICE REVUE *(Ice Show)*
Date Fall 1947
Producer Arthur M. Wirtz
Choreography Catherine Littlefield
Costumes Billy Livingston, Kathryn Kuhn. Ensemble costumes executed by Karinska, others

1948

THE TRIUMPH OF BACCHUS AND ARIADNE *(Ballet)*
Date February 9, 1948, Ballet Society, City Center, New York
Music Vittorio Rieti
Choreography George Balanchine
Costumes Corrado Cagli. Executed by Karinska

FALL RIVER LEGEND *(Ballet)*
Date April 22, 1948, Ballet Theatre, Metropolitan Opera House, New York
Music Morton Gould
Choreography Agnes de Mille
Costumes Miles White. Executed by Karinska

ORPHEUS *(Ballet)*
Date April 28, 1948, Ballet Society, City Center, New York
Music Igor Stravinsky
Choreography George Balanchine
Costumes Isamu Noguchi. Executed by Karinska

THE PIRATE *(Film)*
Date Released May 21, 1948, Metro-Goldwyn-Mayer
Director Vincente Minnelli
Screenplay Albert Hackett, Frances Goodrich
Music and Lyrics Cole Porter
Costumes Tom Keogh. Executed by Karinska

HOWDY MR. ICE *(Ice Show)*
Date June 24, 1948, Center Theatre, Rockefeller Center, New York
Producers Sonja Henie, Arthur M. Wirtz
Choreography Catherine Littlefield, Dorothie Littlefield
Costumes Billy Livingston, Kathryn Kuhn. Executed by Karinska, others

ICE CAPADES OF 1949 *(Ice Show)*
Date September 8, 1948, The Gardens, Pittsburgh
Producer John H. Harris
Choreography Chester Hale
Costumes Billy Livingston. Executed by Karinska

SMALL WONDER *(Musical)*
Date September 15, 1948, Coronet Theatre, New York
Producer George Nichols III
Director Bert Shevelove
Music Baldwin Bergerson, Albert Selden
Lyrics Phyllis McGinley, Billings Brown
Choreography Gower Champion
Costumes John Derro. Executed by Karinska

JOAN OF ARC *(Film)*
Date Released October 20, 1948, RKO Radio Pictures
Producer Walter Wanger
Director Victor Fleming
Screenplay Maxwell Anderson, Andrew Solt, adapted from Anderson's play *Joan of Lorraine*
Costumes Karinska, Dorothy Jeakins
Notes Karinska and Jeakins won the first Academy Award for Costume Design for a Color Film

THE COUNTESS OF MONTE CRISTO *(Film)*
Date Released November 3, 1948, Universal-International
Director Frederick De Cordova
Screenplay William Bowers, based on an original story by Walter Reisch
Costumes Grace Houston. Executed by Karinska

AS THE GIRLS GO *(Musical)*
Date November 13, 1948, Winter Garden Theatre, New York
Producer Michael Todd
Director Howard Bay
Music and Lyrics Jimmy McHugh, Harold Adamson
Choreography Hermes Pan
Costumes Oleg Cassini. Executed by Karinska

THE MADWOMAN OF CHAILLOT *(Drama)*
Date (New Production) December 27, 1948, Belasco Theatre, New York
Producer/Director Alfred de Liagre, Jr.
Script Jean Giraudoux, adapted by Maurice Valency
Costumes Christian Bérard. Executed by Karinska

SONJA HENIE WITH HER 1949 HOLLYWOOD ICE REVUE *(Ice Show)*
Date Fall 1948
Producer Arthur M. Wirtz
Choreography Catherine Littlefield
Costumes Billy Livingston, Kathryn Kuhn, Grace Houston. Ensemble costumes executed by Karinska, others

1949

PRINCESS AURORA *(Ballet)*
Date (New Production) April 2, 1949, Ballet Theatre, Opera House, Chicago
Music Peter Ilyitch Tschaikovsky

Choreography Marius Petipa, adapted by George Balanchine (the "Three Ivans" by Bronislava Nijinska)
Costumes Léon Bakst. Executed by Karinska

HOWDY MR. ICE OF 1950 *(Ice Show)*
Date May 26, 1949, Center Theatre, Rockefeller Center, New York
Producers Sonja Henie, Arthur M. Wirtz
Choreography Catherine Littlefield, Dorothie Littlefield
Costumes Grace Houston, Billy Livingston, Kathryn Kuhn. Executed by Karinska, others

MISS LIBERTY *(Musical)*
Date July 15, 1949, Imperial Theatre, New York
Producers Irving Berlin, Robert E. Sherwood, Moss Hart
Director Moss Hart
Music and Lyrics Irving Berlin
Choreography Jerome Robbins
Costumes Motley. Executed by Karinska, others

BIRTHDAY *(Ballet)*
Date September 27, 1949, Ballet Russe de Monte Carlo², Metropolitan Opera House, New York
Music Gioacchino Rossini
Choreography Tatiana Chamié
Costumes Karinska

ICE CAPADES OF 1950 *(Ice Show)*
Date September 1949
Producer John H. Harris
Choreography Chester Hale
Costumes Billy Livingston. Executed by Karinska, others

BOURRÉE FANTASQUE *(Ballet)*
Date December 1, 1949, New York City Ballet, City Center, New York
Choreography George Balanchine
Music Emmanuel Chabrier
Costumes Karinska
Notes Costumes also used (with additions) in 1967 for *Trois Valses Romantiques* choreographed by George Balanchine to music by Emmanuel Chabrier

SONJA HENIE WITH HER 1950 HOLLYWOOD ICE REVUE *(Ice Show)*
Date Fall 1949
Producer Arthur M. Wirtz
Choreography Catherine Littlefield
Costumes Billy Livingston, Grace Houston, Karinska (ballet costumes). Ensemble costumes executed by Karinska, others

MISCELLANEOUS, 1940s
During the 1940s and possibly the early 1950s, Karinska executed costumes by Edith King for King-Coit Children's Theatre. In the same period she also executed costumes for Lou Walter's Latin Quarter, a popular New York nightclub. Designers with whom she worked on these productions include Kermit Love and Freddy Wittop.

1950

PRODIGAL SON *(Ballet)*
Date (Revival) February 23, 1950, New York City Ballet, City Center, New York
Music Sergei Prokofiev
Choreography George Balanchine
Costumes Georges Rouault. Executed by Karinska

ICE CAPADES OF 1951 *(Ice Show)*
Date September 12, 1950, The Gardens, Pittsburgh
Producer John H. Harris
Choreography Chester Hale
Costumes Billy Livingston. Executed by Karinska

CALL ME MADAM *(Musical)*
Date October 12, 1950, Imperial Theatre, New York

Producer Leland Hayward
Director George Abbott
Music and Lyrics Irving Berlin
Choreography Jerome Robbins
Costumes Raoul Pêne du Bois. Executed by Karinska,
    Mainbocher (Ethel Merman's costume)

PRIMA BALLERINA *(Ballet)*
Date October 25, 1950, Ballet Russe de Monte Carlo[2],
    Opera House, Chicago
Music Charles Lecocq
Choreography Tatiana Chamié
Costumes Karinska

SYMPHONY IN C *(Ballet)*
Date (New production) November 22, 1950, New York
    City Ballet, City Center, New York
Music Georges Bizet
Choreography George Balanchine
Costumes Karinska

MAZURKA FROM ''A LIFE FOR THE
TSAR'' *(Ballet)*
Date November 30, 1950, New York City Ballet, City
    Center, New York
Music Mikhail Glinka
Choreography George Balanchine
Costumes Karinska

SYLVIA: PAS DE DEUX *(Ballet)*
Date December 1, 1950, New York City Ballet, City
    Center, New York
Music Léo Delibes
Choreography George Balanchine
Costumes Karinska

SONJA HENIE WITH HER 1951
HOLLYWOOD ICE REVUE *(Ice Show)*
Date Fall 1950
Producer Arthur M. Wirtz
Choreography Catherine Littlefield
Costumes Billy Livingston. Ensemble costumes executed by
    Karinska, others

1951

THE CARD GAME (FORMERLY THE CARD
PARTY) *(Ballet)*
Date (Revival) February 15, 1951, New York City Ballet,
    City Center, New York
Music Igor Stravinsky
Choreography George Balanchine
Costumes Irene Sharaff. Executed by Karinska

PAS DE TROIS (ALSO MINKUS PAS DE
TROIS) *(Ballet)*
Date February 18, 1951, New York City Ballet, City
    Center, New York
Music Léon Minkus
Choreography George Balanchine
Costumes Karinska

LA VALSE *(Ballet)*
Date February 20, 1951, New York City Ballet, City
    Center, New York
Music Maurice Ravel
Choreography George Balanchine
Costumes Karinska

LADY OF THE CAMELIAS *(Ballet)*
Date February 28, 1951, New York City Ballet, City
    Center, New York
Music Giuseppe Verdi
Choreography Antony Tudor
Costumes Cecil Beaton (from *Camille,* 1946). Executed by
    Karinska

ROMEO AND JULIET *(Drama)*
Date (New Production) March 10, 1951, Broadhurst
    Theatre, New York
Producer Dwight Deere Wiman
Director Peter Glenville
Script William Shakespeare
Costumes Oliver Messel. Executed by Karinska

CAPRICCIO BRILLANT *(Ballet)*
Date June 7, 1951, New York City Ballet, City Center,
    New York
Music Felix Mendelssohn
Choreography George Balanchine
Costumes Karinska

THE CAGE *(Ballet)*
Date June 14, 1951, New York City Ballet, City Center,
    New York
Music Igor Stravinsky
Choreography Jerome Robbins
Costumes Ruth Sobotka. Executed by Karinska

ICE CAPADES OF 1952 *(Ice Show)*
Date September 1951, The Gardens, Pittsburgh
Producer John H. Harris
Choreography Chester Hale
Costumes Billy Livingston. Executed by Karinska

LA TRAVIATA *(Opera)*
Date (New production) October 5, 1951, San Francisco
    Opera Company, San Francisco
Music Giuseppe Verdi
Director Armando Agnini
Costumes Some dresses for Lily Pons by Karinska

TYL ULENSPIEGEL *(Ballet)*
Date November 14, 1951, New York City Ballet, City
    Center, New York
Music Richard Strauss
Choreography George Balanchine
Costumes Esteban Francés. Executed by Karinska

APOLLO, LEADER OF THE MUSES *(Ballet)*
Date (New production) November 15, 1951, New York
    City Ballet, City Center, New York
Music Igor Stravinsky
Choreography George Balanchine
Costumes Karinska

RIGOLETTO *(Opera)*
Date (New production) November 15, 1951, Metropolitan
    Opera Company, New York
Music Giuseppe Verdi
Director Herbert Graf
Costumes Eugene Berman. Executed by Karinska

SONJA HENIE 1952 ICE REVUE *(Ice Show)*
Date November 15, 1951, San Francisco
Producer Sonja Henie
Choreography Robert Sidney
Costumes Billy Livingston. Ensemble costumes executed by
    Karinska, others

SWAN LAKE *(Ballet)*
Date (Revival) November 20, 1951, New York City Ballet,
    City Center, New York
Music Peter Ilyitch Tschaikovsky
Choreography George Balanchine after Lev Ivanov
Costumes Cecil Beaton. Executed by Karinska
Notes A new production in 1964 at the New York State
    Theater had costumes designed by Rouben Ter-
    Arutunian and executed by Karinska

LILAC GARDEN *(Ballet)*
Date (New production) November 30, 1951, New York
    City Ballet, City Center, New York
Music Ernest Chausson
Choreography Antony Tudor
Costumes Karinska

HOLLYWOOD ICE REVUE OF 1952 *(Ice Show)*
Date Fall 1951
Producer Arthur M. Wirtz
Choreography Catherine Littlefield, Dorothie Littlefield
Costumes Grace Houston. Executed by Karinska, others

HOLIDAY ON ICE OF 1952 *(Ice Show)*
Date Fall 1951
Producer George D. Tyson
Choreography Russell Markert, Dolores Pallet
Costumes Billy Livingston. Executed by Karinska

1952

BALLADE *(Ballet)*
Date February 14, 1952, New York City Ballet, City
    Center, New York
Music Claude Debussy
Choreography Jerome Robbins
Costumes Boris Aronson. Executed by Karinska

BAYOU *(Ballet)*
Date February 21, 1952, New York City Ballet,
    City Center, New York
Music Virgil Thomson
Choreography George Balanchine
Costumes Dorothea Tanning. Executed by Karinska

HOLLYWOOD ICE REVUE OF 1953 *(Ice Show)*
Date October 9, 1952, Coliseum, Indianapolis
Producer Arthur M. Wirtz
Choreography Dorothie Littlefield
Costumes Grace Houston. Executed by Karinska, others

SONJA HENIE 1953 ICE REVUE *(Ice Show)*
Date October 20, 1952, Dallas
Producer Sonja Henie
Choreography Elizabeth Kennedy
Costumes Billy Livingston, Humberto Anido. Executed by
    Karinska, others

SERENADE *(Ballet)*
Date (New production) November 4, 1952, New York City
    Ballet, City Center, New York
Music Peter Ilyitch Tschaikovsky
Choreography George Balanchine
Costumes Karinska

SCOTCH SYMPHONY *(Ballet)*
Date November 11, 1952, New York City Ballet, City
    Center, New York
Music Felix Mendelssohn
Choreography George Balanchine
Costumes Karinska, David Ffolkes (men's costumes)

METAMORPHOSES *(Ballet)*
Date November 25, 1952, New York City Ballet, City
    Center, New York
Music Paul Hindemith
Choreography George Balanchine
Costumes Karinska

HANS CHRISTIAN ANDERSEN *(Film)*
Date Released November 26, 1952, RKO Radio Pictures
Director Charles Vidor
Screenplay Moss Hart
Choreography Roland Petit (ballet)
Costumes Clavé, Mary Willis, Karinska (ballet)
Notes Nominated for the 1952 Academy Award for
    Costume Design in a Color Film

HARLEQUINADE PAS DE DEUX *(Ballet)*
Date December 16, 1952, New York City Ballet, City
    Center, New York

Music Riccardo Drigo
Choreography George Balanchine
Costumes Karinska

KALEIDOSCOPE *(Ballet)*
Date December 18, 1952, New York City Ballet, City
  Center, New York
Music Dmitri Kabalevsky
Choreography Ruthanna Boris
Costumes Alvin Colt. Executed by Karinska

ONE, YULETIDE SQUARE *(Ballet)*
Date December 25, 1952, made for television, NBC
Producer L. Leonidoff
Music Léo Delibes (from *Coppelia*)
Choreography George Balanchine
Costumes Karinska

CONCERTINO *(Ballet)*
Date December 30, 1952, New York City Ballet, City
  Center, New York
Music Jean Françaix
Choreography George Balanchine
Costumes Karinska

1953

VALSE FANTAISIE *(Ballet)*
Date January 6, 1953, New York City Ballet, City Center,
  New York
Music Mikhail Glinka
Choreography George Balanchine
Costumes Karinska

CAN-CAN *(Musical)*
Date May 7, 1953, Shubert Theatre, New York
Producers Cy Feuer, Ernest Martin
Book and Direction Abe Burrows
Music and Lyrics Cole Porter
Choreography Michael Kidd
Costumes Motley. Executed by Karinska

ME AND JULIET *(Musical)*
Date May 28, 1953, Majestic Theatre, New York
Producer Richard Rodgers, Oscar Hammerstein
Director George Abbott
Book and Lyrics Oscar Hammerstein
Music Richard Rodgers
Choreography Robert Alton
Costumes Irene Sharaff. Executed by Karinska

FANFARE *(Ballet)*
Date June 2, 1953, New York City Ballet, City Center,
  New York
Music Benjamin Britten
Choreography Jerome Robbins
Costumes Irene Sharaff. Executed by Karinska

1954

THE NUTCRACKER *(Ballet)*
Date February 2, 1954, New York City Ballet with students
  from the School of American Ballet, City Center,
  New York
Music Peter Ilyitch Tschaikovsky
Choreography George Balanchine, with parts by Lev Ivanov
  and Jerome Robbins
Costumes Karinska (mice by Lawrence Vlady)
Notes The new production of 1964 at the New York State
  Theater had some new costumes by Karinska

QUARTET *(Ballet)*
Date February 14, 1954, New York City Ballet, City
  Center, New York
Music Sergei Prokofiev

Choreography Jerome Robbins
Costumes Karinska

IL BARBIERE DI SIVIGLIA *(Opera)*
Date (New production) February 19, 1954, Metropolitan
  Opera Association, New York
Music Gioacchino Rossini
Director Cyril Ritchard
Costumes Eugene Berman. Executed by Karinska

THE GIRL IN PINK TIGHTS *(Musical)*
Date March 5, 1954, Mark Hellinger Theatre, New York
Producer/Director Shepard Traube
Music and Lyrics Sigmund Romberg
Choreography Agnes de Mille
Costumes Miles White. Executed by Karinska, others

THE MIKADO *(Ballet)*
Date October 1, 1954, Ballet Russe de Monte Carlo²,
  Baltimore, Maryland
Music Anthony Sullivan, orchestrated by Vittorio Rieti
Choreography Antonia Cobos
Costumes Bernard Lamotte. Executed by Karinska

ON YOUR TOES *(Musical)*
Date (Revival) October 11, 1954, Forty-sixth Street
  Theatre, New York
Producer/Director George Abbott
Music and Lyrics Richard Rodgers, Lorenz Hart
Choreography George Balanchine assisted by George Church
Costumes Irene Sharaff. Executed by Karinska

VITTORIO *(Ballet)*
Date December 15, 1954, Metropolitan Opera Association,
  New York
Music Giuseppe Verdi
Choreography Zachary Solov
Costumes Esteban Francés. Executed by Karinska

HOLLYWOOD ICE REVUE OF 1955 *(Ice Show)*
Date Fall 1954
Producer Arthur M. Wirtz
Choreography Donn Arden
Costumes Raoul Pêne du Bois. Executed by Karinska,
  others

1955

ARABELLA *(Opera)*
Date (New production) February 10, 1955, Metropolitan
  Opera Association, New York
Music Richard Strauss
Director Herbert Graf
Costumes Rolf Gérard. Executed by Karinska

ROMA *(Ballet)*
Date February 23, 1955, New York City Ballet, City
  Center, New York
Music Georges Bizet
Choreography George Balanchine
Costumes Eugene Berman. Executed by Karinska

SILK STOCKINGS *(Musical)*
Date February 24, 1955, Imperial Theatre, New York
Producers Cy Feuer, Ernest Martin
Director Cy Feuer
Music and Lyrics Cole Porter
Choreography Eugene Loring
Costumes Lucinda Ballard, Robert MacKintosh. Executed
  by Karinska

PAS DE TROIS *(Ballet)*
Date March 1, 1955, New York City Ballet, City Center,
  New York
Music Mikhail Glinka
Choreography George Balanchine
Costumes Karinska

DADDY LONG LEGS *(Film)*
Date Released May 5, 1955, Twentieth Century-Fox
Director Jean Negulesco
Screenplay Phoebe and Henry Ephron
Choreography Fred Astaire, Dave Robel, Roland Petit
  (ballet)
Costumes Tom Keogh (ballet). Executed by Karinska

SEVENTH HEAVEN *(Musical)*
Date May 26, 1955, ANTA Theatre, New York
Producers Gant Gaither, William Bacher
Director John C. Wilson
Music and Lyrics Victor Young, Stella Unger
Choreography Peter Gennaro
Costumes Marcel Vertès. Executed by Karinska

LA DAME À LA LICORNE *(Ballet)*
Date October 14, 1955, Ballet Russe de Monte Carlo²,
  Toronto, Canada
Music Jacques Chailly
Libretto Jean Cocteau
Choreography Heinz Rosen
Costumes Jean Cocteau. Executed by Karinska

WESTERN SYMPHONY *(Ballet)*
Date (New production) November 8, 1955, New York City
  Ballet, City Center, New York
Music Hershy Kay
Choreography George Balanchine
Costumes Karinska

LES CONTES D'HOFFMANN *(Opera)*
Date (New production) November 14, 1955, Metropolitan
  Opera Association, New York
Music Jacques Offenbach
Director Cyril Ritchard
Costumes Rolf Gérard. Executed by Karinska

VILIA (THE MERRY WIDOW) *(Ballet)*
Date (New production) November 16, 1955, Lyric Opera,
  Chicago
Music Franz Lehár
Choreography Ruth Page
Costumes Rolf Gérard. Executed by Barbara and Irene
  Karinska

PIPE DREAM *(Musical)*
Date November 30, 1955, Shubert Theatre, New York
Producers Richard Rodgers, Oscar Hammerstein
Director Harold Clurman
Music and Lyrics Richard Rodgers, Oscar Hammerstein
Choreography Boris Runanine
Costumes Alvin Colt. Executed by Karinska (for Helen
  Traubel only)

SOIRÉE *(Ballet)*
Date December 23, 1955, Metropolitan Opera Association,
  New York
Music Gioacchino Rossini, Benjamin Britten
Choreography Zachary Solov
Costumes Cecil Beaton. Executed by Karinska

HOLLYWOOD ICE REVUE OF 1956 *(Ice Show)*
Date Fall 1955
Producer Arthur M. Wirtz
Choreography Donn Arden
Costumes Raoul Pêne du Bois. Executed by Karinska,
  others

1956

DER ROSENKAVALIER *(Opera)*
Date (New production) February 6, 1956, Metropolitan
  Opera Association, New York
Music Richard Strauss
Director Herbert Graf
Costumes Rolf Gérard. Executed by Karinska

DIE ZAUBERFLÖTE (THE MAGIC
FLUTE) (Opera)
Date   (New production) February 23, 1956, Metropolitan
   Opera Association, New York
Music   Wolfgang Amadeus Mozart
Director   Herbert Graf
Costumes   Harry Horner. Executed by Karinska

ALLEGRO BRILLANTE (Ballet)
Date   March 1, 1956, New York City Ballet, City Center,
   New York
Music   Peter Ilyitch Tschaikovsky
Choreography   George Balanchine
Costumes   Karinska

THE CONCERT (or THE PERILS OF
EVERYBODY) (Ballet)
Date   March 6, 1956, New York City Ballet, City Center,
   New York
Music   Frédéric Chopin
Choreography   Jerome Robbins
Costumes   Irene Sharaff. Executed by Karinska

A MUSICAL JOKE (Ballet)
Date   May 31, 1956, New York City Ballet (Mozart
   Festival), American Shakespeare Festival Theatre,
   Stratford, Connecticut
Music   Wolfgang Amadeus Mozart
Choreography   George Balanchine
Costumes   Karinska

DIVERTIMENTO NO. 15 (Ballet)
Date   May 31, 1956, New York City Ballet (Mozart
   Festival), American Shakespeare Festival Theatre,
   Stratford, Connecticut
Music   Wolfgang Amadeus Mozart
Choreography   George Balanchine
Costumes   Karinska
Notes   New production for the New York City Ballet in
   1966 had new costumes by Karinska

SHANGRI-LA (Musical)
Date   June 13, 1956, Winter Garden Theatre, New York
Producers   Robert Fryer, Lawrence Carr
Director   Albert Marre
Book and Lyrics   James Hilton, Jerome Lawrence, Robert E.
   Lee (based on novel Lost Horizon by Hilton)
Music   Henry Warren
Choreography   Donald Saddler
Costumes   Irene Sharaff. Executed by Karinska

NEW FACES OF 1956 (Musical Revue)
Date   June 14, 1956, Ethel Barrymore Theatre, New York
Producers   Leonard Sillman, John Roberts, Yvette Schumer
Directors   David Tihmar, Paul Lynde
Music   Various composers
Costumes   Thomas Becher. Executed by Karinska ("A Doll's
   House" sketch)

SOMBREROS (Ballet)
Date   June 18, 1956, Ballet Russe de Monte Carlo², Carter
   Barron Amphitheatre, Washington, D.C.
Music   Mexican folk tunes arranged by Ivan Boutnikov
Choreography   Leon Danielian
Costumes   William Cecil. Executed by Karinska

THE SLEEPING PRINCE (Drama)
Date   (New Production) November 1, 1956, Coronet
   Theatre, New York
Producers   Producers Theatre, Gilbert Miller
Director   Michael Redgrave
Script   Terence Rattigan
Costumes   Alvin Colt. Executed by Karinska, Valentina
   (Barbara Bel Geddes's gown)

L'IL ABNER (Musical)
Date   November 5, 1956, St. James Theatre, New York
Producers   Norman Panama, Melvin Frank, Michael Kidd
Director/Choreographer   Michael Kidd

Music and Lyrics   Gene De Paul, Johnny Mercer
Costumes   Alvin Colt. Executed by Karinska

ERNANI (Opera)
Date   (New production) November 23, 1956, Metropolitan
   Opera Association, New York
Music   Giuseppe Verdi
Director   Dino Yannopoulos
Costumes   Esteban Francés. Executed by Karinska

CANDIDE (Musical)
Date   December 1, 1956, Martin Beck Theatre, New York
Producers   Ethel Linder Reiner, Lester Osterman, Jr.
Director   Tyrone Guthrie
Book   Lillian Hellman (based on Voltaire)
Music   Leonard Bernstein
Lyrics   Richard Wilbur, John Latouche, Dorothy Parker
Choreography   Wallace Seibert, Anna Sokolow
Costumes   Irene Sharaff. Executed by Karinska

LA PERICHOLE (Opera)
Date   (New Production) December 21, 1956, Metropolitan
   Opera Association, New York
Music   Jacques Offenbach
Director   Cyril Ritchard
Costumes   Rolf Gérard. Executed by Karinska

HOLIDAY ON ICE OF 1957 (Ice Show)
Date   Fall 1956
Producer   George D. Tyson
Choreography   Chester Hale
Costumes   Robert MacKintosh. Executed by Karinska,
   others

1957

THE UNICORN, THE GORGON AND THE
MANTICORE (Ballet)
Date   (New Production) January 15, 1957, New York City
   Ballet, City Center, New York
Music and Libretto   Gian Carlo Menotti
Choreography   John Butler
Costumes   Robert Fletcher. Executed by Karinska

LA TRAVIATA (Opera)
Date   (New production) February 21, 1957, Metropolitan
   Opera Association, New York
Music   Giuseppe Verdi
Director   Tyrone Guthrie
Costumes   Rolf Gérard. Executed by Karinska

MAIDEN VOYAGE (Comedy)
Date   February 28, 1957, Forrest Theatre, Philadelphia
Producers   Kermit Bloomgarden, Anna Deere Wiman
Director   Joseph Anthony
Script   Paul Osborn
Costumes   Alvin Colt. Executed by Karinska

VARIATIONS CLASSIQUES (Ballet)
Date   October 6, 1957, Ballet Russe de Monte Carlo²
   (Casals Festival), San Juan, Puerto Rico
Music   Johannes Brahms
Choreography   Nina Novak
Costumes   Karinska

MARY STUART (Drama)
Date   October 8, 1957, Phoenix Theatre, New York
Producers   T. Edward Hambleton, Norris Houghton
Director   Tyrone Guthrie
Script   Friedrich Schiller
Costumes   Alvin Colt. Executed by Karinska

COPPER AND BRASS (Musical)
Date   October 17, 1957, Martin Beck Theatre, New York
Producers   Lyn Austin, Thomas Noyes, Anderson Lawler
Director   Marc Daniels
Music and Lyrics   David Baker, David Craig

Choreography   Anna Sokolow, Bob Fosse
Costumes   Alvin Colt. Executed by Karinska

HOLIDAY ON ICE OF 1958 (Ice Show)
Date   October 19, 1957, Coliseum, Fort Wayne, Indiana
Producer   George D. Tyson
Choreography   Chester Hale
Costumes   Robert MacKintosh. Executed by Karinska,
   others

EUGENE ONEGIN (Opera)
Date   (New production) October 28, 1957, Metropolitan
   Opera Association, New York
Music   Peter Ilyitch Tschaikovsky
Director   Peter Brook
Costumes   Rolf Gérard. Executed by Karinska

DON GIOVANNI (Opera)
Date   (New production) October 31, 1957, Metropolitan
   Opera Association, New York
Music   Wolfgang Amadeus Mozart
Director   Herbert Graf
Costumes   Eugene Berman. Executed by Karinska

LE NOZZE DI FIGARO (Opera)
Date   (New Production) 1957, NBC Opera Company
   National Tour (presented by NBC and RCA)
Music   Wolfgang Amadeus Mozart
Director   Peter Herman Adler
Costumes   Alvin Colt. Executed by Karinska

MADAMA BUTTERFLY (Opera)
Date   (New Production) 1957, NBC Opera Company
   National Tour (presented by NBC and RCA)
Music   Giacomo Puccini
Director   Peter Herman Adler
Costumes   Alvin Colt. Executed by Karinska

1958

GOUNOD SYMPHONY (Ballet)
Date   January 8, 1958, New York City Ballet, City Center,
   New York
Music   Charles Gounod
Choreography   George Balanchine
Costumes   Karinska

STARS AND STRIPES (Ballet)
Date   January 17, 1958, New York City Ballet, City Center,
   New York
Music   John Philip Sousa, adapted by Hershy Kay
Choreography   George Balanchine
Costumes   Karinska

THE INFERNAL MACHINE (Drama)
Date   (New production) February 3, 1958, Phoenix
   Theatre, New York
Producers   T. Edward Hambleton, Norris Houghton
Director   Herbert Berghof
Script   Jean Cocteau, adapted by Albert Bermel
Costumes   Alvin Colt. Executed by Karinska

WALTZ-SCHERZO (Ballet)
Date   September 9, 1958, New York City Ballet, City
   Center, New York
Music   Peter Ilyitch Tschaikovsky
Choreography   George Balanchine
Costumes   Karinska

CAVALLERIA RUSTICANA (Opera)
Date   (New production) November 7, 1958, Metropolitan
   Opera Association, New York
Music   Pietro Mascagni
Director   José Quintero
Costumes   Rolf Gérard. Executed by Karinska

PAGLIACCI (Opera)
Date (New production) November 7, 1958, Metropolitan
  Opera Association, New York
Music Ruggiero Leoncavallo
Director José Quintero
Costumes Rolf Gérard. Executed by Karinska

OCTET (Ballet)
Date December 2, 1958, New York City Ballet, City
  Center, New York
Music Igor Stravinsky
Choreography Willam Christensen
Costumes Lewis Brown, Karinska (Part I)

THE SEVEN DEADLY SINS (Ballet)
Date (New production) December 4, 1958, New York City
  Ballet, City Center, New York
Music Kurt Weill
Lyrics Bertolt Brecht
Choreography George Balanchine
Costumes Rouben Ter-Arutunian. Executed by Karinska

1959

MACBETH (Opera)
Date (New production) February 5, 1959, Metropolitan
  Opera Association, New York
Music Giuseppe Verdi
Director Carl Ebert
Costumes Caspar Rudolph Neher. Executed by Karinska

LOOK AFTER LULU (Comedy)
Date March 3, 1959, Henry Miller's Theatre, New York
Producers Playwrights' Company, Gilbert Miller
Director Cyril Ritchard
Script Noel Coward adapted from Georges Feydeau's play,
  Occupe-toi d'Amélie
Costumes Cecil Beaton. Executed by Karinska, others

FIRST IMPRESSIONS (Musical)
Date March 19, 1959, Alvin Theatre, New York
Producers George Gilbert, Edward Specter
Director Abe Burrows
Music Robert Goldman, Glenn Paxton, George Weiss
Choreography Jonathan Lucas
Costumes Alvin Colt. Executed by Karinska

LES DIAMANTS (Ballet)
Date March 22, 1959, Metropolitan Opera Association,
  New York
Music Charles de Bériot
Choreography Alexandra Danilova
Costumes Karinska

EPISODES (Ballet)
Date May 14, 1959, New York City Ballet, City Center,
  New York
Music Anton Webern
Choreography Martha Graham (Part I), George Balanchine
  (Part II)
Costumes Karinska
Notes Martha Graham was involved with the design of her
  own costumes in collaboration with Karinska. Cecil
  Beaton was originally commissioned for the project and
  some of his ideas were reworked

IL TROVATORE (Opera)
Date (New production) October 26, 1959, Metropolitan
  Opera Association, New York
Music Giuseppe Verdi
Director Herbert Graf
Costumes Motley. Executed by Karinska

LE NOZZE DI FIGARO (Opera)
Date (New production) October 30, 1959, Metropolitan
  Opera Association, New York
Music Wolfgang Amadeus Mozart

Director Cyril Ritchard
Costumes Oliver Messel. Executed by Karinska

DER ZIGEUNERBARON (THE GYPSY
BARON) (Opera)
Date (New production) November 25, 1959, Metropolitan
  Opera Association, New York
Music Johann Strauss the Younger
Director Cyril Ritchard
Costumes Rolf Gérard. Executed by Karinska

HOLIDAY ON ICE OF 1960 (Ice Show)
Date Fall 1959
Producer Ruth Tyson
Choreography Chester Hale
Costumes Freddy Wittop. Executed by Karinska, others

1960

PANAMERICA (Ballet)
Date January 20, 1960, New York City Ballet, City Center,
  New York
Music Various Latin-American composers
Choreography Gloria Contreras, George Balanchine,
  Francisco Moncion, John Taras, Jacques d'Amboise
Costumes Esteban Francés, Karinska (section IV). Most
  sections executed by Karinska

GREENWILLOW (Musical)
Date March 8, 1960, Alvin Theatre, New York
Producers Robert A. Willey, Frank Productions Inc.
Director George Roy Hill
Music and Lyrics Frank Loesser
Choreography Joe Layton
Costumes Alvin Colt. Executed by Karinska

PAS DE DEUX (later TSCHAIKOVSKY PAS
DE DEUX) (Ballet)
Date March 29, 1960, New York City Ballet, City Center,
  New York
Music Peter Ilyitch Tschaikovsky
Choreography George Balanchine
Costumes Karinska

THE FIGURE IN THE CARPET (Ballet)
Date April 13, 1960, New York City Ballet, City Center,
  New York
Music George Frederic Handel
Choreography George Balanchine
Costumes Esteban Francés. Executed by Karinska

TWELFTH NIGHT (Comedy)
Date (New Production) June 3, 1960, American
  Shakespeare Festival, Stratford, Connecticut
Director Jack Landau
Script William Shakespeare
Costumes Rouben Ter-Arutunian. Executed by Karinska

BECKET (Drama)
Date (New Production) October 5, 1960, St. James
  Theatre, New York
Producer David Merrick
Director Peter Glenville
Script Jean Anouilh
Costumes Motley. Executed by Karinska

VARIATIONS FROM DON SEBASTIAN (later
DONIZETTI VARIATIONS) (Ballet)
Date November 16, 1960, New York City Ballet, City
  Center, New York
Music Gaetano Donizetti
Choreography George Balanchine
Costumes Karinska (women's costumes), Esteban Francés
  (men's costumes from Panamerica)
Notes All costumes by Karinska in new production, 1971

LIEBESLIEDER WALZER (Ballet)
Date November 22, 1960, New York City Ballet, City
  Center, New York

Music Johannes Brahms
Choreography George Balanchine
Costumes Karinska

L'ELISIR D'AMORE (Opera)
Date (New production) November 25, 1960, Metropolitan
  Opera Association, New York
Music Gaetano Donizetti
Director Nathaniel Merrill
Costumes Robert O'Hearn. Executed by Karinska

EBONY CONCERTO (Ballet)
Date December 7, 1960, New York City Ballet, City
  Center, New York
Music Igor Stravinsky
Choreography John Taras
Costumes Karinska

RAGTIME (I) (Ballet)
Date December 7, 1960, New York City Ballet, City
  Center, New York
Music Igor Stravinsky
Choreography George Balanchine
Costumes Karinska

WILDCAT (Musical)
Date December 16, 1960, Alvin Theatre, New York
Producers Michael Kidd, N. Richard Nash
Director/Choreographer Michael Kidd
Music and Lyrics Cy Coleman, Carolyn Leigh
Costumes Alvin Colt. Executed by Karinska

HOLIDAY ON ICE OF 1961 (Ice Show)
Date Fall 1960
Producer Ruth Tyson
Choreography Chester Hale
Costumes Freddy Wittop. Executed by Karinska, others

MISCELLANEOUS, 1960
Karinska executed reproductions of First Ladies' gowns for
a gala fashion show presented during the Republican
Convention in Chicago. These gowns were exhibited at the
Smithsonian Institution in Washington, D.C., and at
museums throughout the United States.

1961

MARTHA (Opera)
Date (New production) January 26, 1961, Metropolitan
  Opera Association, New York
Music Friedrich von Flotow
Director Carl Ebert
Costumes Motley. Executed by Karinska

TURANDOT (Opera)
Date (New production) February 24, 1961, Metropolitan
  Opera Association, New York
Music Giacomo Puccini
Director Yoshio Aoyama, Nathaniel Merrill
Costumes Cecil Beaton. Executed by Karinska

ÉTUDES (Ballet)
Date (New production) October 5, 1961, American Ballet
  Theatre, Fifty-fourth Street Theatre, New York
Music Karl Czerny, arranged by Knudaage Riisager
Choreography Harald Lander
Costumes Rolf Gérard. Executed by Karinska

ELIZABETH THE QUEEN (Drama)
Date October 19, 1961, National Repertory Theatre,
  Academy of Music, Northampton, Massachusetts
Producers Frances Ann Hersey, Michael Dewell
Director Jack Sydow
Script Maxwell Anderson
Costumes Alvin Colt. Executed by Karinska (for Eva Le
  Gallienne and Faye Emerson)

VALSES ET VARIATIONS (later RAYMONDA
VARIATIONS) *(Ballet)*
Date December 7, 1961, New York City Ballet, City
    Center, New York
Music Alexander Glazounov
Choreography George Balanchine
Costumes Karinska

1962

A MIDSUMMER NIGHT'S DREAM *(Ballet)*
Date January 17, 1962, New York City Ballet with children
    from the School of American Ballet, City Center, New
    York
Music Felix Mendelssohn
Choreography George Balanchine
Costumes Karinska (Bottom's donkey head executed by
    Lawrence Vlady)
Notes Costumes redesigned in 1964 by Karinska for a new
    production for New York City Ballet at the New York
    State Theater

TURN OF THE SCREW *(Opera)*
Date (New Production) March 25, 1962, New York City
    Opera, City Center, New York
Music Benjamin Britten
Libretto Myfanwy Piper after Henry James
Director Allen Fletcher
Costumes Alvin Colt. Executed by Karinska

KING RICHARD II *(Drama)*
Date (New Production) June 12, 1962, American
    Shakespeare Festival, Stratford, Connecticut
Producer Joseph V. Reed
Director Allen Fletcher
Script William Shakespeare
Costumes Motley. Executed by Karinska

MISCELLANEOUS, 1962
Karinska made the tutu for a ballerina doll presented in
1962 to President John F. Kennedy's daughter, Caroline, by
American Ballet Theatre.

1963

LA SONNAMBULA *(Opera)*
Date (New production) February 21, 1963, Metropolitan
    Opera Association, New York
Music Vincenzo Bellini
Director Henry Butler
Costumes Rolf Gérard. Executed by Karinska

OTELLO *(Opera)*
Date (New production) March 10, 1963, Metropolitan
    Opera Association, New York
Music Giuseppe Verdi
Director Herbert Graf
Costumes Eugene Berman. Executed by Karinska

TOVARICH *(Musical)*
Date March 18, 1963, Broadway Theatre, New York
Producers Abel Farbman, Sylvia and Joseph Harris
Director Peter Glenville
Music Lee Pockriss
Choreography Herbert Ross
Costumes Motley. Executed by Karinska

BUGAKU *(Ballet)*
Date March 20, 1963, New York City Ballet, City Center,
    New York
Music Toshiro Mayuzumi
Choreography George Balanchine
Costumes Karinska

ARCADE *(Ballet)*
Date March 28, 1963, New York City Ballet, City Center,
    New York

Music Igor Stravinsky
Choreography John Taras
Costumes Ruth Sobotka. Executed by Karinska

THE CHASE (or, THE VIXEN'S
CHOICE) *(Ballet)*
Date September 18, 1963, New York City Ballet, City
    Center, New York
Music Wolfgang Amadeus Mozart
Choreography Jacques d'Amboise
Costumes Karinska

THE SEAGULL *(Drama)*
Date (New Production) October 10, 1963, National
    Repertory Theatre, Aycock Auditorium, Greensboro,
    North Carolina
Producers Frances Ann Dougherty, Michael Dewell
Director Eva Le Gallienne
Script Anton Chekhov (translated by Eva Le Gallienne)
Costumes Alvin Colt. Executed by Karinska (for Eva Le
    Gallienne)
Notes Opened on Broadway April 5, 1964

RING AROUND THE MOON *(Drama)*
Date (New Production) October 11, 1963, National
    Repertory Theatre, Aycock Auditorium, Greensboro,
    North Carolina
Producers Frances Ann Dougherty, Michael Dewell
Director Jack Sydow
Script Jean Anouilh
Costumes Alvin Colt. Executed by Karinska (for Eva Le
    Gallienne)

AIDA *(Opera)*
Date (New production) October 14, 1963, Metropolitan
    Opera Association, New York
Music Giuseppe Verdi
Director Nathaniel Merrill
Choreography Katherine Dunham
Costumes Robert O'Hearn. Executed by Karinska

MEDITATION *(Ballet)*
Date December 10, 1963, New York City Ballet, City
    Center, New York
Music Peter Ilyitch Tschaikovsky
Choreography George Balanchine
Costumes Karinska

MISCELLANEOUS, 1963
Karinska executed costumes for Harry Belafonte and his
company for his national concert tour.

1964

TARANTELLA *(Ballet)*
Date January 7, 1964, New York City Ballet, City Center,
    New York
Music Louis Moreau Gottschalk
Choreography George Balanchine
Costumes Karinska

FALSTAFF *(Opera)*
Date (New production) March 6, 1964, Metropolitan
    Opera Association, New York
Music Giuseppe Verdi
Director Franco Zeffirelli
Costumes Franco Zeffirelli. Executed by Karinska

CLARINADE *(Ballet)*
Date April 29, 1964, New York City Ballet, New York State
    Theater
Music Morton Gould
Choreography George Balanchine
Costumes Karinska

DIM LUSTRE *(Ballet)*
Date May 6, 1964, New York City Ballet, New York State
    Theater

Music Richard Strauss
Choreography Antony Tudor
Costumes Beni Montresor. Executed by Karinska

IRISH FANTASY *(Ballet)*
Date August 12, 1964, Greek Theater, Los Angeles,
    California
Music Camille Saint-Saëns
Choreography Jacques d'Amboise
Costumes Karinska

.BALLET IMPERIAL *(Ballet)*
Date (New production) October 15, 1964, New York City
    Ballet, New York State Theater
Music Peter Ilyitch Tschaikovsky
Choreography George Balanchine
Costumes Karinska
Notes In 1973 (retitled *Piano Concerto No. 2*, then
    Tschaikovsky Piano Concerto No. 2) redone with new
    costumes by Karinska; tutus replaced by chiffon dresses

1965

PAS DE DEUX AND
DIVERTISSEMENT *(Ballet)*
Date January 14, 1965, New York City Ballet, New York
    State Theater
Music Léo Delibes
Choreography George Balanchine
Costumes Karinska

SHADOW'D GROUND *(Ballet)*
Date January 21, 1965, New York City Ballet, New York
    State Theater
Music Aaron Copland
Choreography John Taras
Costumes John Braden. Executed by Karinska

HARLEQUINADE *(Ballet)*
Date February 4, 1965, New York City Ballet with
    children from the School of American Ballet, New York
    State Theater
Music Riccardo Drigo
Choreography George Balanchine
Costumes Rouben Ter-Arutunian. Executed by Karinska

DON QUIXOTE *(Ballet)*
Date May 28, 1965, New York City Ballet with children
    from School of American Ballet, New York State Theater
Music Nicolas Nabokov
Choreography George Balanchine
Costumes Esteban Francés. Executed by Karinska (giant by
    Kermit Love, Peter Saklin; masks and armor by
    Lawrence Vlady)

1966

SUMMERSPACE *(Ballet)*
Date April 14, 1966, New York City Ballet, New York State
    Theater
Music Morton Feldman
Choreography Merce Cunningham
Costumes Robert Rauschenberg. Executed by Karinska

BRAHMS-SCHOENBERG QUARTET *(Ballet)*
Date April 21, 1966, New York City Ballet, New York State
    Theater
Music Johannes Brahms, orchestrated by Arnold
    Schoenberg
Choreography George Balanchine
Costumes Karinska

JEUX *(Ballet)*
Date April 28, 1966, New York City Ballet, New York State
    Theater

Music Claude Debussy
Choreography John Taras
Costumes Raoul Pêne du Bois. Executed by Karinska

LA TRAVIATA *(Opera)*
Date (New production) September 24, 1966, Metropolitan
Opera Association, New York
Music Giuseppe Verdi
Director Alfred Lunt
Costumes Cecil Beaton. Executed by Karinska

LA GUIRLANDE DE CAMPRA *(Ballet)*
Date December 1, 1966, New York City Ballet, New York
State Theater
Music Various, after a theme by André Campra (1717)
Choreography John Taras
Costumes Esteban Francés, Peter Harvey. Executed by
Karinska

1967

PROLOGUE *(Ballet)*
Date January 12, 1967, New York City Ballet, New York
State Theater
Music William Byrd, Giles Farnby, others
Choreography Jacques d'Amboise
Costumes Peter Larkin. Executed by Karinska

JEWELS *(Ballet)*
Date April 13, 1967, New York City Ballet, New York State
Theater
Music Gabriel Fauré, Igor Stravinsky, Peter Ilyitch
Tschaikovsky
Choreography George Balanchine
Costumes Karinska

GLINKIANA (later VALSE FANTAISIE) *(Ballet)*
Date November 23, 1967, New York City Ballet, New York
State Theater
Music Mikhail Glinka
Choreography George Balanchine
Costumes Esteban Francés. Executed by Karinska

MISCELLANEOUS, 1967
Karinska made a gown for the role of Mary Todd Lincoln
in "White House Happening," Lincoln Kirstein's dramatic
play of the Civil War, at Loeb Center, Harvard University.
The dress was based on a photograph by Mathew Brady of
Mrs. Lincoln in her inaugural gown (1861).

1968

METASTASEIS & PITHOPRAKTA *(Ballet)*
Date January 18, 1968, New York City Ballet, New York
State Theater
Music Iannis Xenakis
Choreography George Balanchine
Costumes Karinska

HAYDN CONCERTO *(Ballet)*
Date January 25, 1968, New York City Ballet, New York
State Theater
Music Franz Joseph Haydn
Choreography John Taras
Costumes Raoul Pêne du Bois. Executed by Karinska

SLAUGHTER ON TENTH AVENUE *(Ballet)*
Date May 2, 1968, New York City Ballet, New York State
Theater
Music Richard Rodgers (from *On Your Toes*, 1936)
Choreography George Balanchine
Costumes Irene Sharaff. Executed by Karinska

STRAVINSKY: SYMPHONY IN C *(Ballet)*
Date May 9, 1968, New York City Ballet, New York State
Theater
Music Igor Stravinsky
Choreography John Clifford
Costumes John Braden. Executed by Karinska

LA SOURCE *(Ballet)*
Date November 23, 1968, New York City Ballet, New York
State Theater
Music Léo Delibes
Choreography George Balanchine
Costumes Karinska

1969

TSCHAIKOVSKY SUITE (later
TSCHAIKOVSKY SUITE NO. 2) *(Ballet)*
Date January 9, 1969, New York City Ballet, New York
State Theater
Music Peter Ilyitch Tschaikovsky
Choreography Jacques d'Amboise
Costumes John Braden. Executed by Karinska

FANTASIES *(Ballet)*
Date January 23, 1969, New York City Ballet, New York
State Theater
Music Ralph Vaughan Williams
Choreography John Clifford
Costumes Robert O'Hearn. Executed by Karinska

DANCES AT A GATHERING *(Ballet)*
Date May 8, 1969, New York City Ballet, New York State
Theater
Music Frédéric Chopin
Choreography Jerome Robbins
Costumes Joe Eula. Executed by Karinska

MISCELLANEOUS, 1960s
Karinska made clothes for a number of colleagues and
friends: Gloria Vanderbilt (an Edwardian gown of lavender
satin), Suzanne Farrell (her wedding dress and headdress),
Allegra Kent (bell-bottom, navy blue wool jersey pants),
Patricia McBride (a black velvet strapless dress), Mrs.
Robert Merrill (dress for the 1966 *La Traviata* opening),
Mrs. Herman Krawitz (a dress made of garnet-colored
velvet left over from the *Mary Stuart* of 1957), and Mrs.
Lytle Hull (a boa of silver leaves for the Bal de Tête).

1970

WHO CARES? *(Ballet)*
Date February 5, 1970, New York City Ballet, New York
State Theater
Music George Gershwin
Choreography George Balanchine
Costumes Karinska

FIREBIRD *(Ballet)*
Date (New production) May 28, 1970, New York City
Ballet, New York State Theater
Music Igor Stravinsky
Choreography George Balanchine, Jerome Robbins
Costumes Marc Chagall. Executed by Karinska
Notes In 1972, Karinska executed a new Firebird costume
with long train and large wings, (modified in 1974)

TSCHAIKOVSKY SUITE NO. 3 *(Ballet)*
Date December 3, 1970, New York City Ballet, New York
State Theater
Music Peter Ilyitch Tschaikovsky
Choreography George Balanchine
Costumes Nicolas Benois. Executed by Karinska

1971

KODÁLY DANCES *(Ballet)*
Date January 14, 1971, New York City Ballet, New York
State Theater
Music Zoltán Kodály
Choreography John Clifford
Costumes Stanley Simmons. Executed by Karinska

FOUR LAST SONGS *(Ballet)*
Date January 21, 1971, New York City Ballet, New York
State Theater
Music Richard Strauss
Choreography Lorca Massine
Costumes Joe Eula. Executed by Karinska

THE GOLDBERG VARIATIONS *(Ballet)*
Date May 27, 1971, New York City Ballet, New York State
Theater
Music Johann Sebastian Bach
Choreography Jerome Robbins
Costumes Joe Eula. Executed by Karinska

PAMTGG *(Ballet)*
Date June 17, 1971, New York City Ballet, New York State
Theater
Music Roger Kellaway
Choreography George Balanchine
Costumes Irene Sharaff. Executed by Karinska

1972

A CONCERTO FOR PIANO AND WINDS *(Ballet)*
Date June 20, 1972, New York City Ballet, New York State
Theater (Stravinsky Festival)
Music Igor Stravinsky
Choreography John Taras
Costumes Rouben Ter-Arutunian. Executed by Karinska

DIVERTIMENTO FROM BAISER DE LA
FÉE *(Ballet)*
Date June 21, 1972, New York City Ballet, New York State
Theater (Stravinsky Festival)
Music Igor Stravinsky
Choreography George Balanchine
Costumes Eugene Berman (from *Roma*, 1955). Executed by
Karinska

SCHERZO À LA RUSSE *(Ballet)*
Date June 21, 1972, New York City Ballet, New York State
Theater (Stravinsky Festival)
Music Igor Stravinsky
Choreography George Balanchine
Costumes Karinska

SCÈNES DE BALLET *(Ballet)*
Date June 22, 1972, New York City Ballet, New York State
Theater (Stravinsky Festival)
Music Igor Stravinsky
Choreography John Taras
Costumes Karinska

THE SONG OF THE NIGHTINGALE *(Ballet)*
Date June 22, 1972, New York City Ballet, New York State
Theater (Stravinsky Festival)
Music Igor Stravinsky
Choreography John Taras
Costumes Rouben Ter-Arutunian. Executed by Karinska

PULCINELLA *(Ballet)*
Date June 23, 1972, New York City Ballet, New York State
Theater (Stravinsky Festival)
Music Igor Stravinsky
Choreography George Balanchine, Jerome Robbins
Costumes Eugene Berman. Executed by Karinska. Masks
and props by Kermit Love

1973

CORTÈGE HONGROIS (Ballet)
Date   May 17, 1973, New York City Ballet, New York State Theater
Music   Alexander Glazounov
Choreography   George Balanchine
Costumes   Rouben Ter-Arutunian. Executed by Karinska

1974

DYBBUK (Ballet)
Date   May 16, 1974, New York City Ballet, New York State Theater
Music   Leonard Bernstein
Choreography   Jerome Robbins
Costumes   Patricia Zipprodt. Executed by Karinska

SALTARELLI (Ballet)
Date   May 30, 1974, New York City Ballet, New York State Theater
Music   Antonio Vivaldi
Choreography   Jacques d'Amboise
Costumes   John Braden. Executed by Karinska

COPPELIA (Ballet)
Date   (New production) July 17, 1974, New York City Ballet, Saratoga Performing Arts Center, New York
Music   Léo Delibes
Choreography   Alexandra Danilova and George Balanchine after Marius Petipa
Costumes   Rouben Ter-Arutunian. Executed by Karinska, Barbara Matera, Ltd.
Notes   Act III costumes altered before first New York performance and new children's costumes designed by Karinska

1975

SINFONIETTA (Ballet)
Date   January 9, 1975, New York City Ballet, New York State Theater
Music   Paul Hindemith
Choreography   Jacques d'Amboise
Costumes   John Braden. Executed by Karinska

L'ENFANT ET LES SORTILÈGES (Lyric Fantasy)
Date   (New production) May 15, 1975, New York City Ballet, New York State Theater (Ravel Festival)
Music   Maurice Ravel
Libretto   Colette (translated by Lincoln Kirstein and Jane Barzin)
Choreography   George Balanchine
Costumes   Kermit Love, David Mitchell. Executed by Karinska

ALBORADO DEL GRACIOSA (Ballet)
Date   May 22, 1975, New York City Ballet, New York State Theater (Ravel Festival)
Music   Maurice Ravel
Choreography   Jacques d'Amboise
Costumes   John Braden. Executed by Karinska

DAPHNIS AND CHLOE (Ballet)
Date   May 22, 1975, New York City Ballet, New York State Theater (Ravel Festival)
Music   Maurice Ravel
Choreography   John Taras
Costumes   Joe Eula. Executed by Karinska

GASPARD DE LA NUIT (Ballet)
Date   May 29, 1975, New York City Ballet, New York State Theater (Ravel Festival)
Music   Maurice Ravel
Choreography   George Balanchine
Costumes   Bernard Daydé. Executed by Karinska, supervised by David Mitchell

RAPSODIE ESPAGNOLE (Ballet)
Date   May 29, 1975, New York City Ballet, New York State Theater (Ravel Festival)
Music   Maurice Ravel
Choreography   George Balanchine
Costumes   Michael Avedon. Executed by Karinska

SARABANDE AND DANSE (II) (Ballet)
Date   May 29, 1975, New York City Ballet, New York State Theater (Ravel Festival)
Music   Claude Debussy, orchestrated by Maurice Ravel
Choreography   Jacques d'Amboise
Costumes   John Braden. Executed by Karinska

TZIGANE (Ballet)
Date   May 29, 1975, New York City Ballet, New York State Theater (Ravel Festival)
Music   Maurice Ravel
Choreography   George Balanchine
Costumes   Joe Eula, Stanley Simmons (from Kodály Dances). Executed by Karinska

UN BARQUE SUR L'OCÉAN (Ballet)
Date   May 29, 1975, New York City Ballet, New York State Theater (Ravel Festival)
Music   Maurice Ravel
Choreography   Jerome Robbins
Costumes   Parmelee Welles. Executed by Karinska

1976

CHACONNE (Ballet)
Date   January 22, 1976, New York City Ballet, New York State Theater
Music   Christoph Willibald von Gluck
Choreography   George Balanchine, staged by Brigitte Thom
Costumes   Karinska. Initially danced in practice clothes; costumes added in spring 1976

UNION JACK (Ballet)
Date   May 13, 1976, New York City Ballet, New York State Theater
Music   Hershy Kay
Choreography   George Balanchine
Costumes   Rouben Ter-Arutunian. Executed by Karinska, Sheldon Kasman (Scottish costumes)

1977

VIENNA WALTZES (Ballet)
Date   June 23, 1977, New York City Ballet, New York State Theater
Music   Johann Strauss the Younger, Franz Lehár, Richard Strauss
Choreography   George Balanchine
Costumes   Karinska

CREDITS

ILLUSTRATION CREDITS

Key: r (right), l (left), t (top), c (center), b (bottom)
Courtesy Cris Alexander: 125b; Photograph by Gordon Anthony. Collections of the Theatre Museum. Courtesy of the Board of Trustees. Victoria & Albert Museum: 23t, 36c, 36b, 37t, 37b; Courtesy Edward Bigelow: 114t, 131t, 139tr, 164tr; Courtesy The Billy Rose Theater Collection. New York Public Library for the Performing Arts, Astor, Lenox and Tilden Foundations: 54l, 54r, 55, 58; Courtesy Kenneth Paul Block. Photo by Paul Kolnik: 45; Courtesy John Braden: 172; Courtesy Steven Caras: 145l; Courtesy Alvin Colt: 67b; Courtesy Culver Pictures: 39, 57t, 57b, 59, 60t, 60b, 61, 62t, 64tr, 64tl, 64b, 65, 66, 69, 71, 76t; Photograph by Louise Dahl-Wolfe. Courtesy the Museum at the Fashion Institute of Technology: 53; Courtesy Dance Collection. The New York City Public Library for the Performing Arts, Astor, Lenox and Tilden Foundations: 19t, 27t, 27r, 98b, 145r; Courtesy Arthur Elgort: 109, 129b, 149r, 149l; Photo by Phillipe Halsman © Yvonne Halsman: 62r, 63, 122, 123; © Horst (Courtesy Harper's Bazaar): 30t, 44t, 44b, 47; Courtesy of Karinska Family: 10, 11t, 12, 17, 78t, 78b, 81, 92b, 118, 144t, 144b; Courtesy King World Productions, Inc.: 79; Courtesy Paul Kolnik: 131c, 133tr, 133tl, 133br, 134t, 134c, 134b, 135t, 135b, 136t, 139cl, 139bl, 159, 165; Courtesy Nancy Lassalle: 96; Courtesy Tanaquil Le Clercq: 102, 127t; Courtesy the Library of Congress. Photograph by Mathew Brady: 70t; Courtesy of Kermit Love: 50; Courtesy Estate of George Platt Lynes: 98tl, 100t, 100b, 101t, 101b, 103, 109;

Courtesy of Nola McIlvin: 96; Courtesy Metropolitan Opera Archives: 87t, 87b, 88t, 88b, 89, 90t, 90b, 91tr, 91tl, 91b, 92t, 93t, 94; Courtesy Joel Meyerowitz: 131c, 132tr, 132tl, 132br, 132bl, 133tl, 133br, 154b; Courtesy Judith Michael: 131b, 139br; Courtesy Estate of Jo Mielziner: 51r; Courtesy Museum of Modern Art/Film Stills Archive: 83; Courtesy New York City Ballet: 139tl, 140t; Courtesy Photofest: 73, 74, 75, 76b; Courtesy Wilbur Pippin: 120; Photograph by Courtesy François Poivret. Courtesy Bibliothèque Littéraire Jacques Doucet, Paris: 24; Courtesy Tatiana Riabouchinska; Courtesy Roger-Viollet: 18, 23b, 25tr, 25b, 28, 29, 30b, 31, 32b, 32t; Courtesy Royal Ballet Benevolent Fund: 34; Photograph by Maurice Seymour. Courtesy Ronald Seymour: 19b, 41tr, 41b; Courtesy Stanley Simmons: 1 (Photograph by Paul Kolnik), 21; Photograph by Martha Swope. Courtesy Martha Swope: 2–3, 8, 11, 25tl, 104t, 104b, 112t, 112b, 114r, 115t, 115b, 120, 121, 122br, 122bl, 125t, 129t, 136b, 137t, 137b, 138, 140c, 140b, 142b, 146t, 146b, 147b, 148b, 150t, 150b, 152t, 153, 156, 156c, 156b, 157t, 157b, 158t, 164tl, 164br, 164bl, 166tl, 168tr, 168tl, 168b, 169tr; Courtesy John Taras: 97, 148; Collections of the Theatre Museum. Courtesy of the Board of Trustees. Victoria & Albert Museum: 35; Photographs by Jerry L. Thompson. Courtesy Ballet Society: 70b, 105, 106, 107, 110, 111, 147t, 147r, 152b, 166tr, 166b, 167, 169tl, 271; Courtesy Vogue Copyright © 1945 (renewed 1973) by Irving Penn: 42–3; Courtesy Miles White: endpapers, 49t, 56tr, 56tl, 95t, 95b; Photograph © by Jerome Zerbe. From Happy Times by Brendan Gill, reproduced by permission from Harcourt, Brace & Co.: 46; Courtesy Patricia Zipprodt: 156bl

FILM CREDITS

Frenchman's Creek Copyright © 1944 by Universal City Studios, Inc. Courtesy of MCA Publishing Rights, a Division of MCA, Inc.: 71; Gaslight © 1944 Turner Entertainment Co. All Rights Reserved: 74; Joan of Arc © 1948 Turner Entertainment Co. All Rights Reserved: 79; Kismet © 1944 Turner Entertainment Co. All Rights Reserved: 75; Kitty Copyright © 1944 by Universal City Studios, Inc. Courtesy of MCA Publishing Rights, a Division of MCA, Inc.: 73; Lady in the Dark Copyright © 1944 by Universal City Studios, Inc. Courtesy of MCA Publishing Rights, a Division of MCA, Inc.: 69; The Pirate © 1948 Turner Entertainment Co. All Rights Reserved: 76b; Unconquered Copyright © 1947 by Universal City Studios, Inc. Courtesy of MCA Publishing Rights, a Division of MCA, Inc.: 76t

TEXT CREDITS

Grateful acknowledgment is made for permission to reproduce excerpts from the following texts.
Cecil Beaton. Ballet. Garden City, NY: Doubleday, 1953: pp. 34–6. © Estate of Cecil Beaton; Edith Head and Paddy Calistro. Edith Head's Hollywood. New York: E. P. Dutton, 1983: pp. 70, 81. © Paddy Calistro and Estate of Edith Head; Sono Osato. Distant Dances. New York: Alfred A. Knopf, 1980: pp. 36–8. © Sono Osato; Irene Sharaff. Broadway and Hollywood: Costumes Designed by Irene Sharaff. New York: Van Nostrand Reinhold Co., 1976: pp. 52, 96–8. © Estate of Irene Sharaff

INDEX

Italic page numbers indicate captions to illustrations.